STAR WARS®

JANGO FETT

OPEN SEASONS

VE I SLAVE I SLAVE I SLAV

PUBLISHER
MIKE RICHARDSON

DESIGNER
DARIN FABRICK

ART DIRECTOR
MARK COX

ASSISTANT EDITOR
JEREMY BARLOW

EDITOR
RANDY STRADLEY

SPECIAL THANKS TO
CHRIS CERASI &
LUCY AUTREY WILSON
AT LUCAS LICENSING

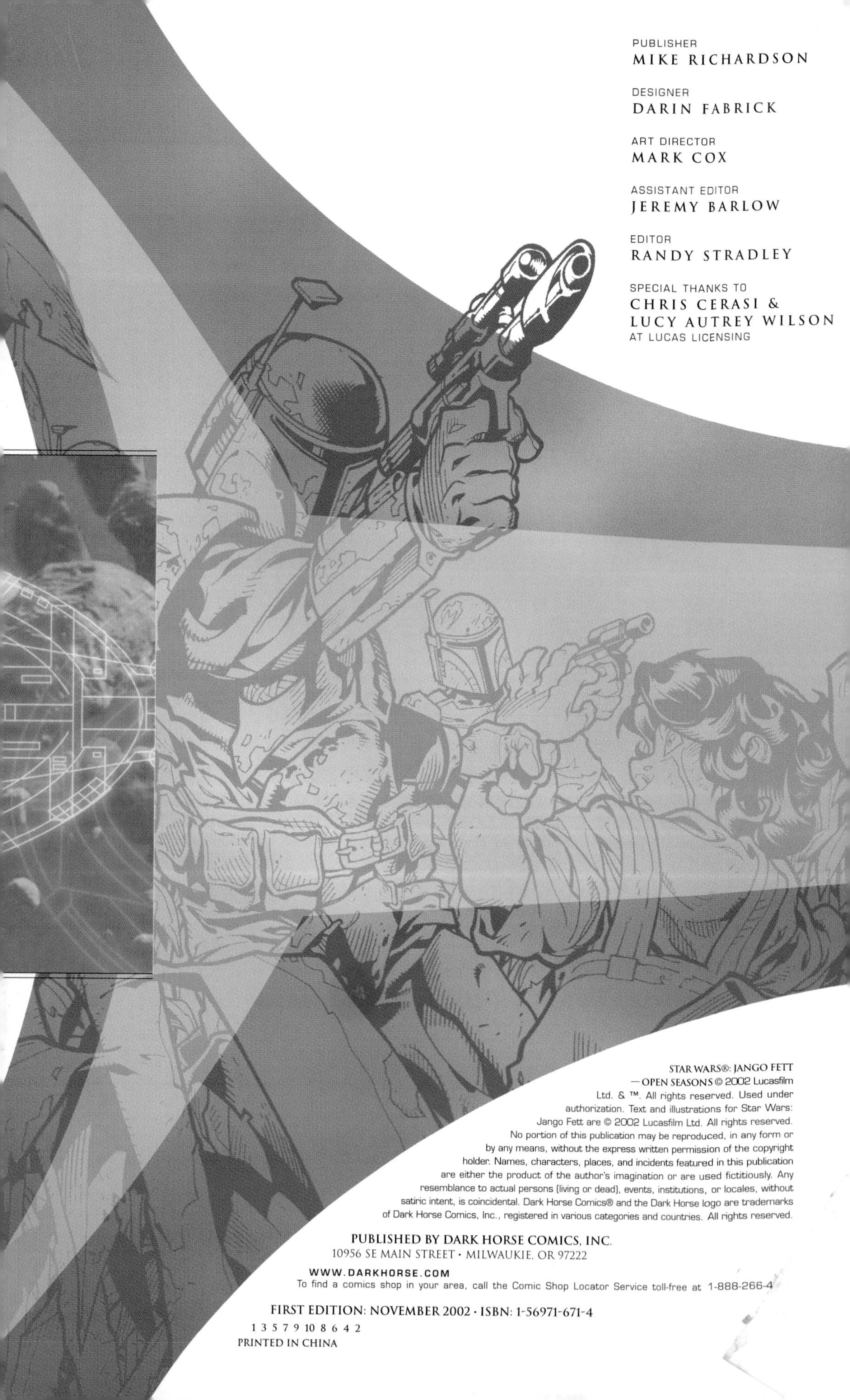

PUBLISHED BY DARK HORSE COMICS, INC.
10956 SE MAIN STREET • MILWAUKIE, OR 97222

WWW.DARKHORSE.COM
To find a comics shop in your area, call the Comic Shop Locator Service toll-free at 1-888-266-4

FIRST EDITION: NOVEMBER 2002 • ISBN: 1-56971-671-4

1 3 5 7 9 10 8 6 4 2
PRINTED IN CHINA

STAR WARS

JANGO FETT

OPEN SEASONS

WRITTEN BY	HAYDEN BLACKMAN
PENCIL ART BY	RAMON BACHS
INKS BY	RAUL FERNANDEZ
COLORS BY	BRAD ANDERSON WITH ADDITIONAL COLORS BY STUDIO F
LETTERING BY	DIGITAL CHAMELEON

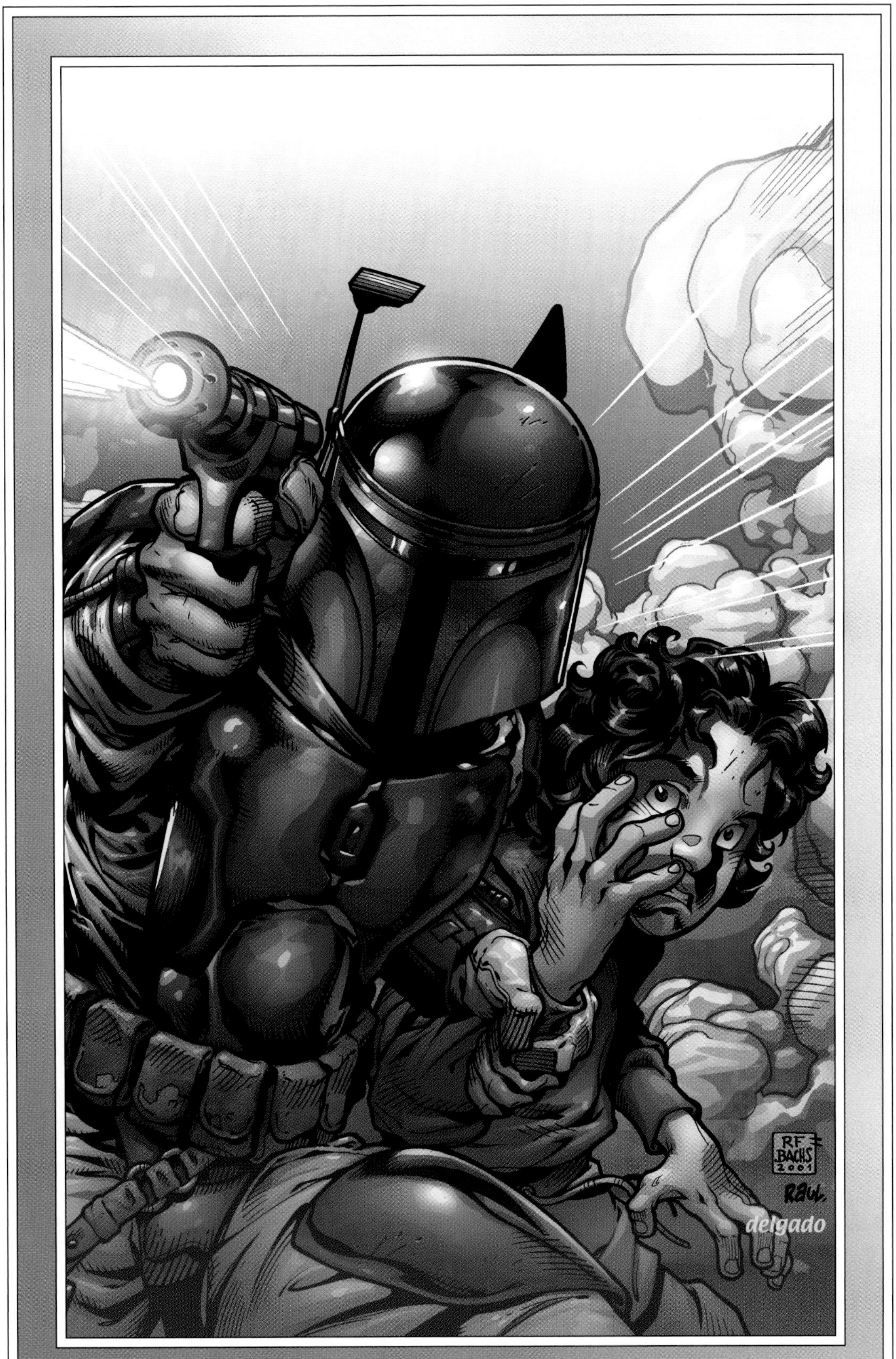
RF BACHS 2001
RAUL
delgado

S U M M E R

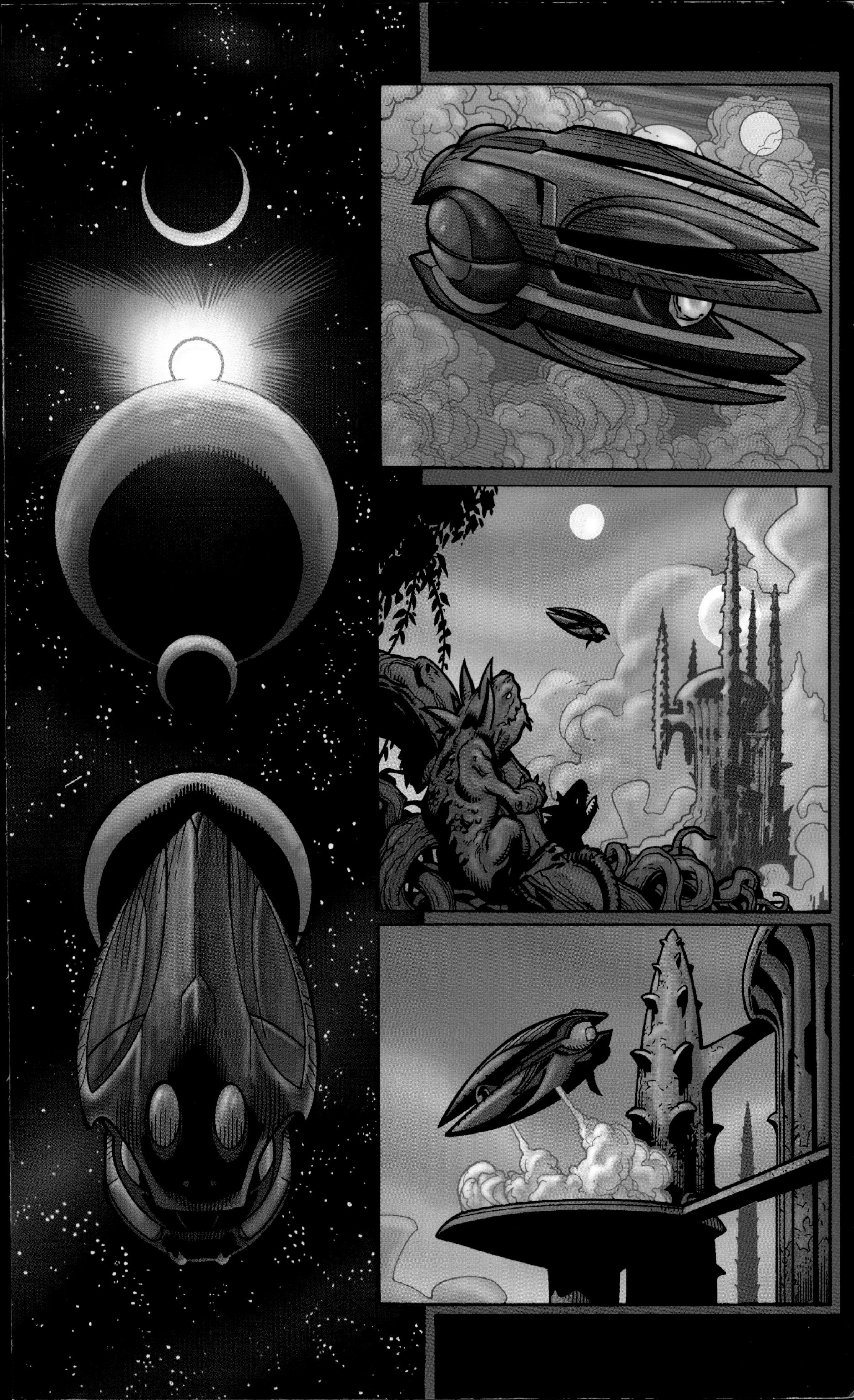

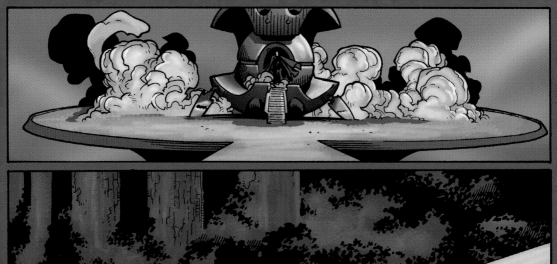

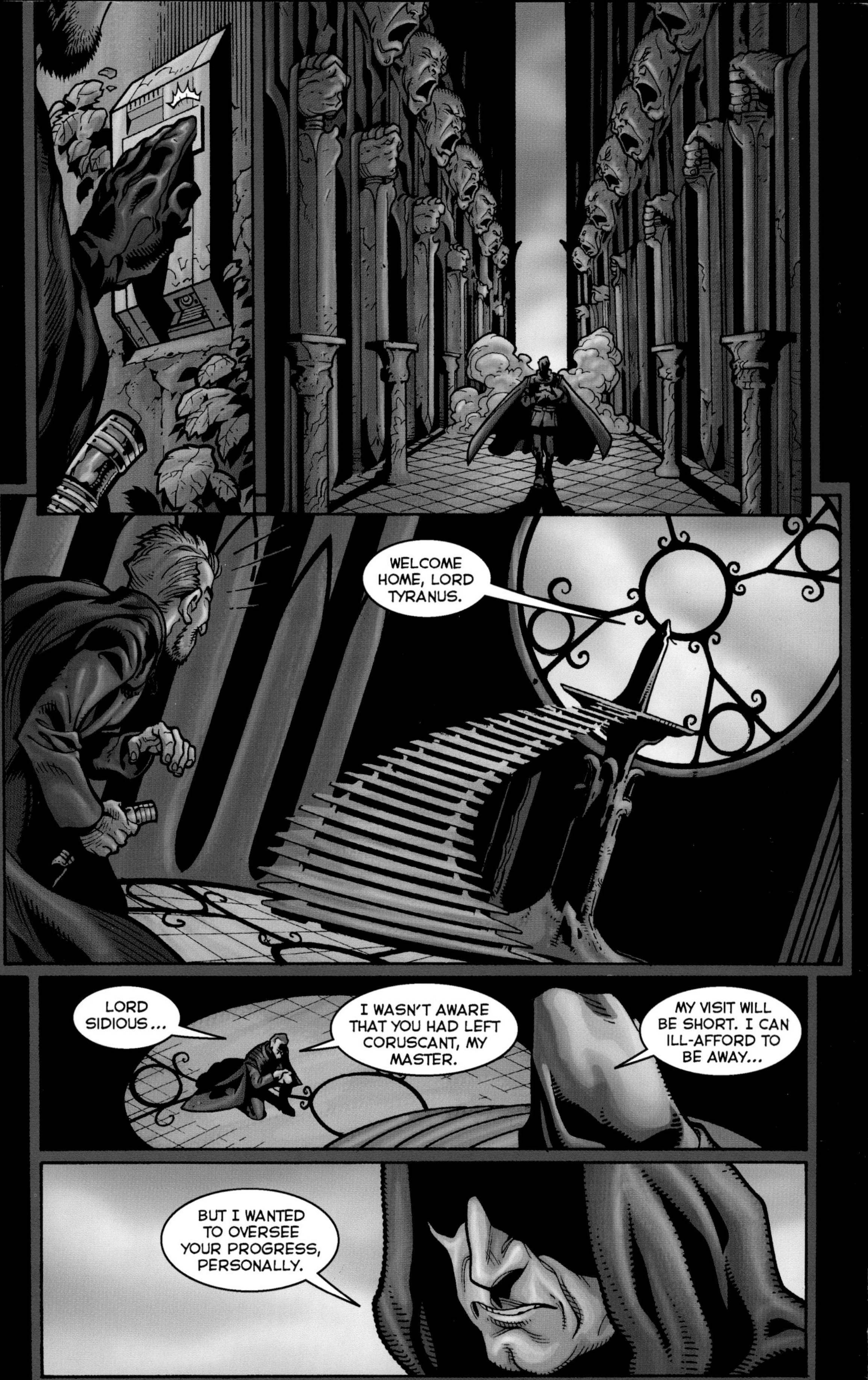
WELCOME HOME, LORD TYRANUS.
LORD SIDIOUS...
I WASN'T AWARE THAT YOU HAD LEFT CORUSCANT, MY MASTER.
MY VISIT WILL BE SHORT. I CAN ILL-AFFORD TO BE AWAY...
BUT I WANTED TO OVERSEE YOUR PROGRESS, PERSONALLY.

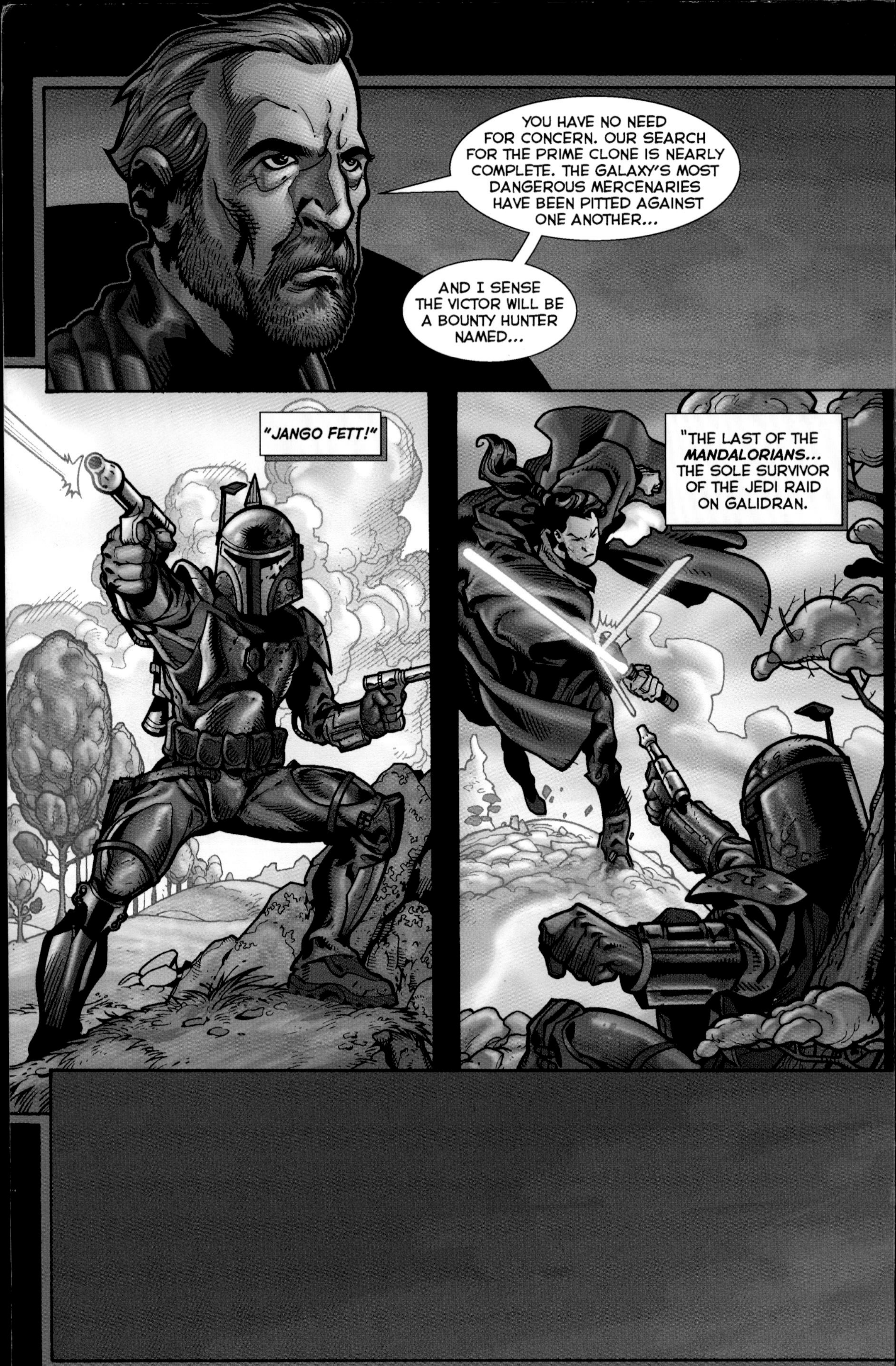
YOU HAVE NO NEED FOR CONCERN. OUR SEARCH FOR THE PRIME CLONE IS NEARLY COMPLETE. THE GALAXY'S MOST DANGEROUS MERCENARIES HAVE BEEN PITTED AGAINST ONE ANOTHER...
AND I SENSE THE VICTOR WILL BE A BOUNTY HUNTER NAMED...
"JANGO FETT!"
"THE LAST OF THE MANDALORIANS... THE SOLE SURVIVOR OF THE JEDI RAID ON GALIDRAN.

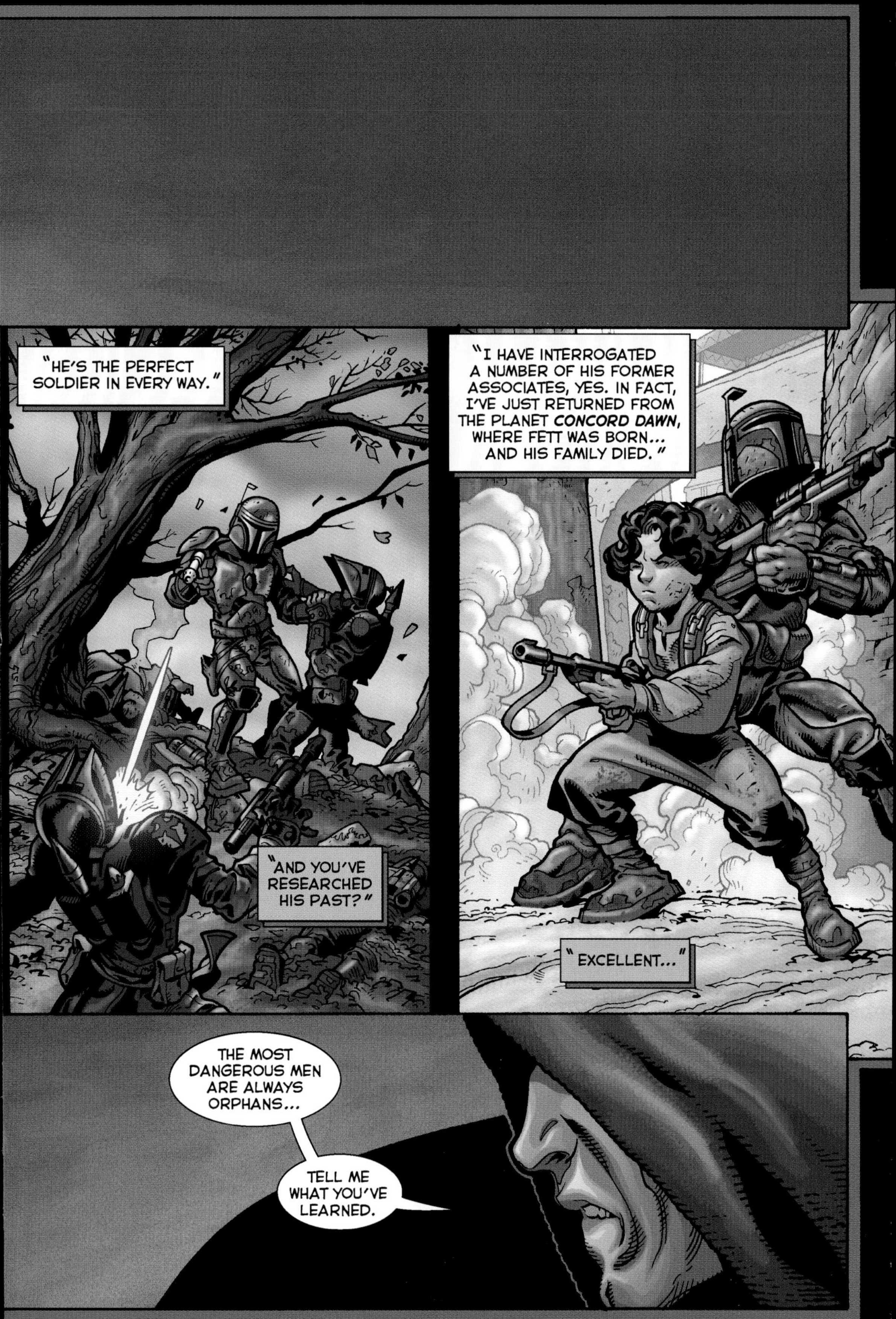
"HE'S THE PERFECT SOLDIER IN EVERY WAY."
"AND YOU'VE RESEARCHED HIS PAST?"
"I HAVE INTERROGATED A NUMBER OF HIS FORMER ASSOCIATES, YES. IN FACT, I'VE JUST RETURNED FROM THE PLANET CONCORD DAWN, WHERE FETT WAS BORN... AND HIS FAMILY DIED."
"EXCELLENT..."
THE MOST DANGEROUS MEN ARE ALWAYS ORPHANS...
TELL ME WHAT YOU'VE LEARNED.

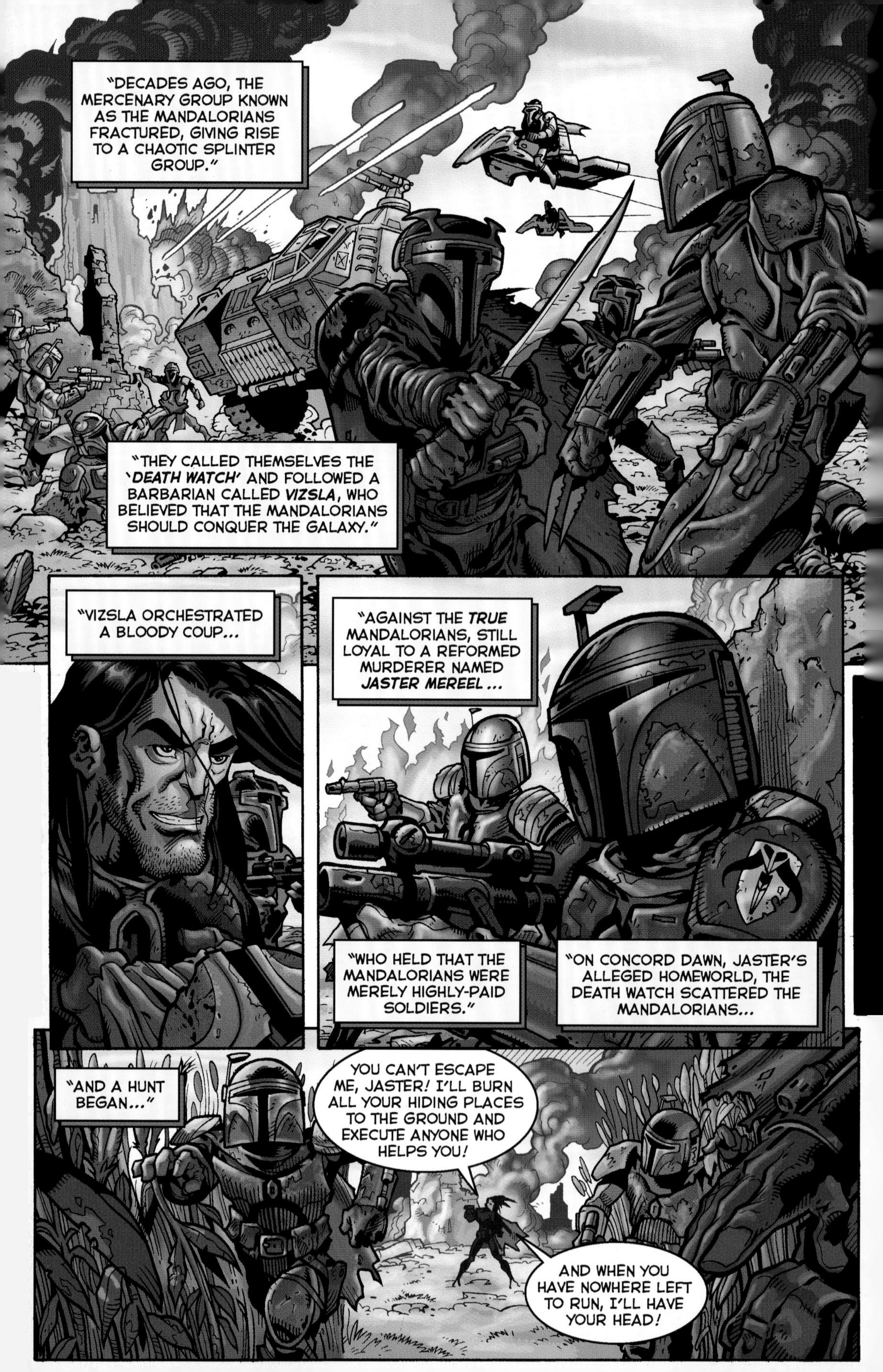
"DECADES AGO, THE MERCENARY GROUP KNOWN AS THE MANDALORIANS FRACTURED, GIVING RISE TO A CHAOTIC SPLINTER GROUP."
"THEY CALLED THEMSELVES THE '*DEATH WATCH*' AND FOLLOWED A BARBARIAN CALLED *VIZSLA*, WHO BELIEVED THAT THE MANDALORIANS SHOULD CONQUER THE GALAXY."
"VIZSLA ORCHESTRATED A BLOODY COUP...
"AGAINST THE *TRUE* MANDALORIANS, STILL LOYAL TO A REFORMED MURDERER NAMED *JASTER MEREEL*...
"WHO HELD THAT THE MANDALORIANS WERE MERELY HIGHLY-PAID SOLDIERS."
"ON CONCORD DAWN, JASTER'S ALLEGED HOMEWORLD, THE DEATH WATCH SCATTERED THE MANDALORIANS...
"AND A HUNT BEGAN..."
YOU CAN'T ESCAPE ME, JASTER! I'LL BURN ALL YOUR HIDING PLACES TO THE GROUND AND EXECUTE ANYONE WHO HELPS YOU!
AND WHEN YOU HAVE NOWHERE LEFT TO RUN, I'LL HAVE YOUR HEAD!

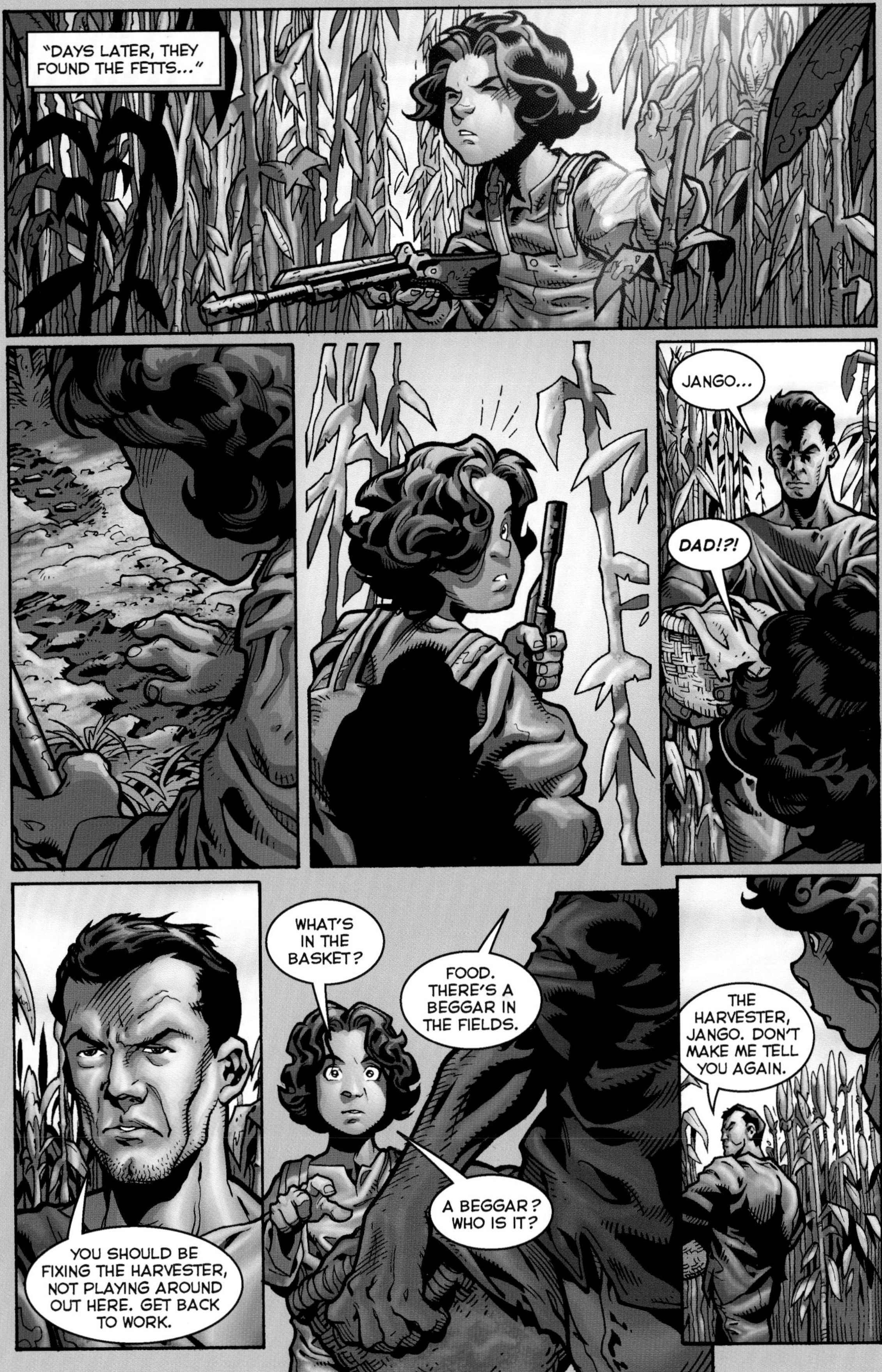
"DAYS LATER, THEY FOUND THE FETTS..."
JANGO...
DAD!?!
YOU SHOULD BE FIXING THE HARVESTER, NOT PLAYING AROUND OUT HERE. GET BACK TO WORK.
WHAT'S IN THE BASKET?
FOOD. THERE'S A BEGGAR IN THE FIELDS.
A BEGGAR? WHO IS IT?
THE HARVESTER, JANGO. DON'T MAKE ME TELL YOU AGAIN.

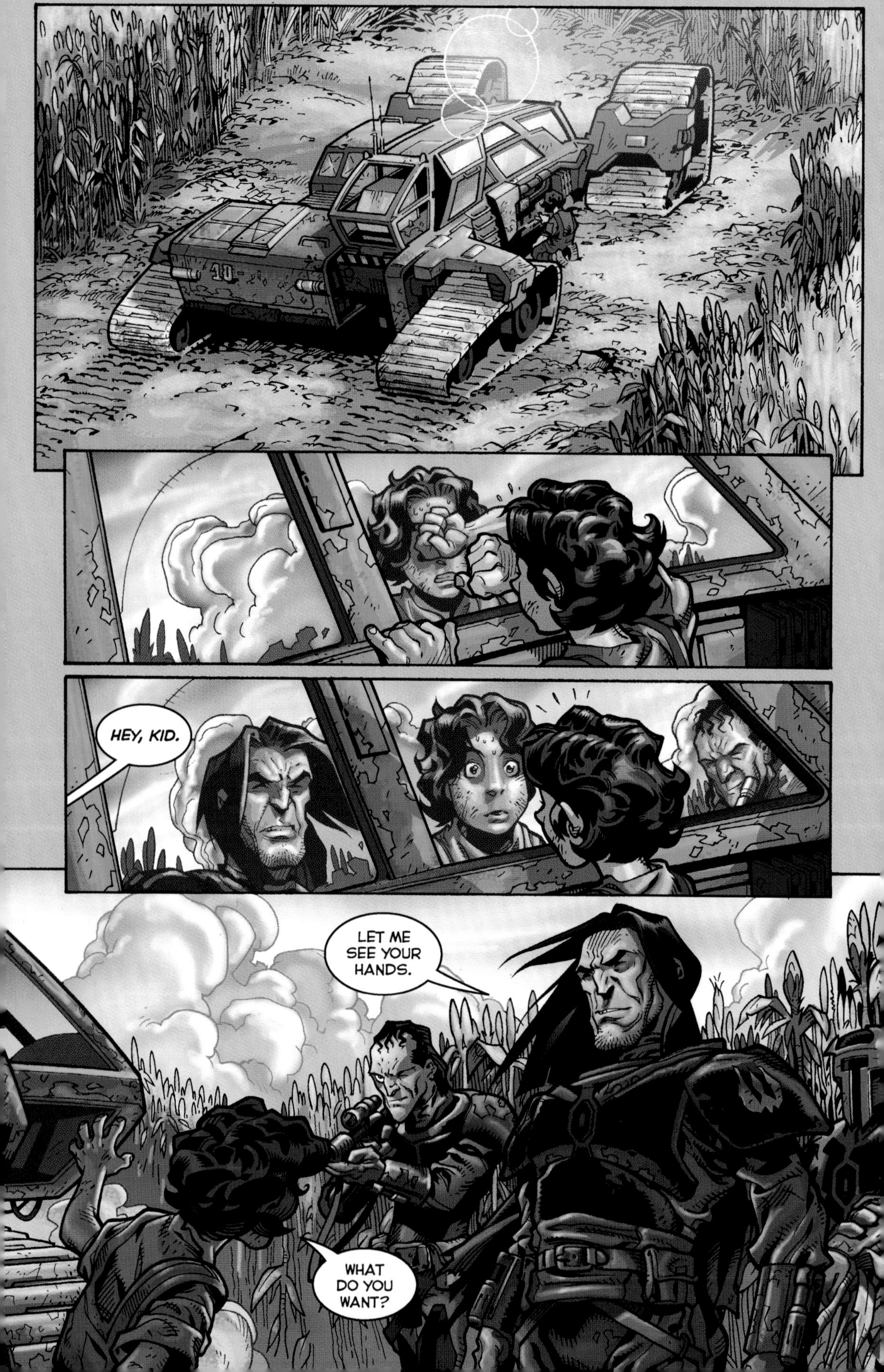
HEY, KID.
LET ME SEE YOUR HANDS.
WHAT DO YOU WANT?

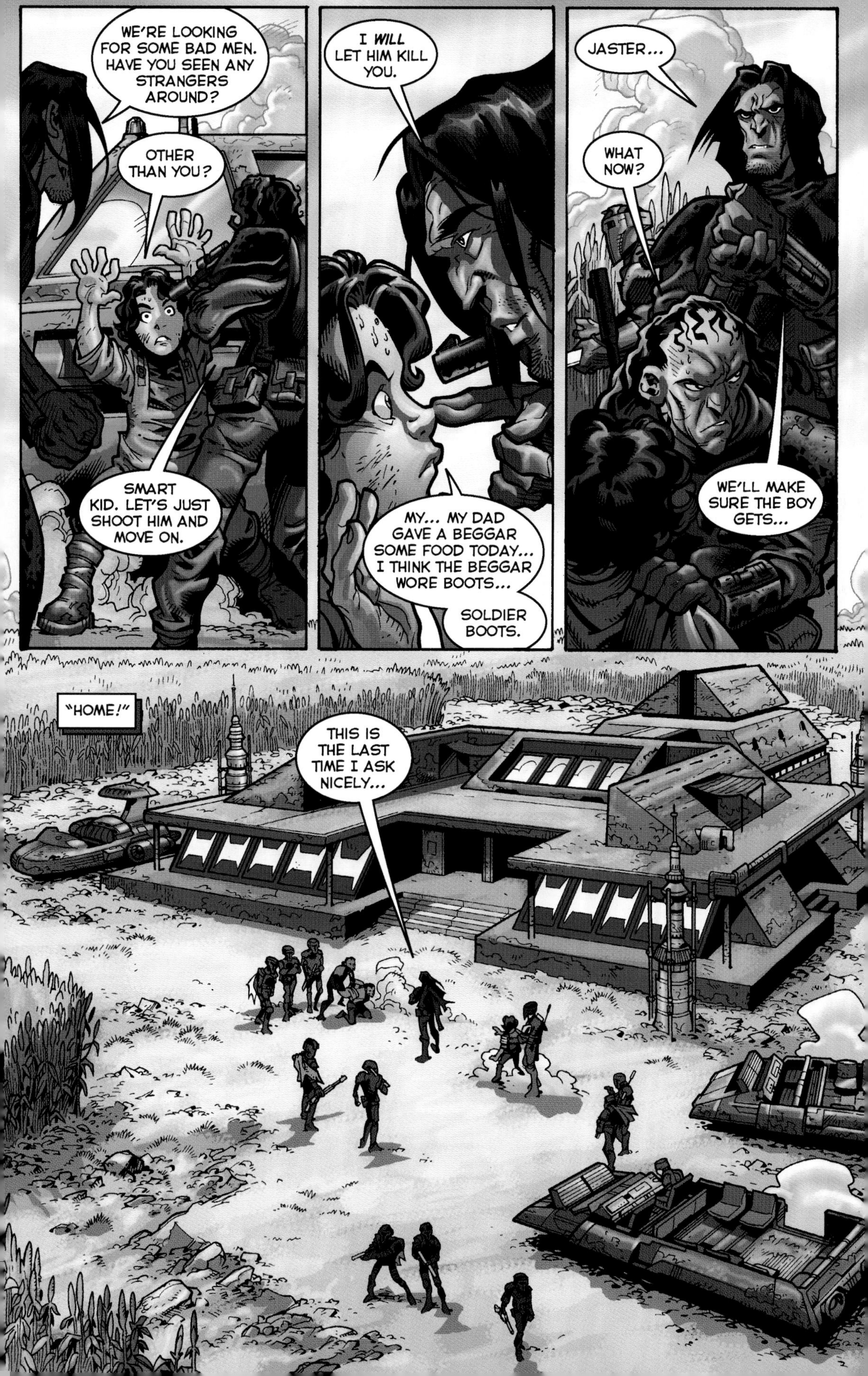
WE'RE LOOKING FOR SOME BAD MEN. HAVE YOU SEEN ANY STRANGERS AROUND?
OTHER THAN YOU?
SMART KID. LET'S JUST SHOOT HIM AND MOVE ON.
I *WILL* LET HIM KILL YOU.
MY... MY DAD GAVE A BEGGAR SOME FOOD TODAY... I THINK THE BEGGAR WORE BOOTS...
SOLDIER BOOTS.
JASTER...
WHAT NOW?
WE'LL MAKE SURE THE BOY GETS...
"HOME!"
THIS IS THE LAST TIME I ASK NICELY...

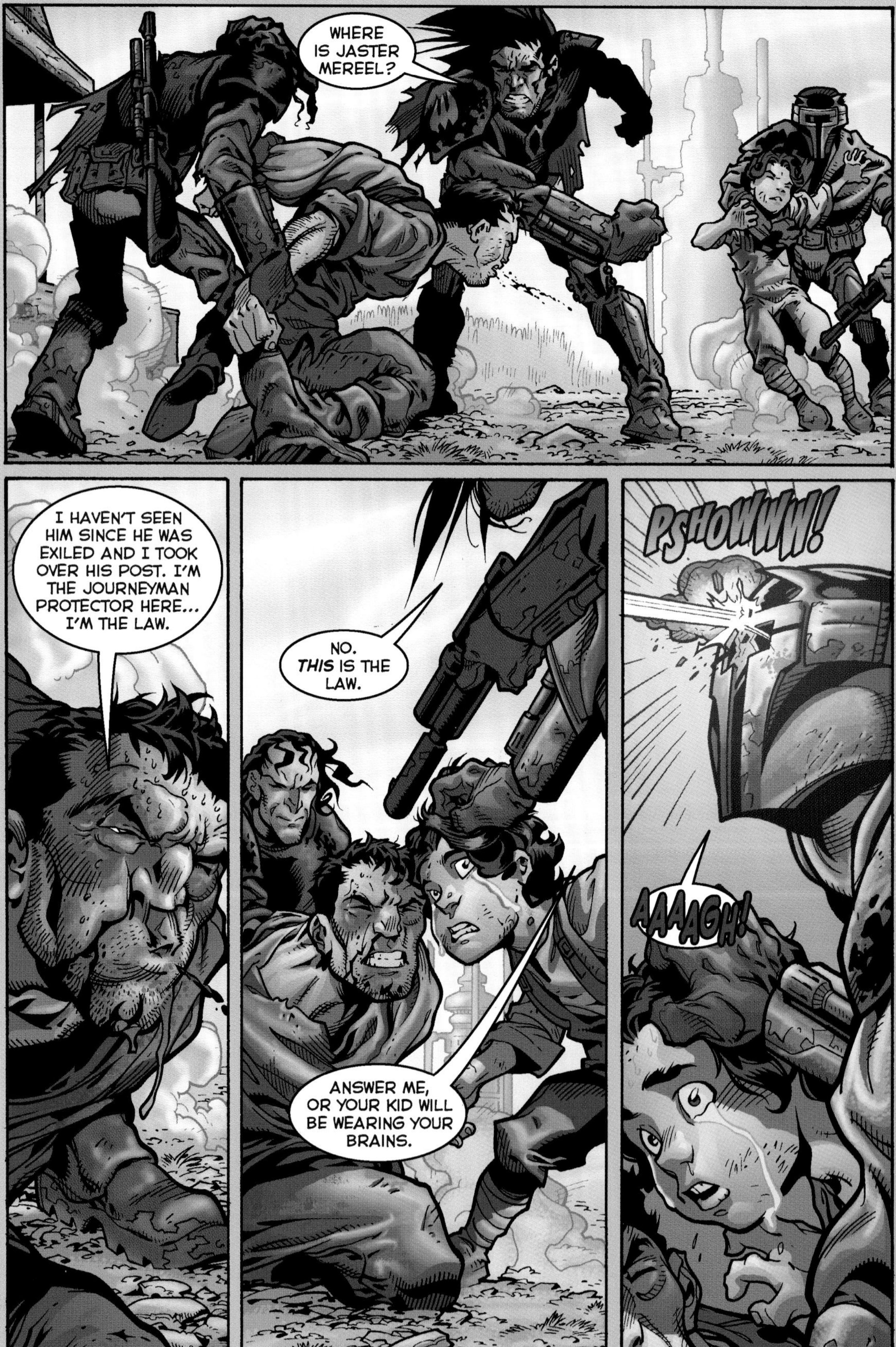
WHERE IS JASTER MEREEL?
I HAVEN'T SEEN HIM SINCE HE WAS EXILED AND I TOOK OVER HIS POST. I'M THE JOURNEYMAN PROTECTOR HERE... I'M THE LAW.
NO. *THIS* IS THE LAW.
ANSWER ME, OR YOUR KID WILL BE WEARING YOUR BRAINS.
PSHOWWW!
AAAAGH!

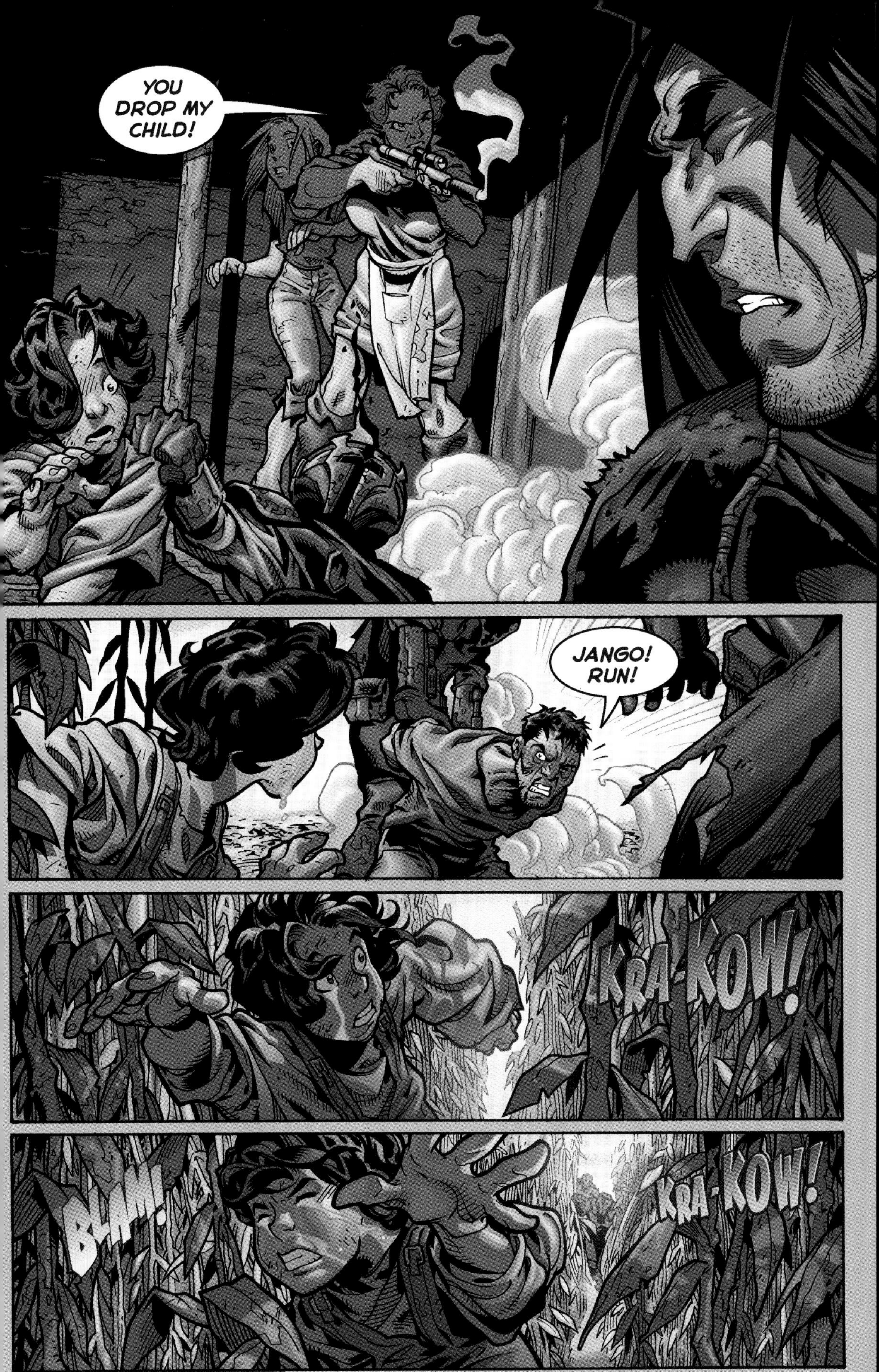
YOU DROP MY CHILD!
JANGO! RUN!
KRA-KOW!
BLAM!
KRA-KOW!

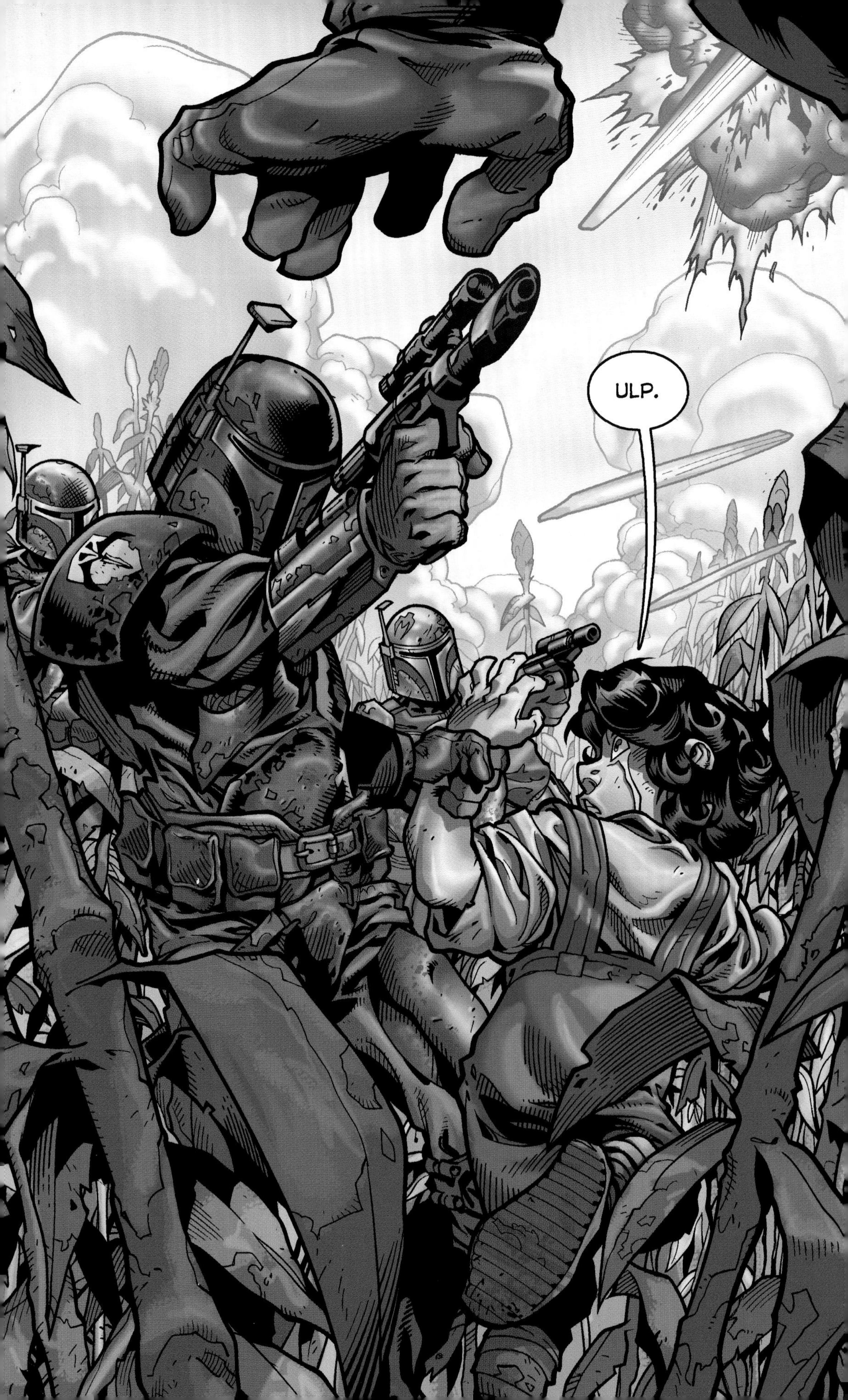
ULP.

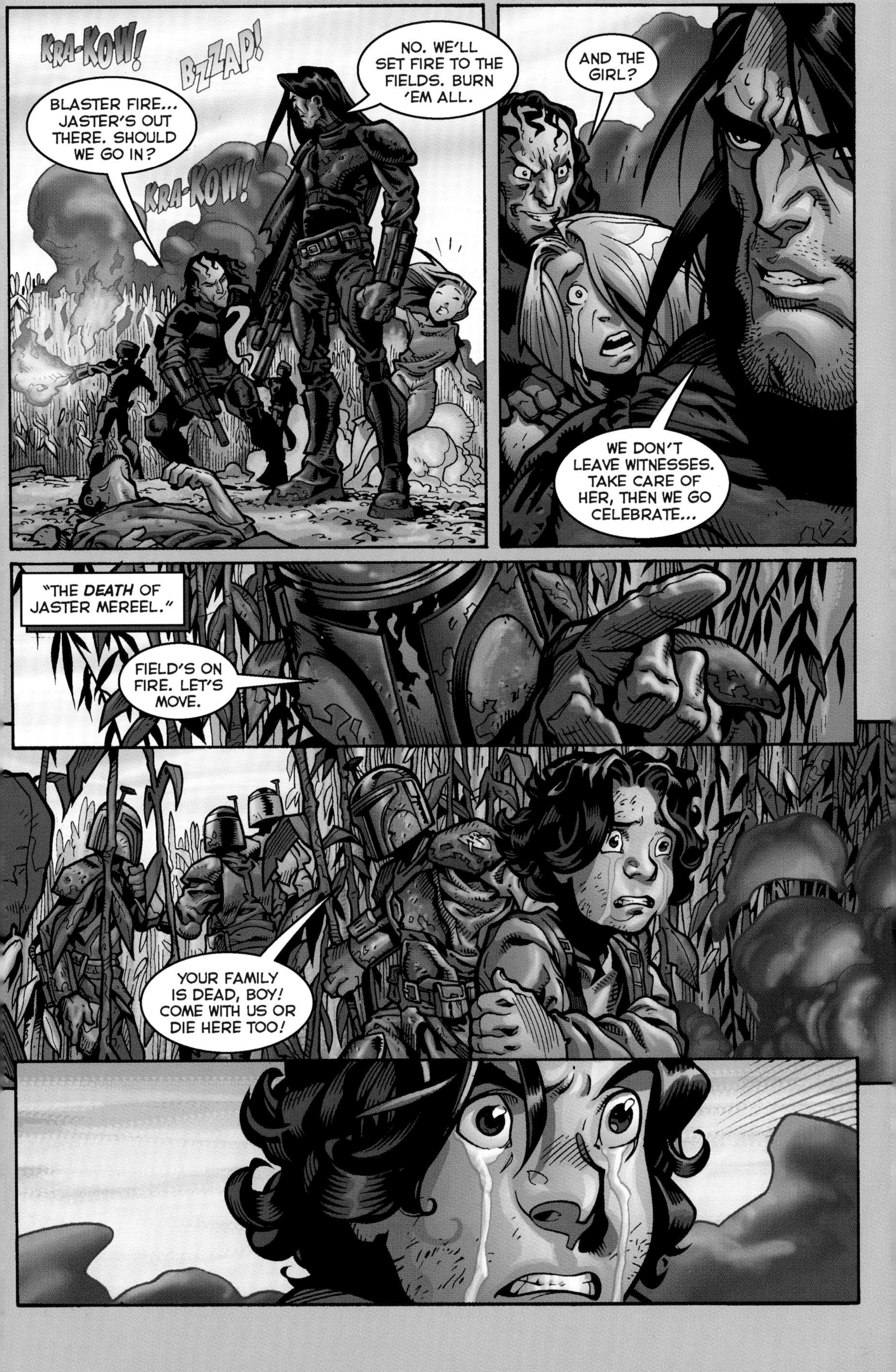
KRA-KOW!
BZZAP!
BLASTER FIRE... JASTER'S OUT THERE. SHOULD WE GO IN?
KRA-KOW!
NO. WE'LL SET FIRE TO THE FIELDS. BURN 'EM ALL.
AND THE GIRL?
WE DON'T LEAVE WITNESSES. TAKE CARE OF HER, THEN WE GO CELEBRATE...
"THE DEATH OF JASTER MEREEL."
FIELD'S ON FIRE. LET'S MOVE.
YOUR FAMILY IS DEAD, BOY! COME WITH US OR DIE HERE TOO!

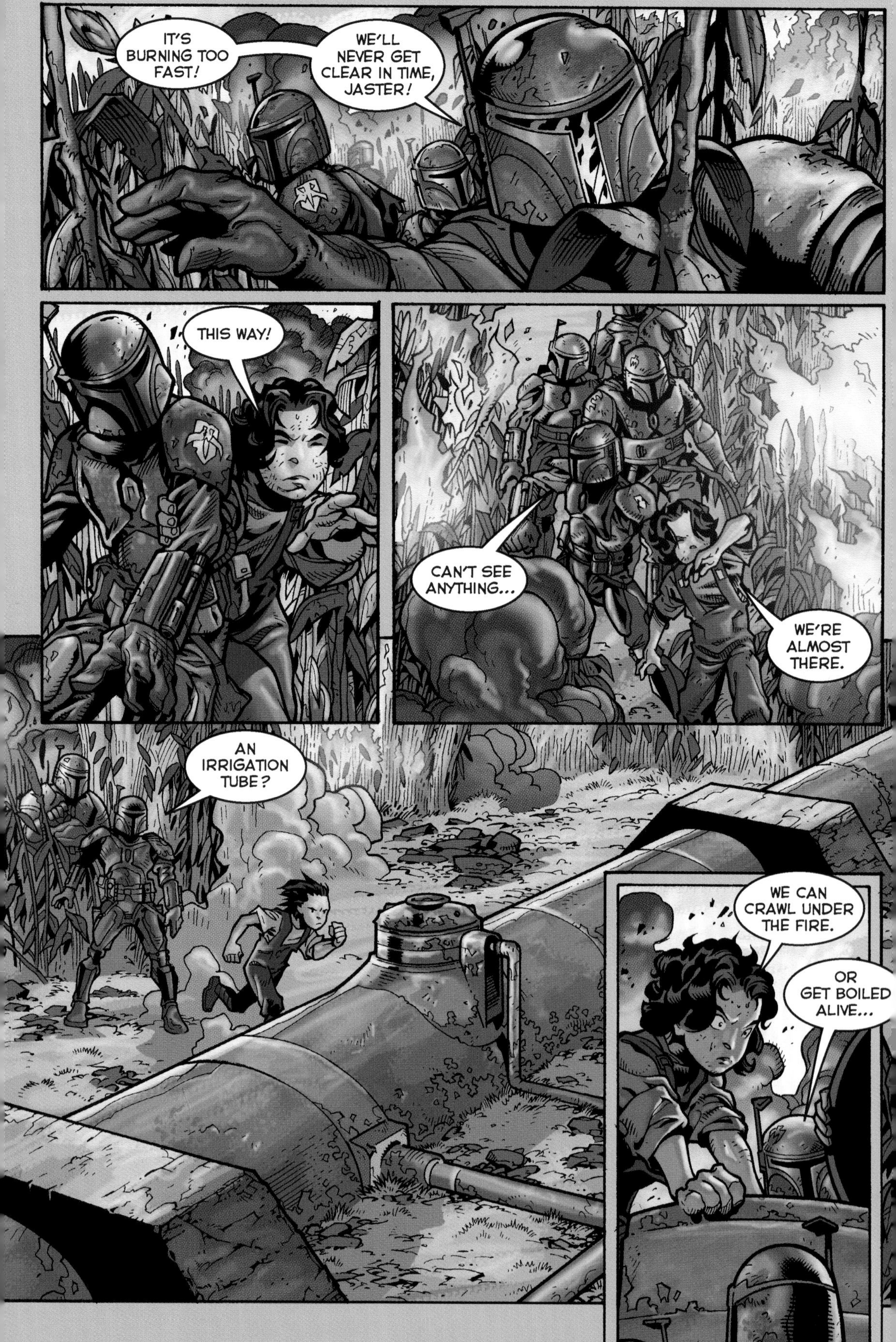
IT'S BURNING TOO FAST!
WE'LL NEVER GET CLEAR IN TIME, JASTER!
THIS WAY!
CAN'T SEE ANYTHING...
WE'RE ALMOST THERE.
AN IRRIGATION TUBE?
WE CAN CRAWL UNDER THE FIRE.
OR GET BOILED ALIVE...

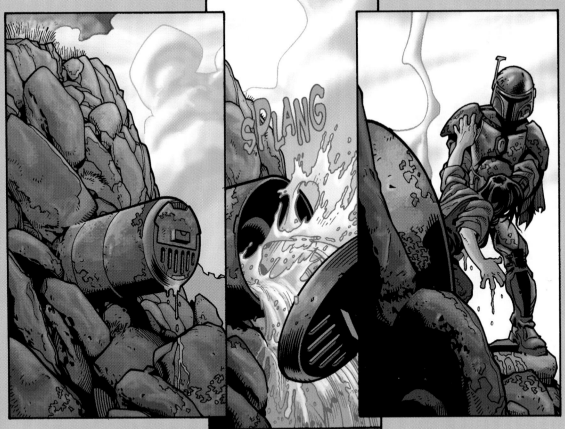

SPLANG

CHECK YOUR WEAPONS AND CATCH YOUR BREATH. WE'RE MOVING OUT AS SOON AS IT GETS DARK.

NOW, WE JUST HAVE TO FIND VIZSLA. HE'LL NEED TO RESUPPLY...

I CAN TAKE YOU TO THE CLOSEST TOWN. THEY SELL FOOD AND POWER CELLS. HE'LL BE THERE.

YOU KNOW HOW TO USE A BLASTER, BOY?

YES. MY DAD... HE TAUGHT ME TO SHOOT.

THEN HE WAS A GOOD MAN.

THE BOY COMES WITH US.

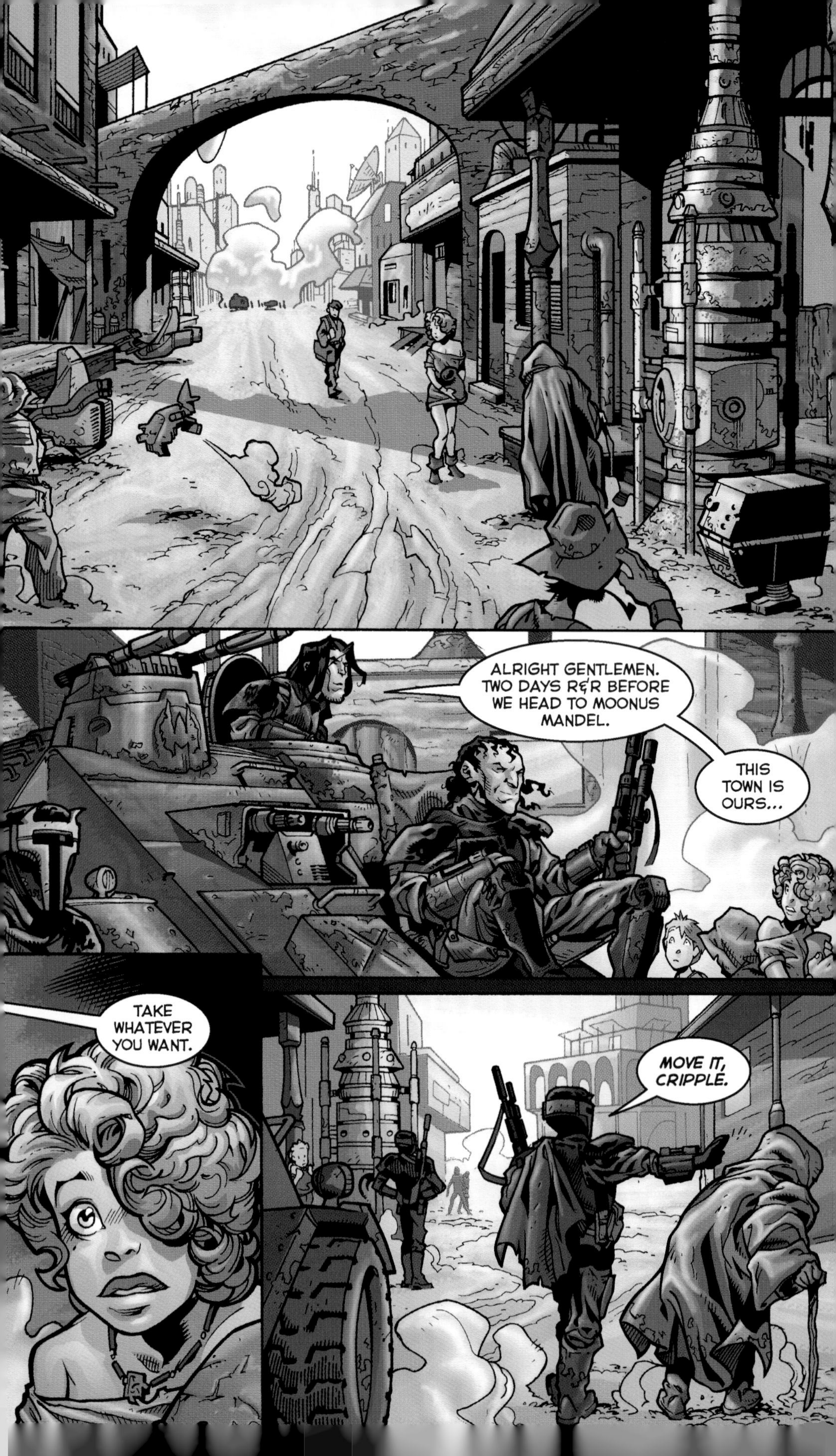
ALRIGHT GENTLEMEN. TWO DAYS R&R BEFORE WE HEAD TO MOONUS MANDEL.
THIS TOWN IS OURS...
TAKE WHATEVER YOU WANT.
MOVE IT, CRIPPLE.

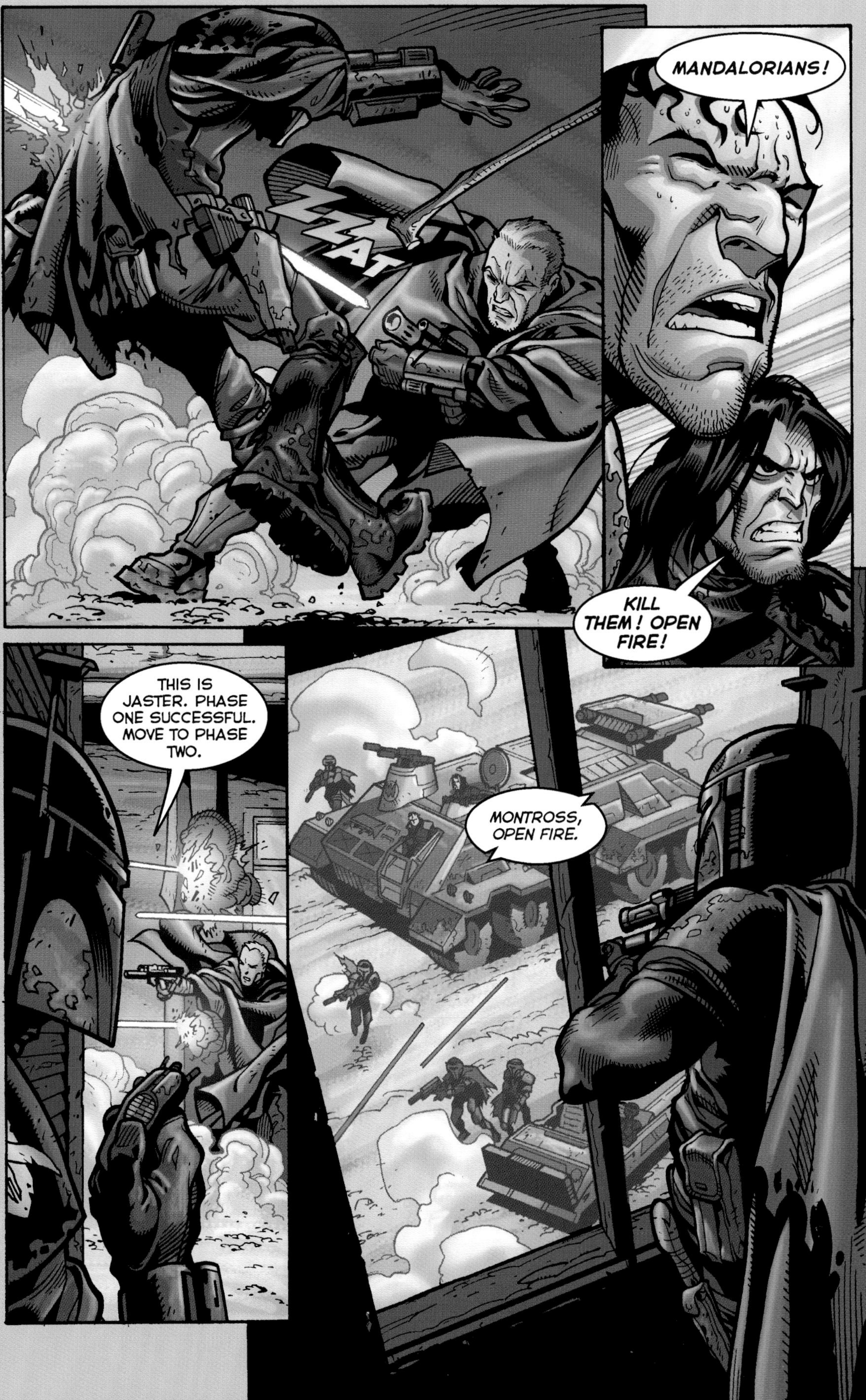

ZZAT
MANDALORIANS!
KILL THEM! OPEN FIRE!
THIS IS JASTER. PHASE ONE SUCCESSFUL. MOVE TO PHASE TWO.
MONTROSS, OPEN FIRE.

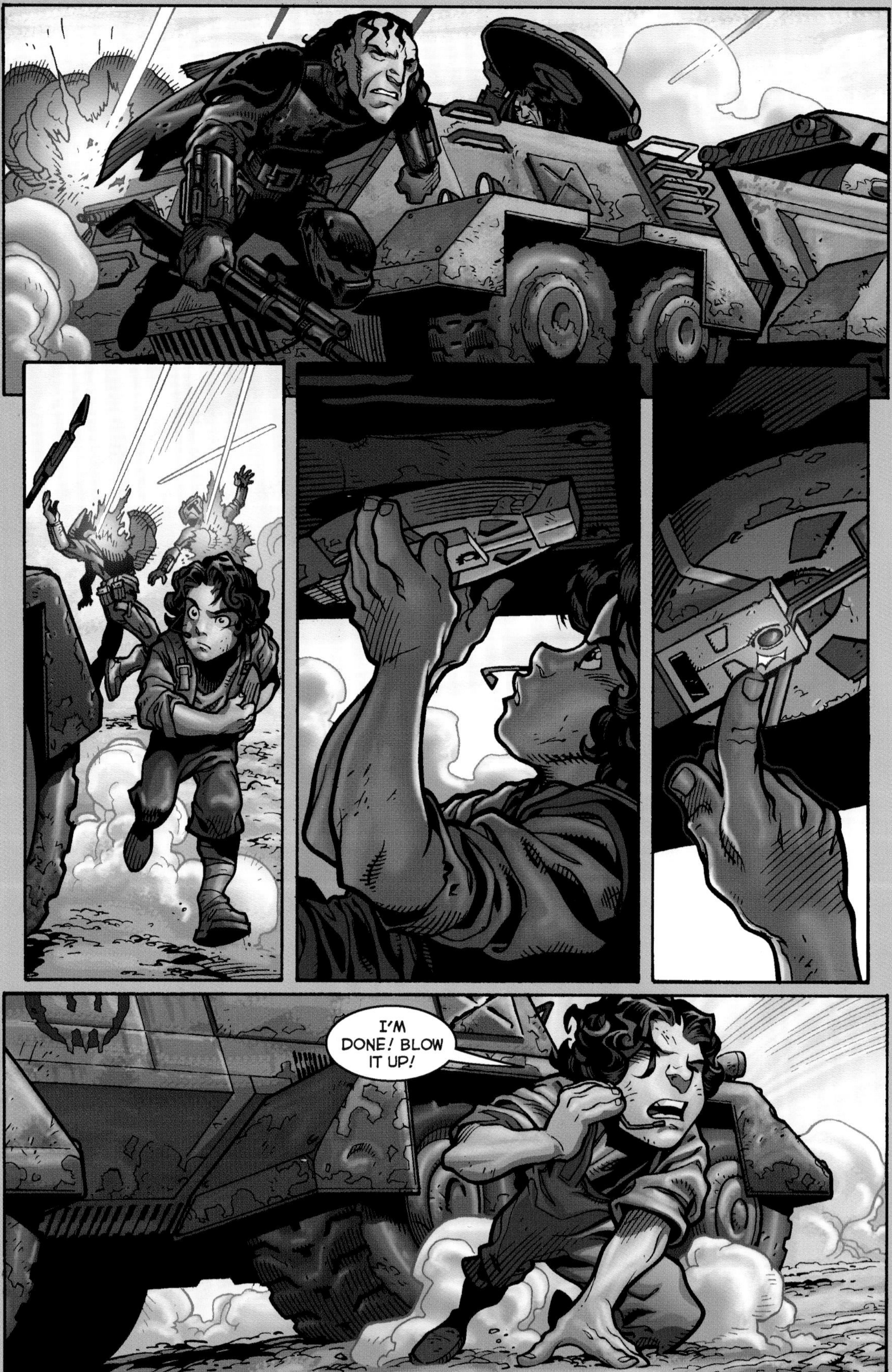
I'M DONE! BLOW IT UP!

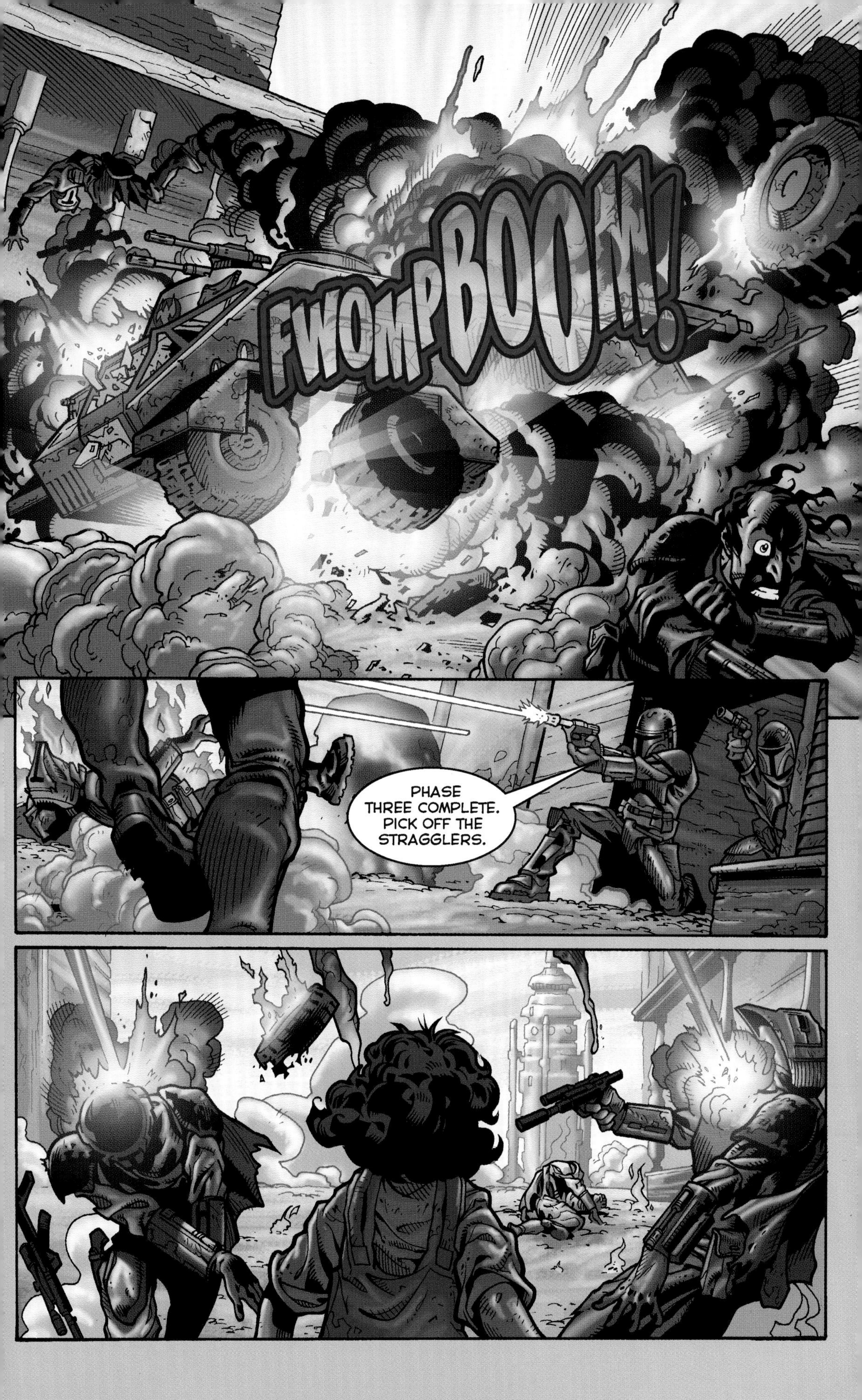
FWOMPBOOM!
PHASE THREE COMPLETE. PICK OFF THE STRAGGLERS.

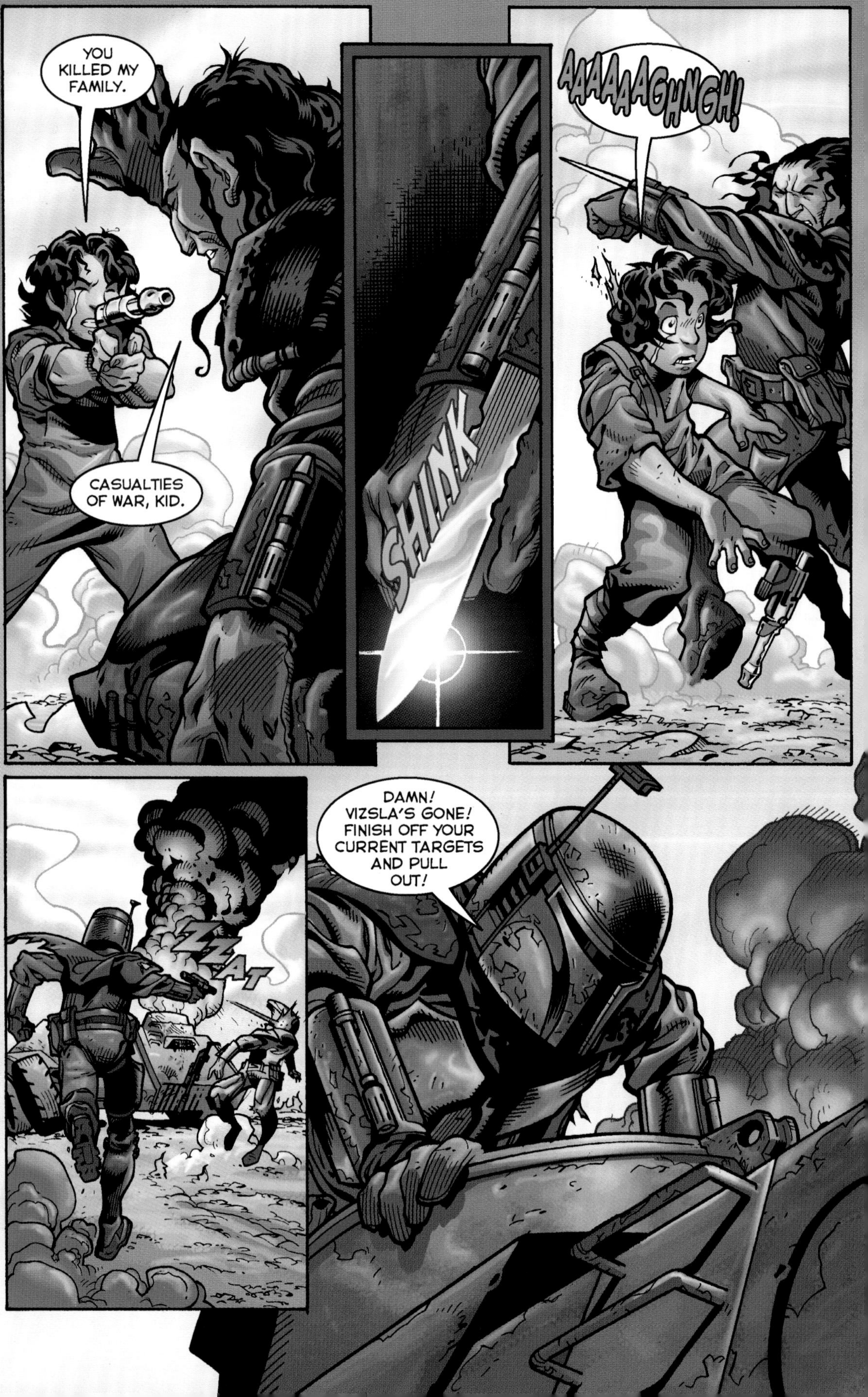
YOU KILLED MY FAMILY.
CASUALTIES OF WAR, KID.
SHINK
AAAAAAGHNGH!
ZZZAT
DAMN! VIZSLA'S GONE! FINISH OFF YOUR CURRENT TARGETS AND PULL OUT!

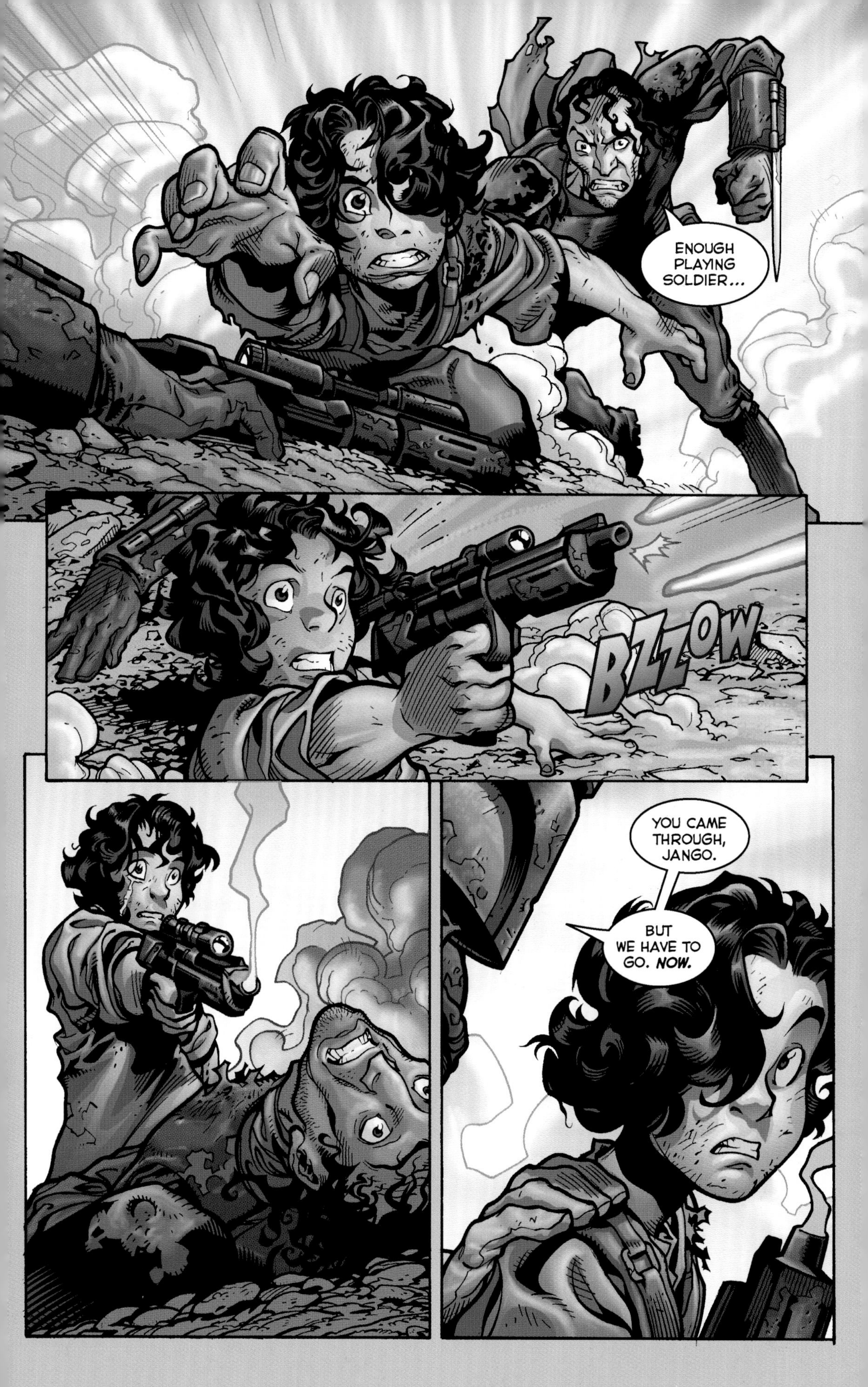
ENOUGH PLAYING SOLDIER...
BZZOW
YOU CAME THROUGH, JANGO.
BUT WE HAVE TO GO. *NOW.*

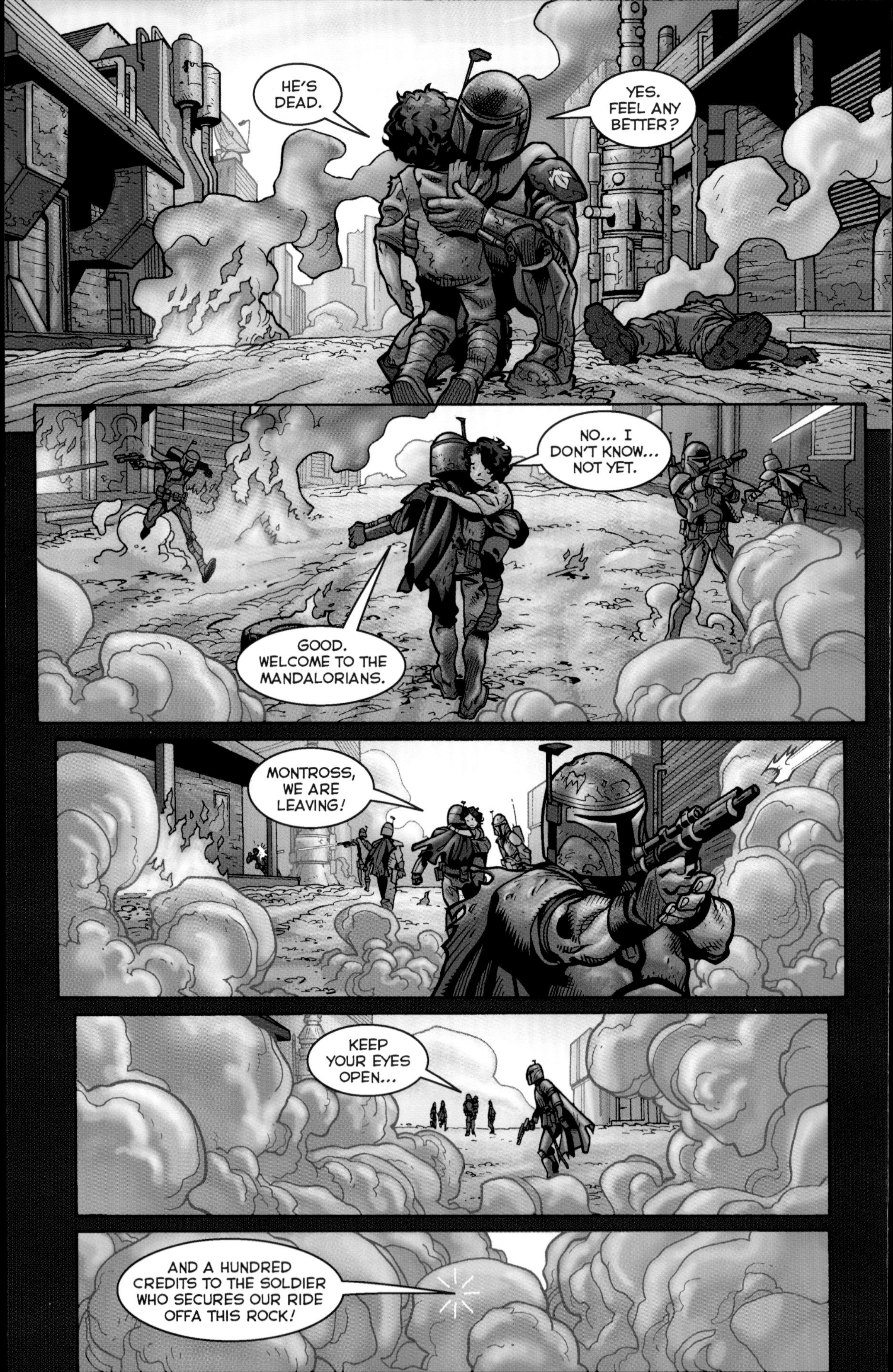
HE'S DEAD.
YES. FEEL ANY BETTER?
NO... I DON'T KNOW... NOT YET.
GOOD. WELCOME TO THE MANDALORIANS.
MONTROSS, WE ARE LEAVING!
KEEP YOUR EYES OPEN...
AND A HUNDRED CREDITS TO THE SOLDIER WHO SECURES OUR RIDE OFFA THIS ROCK!

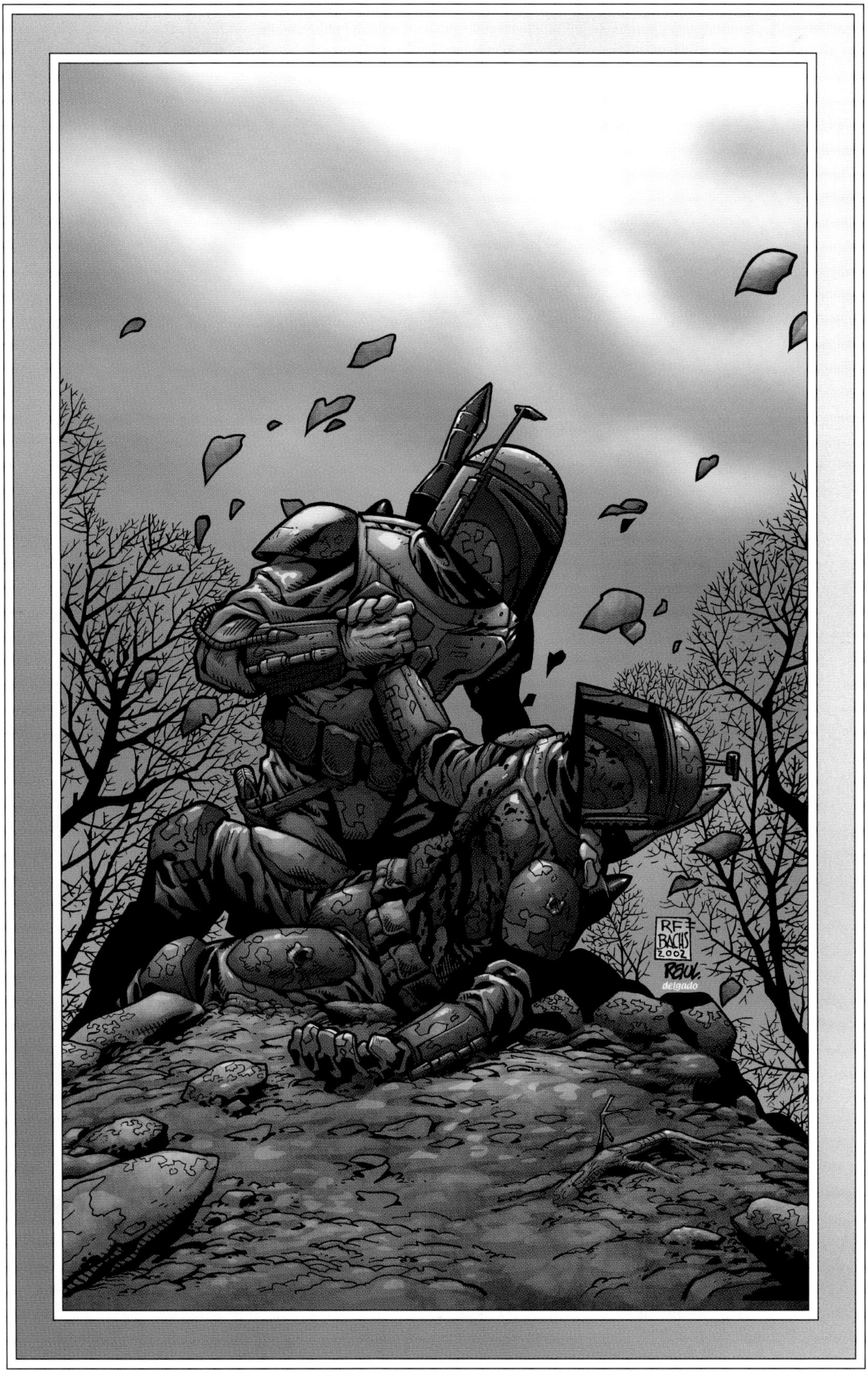
RF
BACHS
2002
RAUL
delgado

F A L L

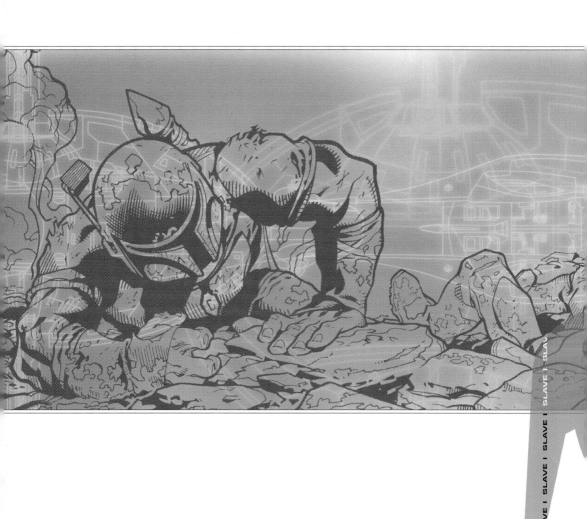

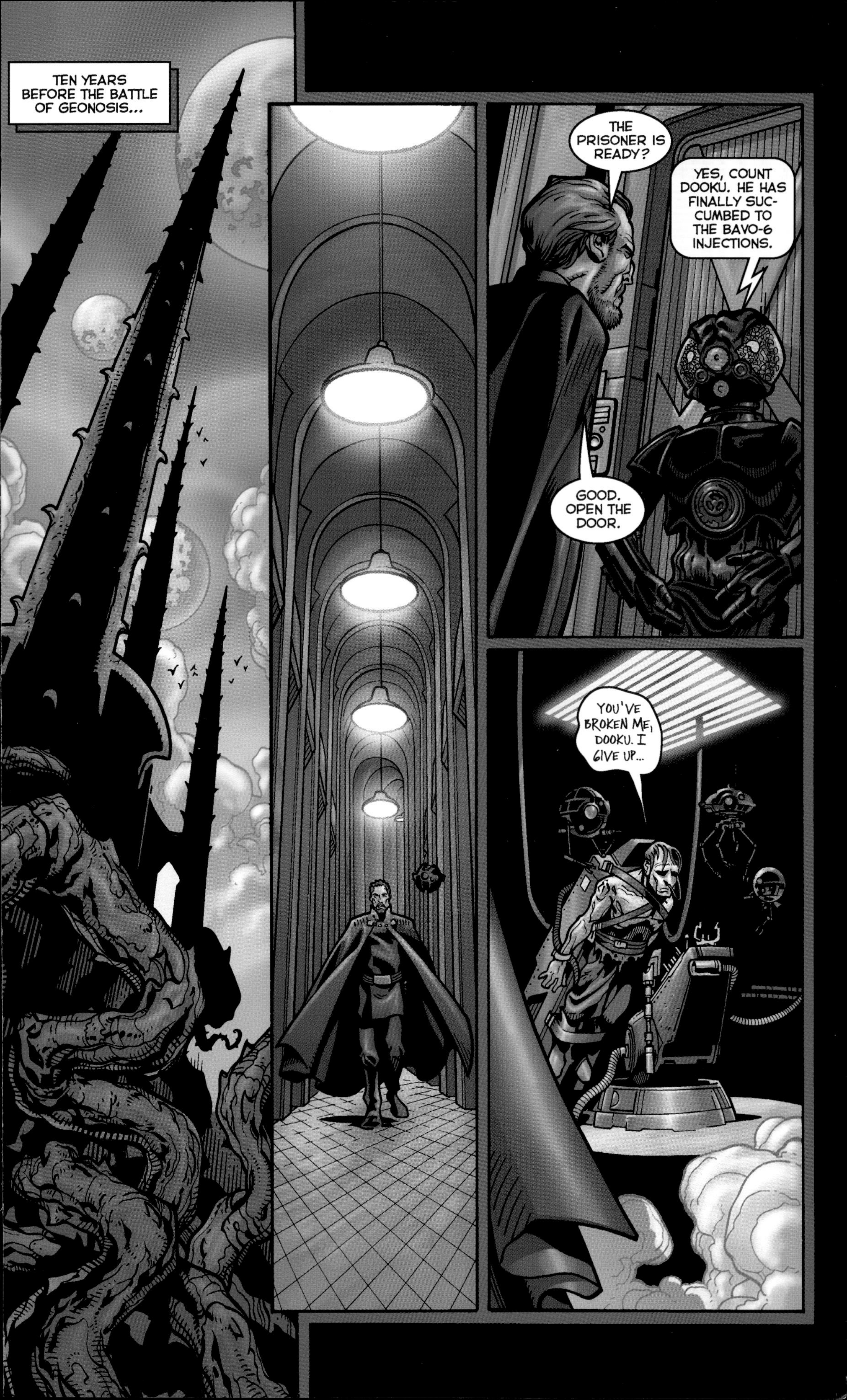
TEN YEARS BEFORE THE BATTLE OF GEONOSIS...
THE PRISONER IS READY?
YES, COUNT DOOKU. HE HAS FINALLY SUC-CUMBED TO THE BAVO-6 INJECTIONS.
GOOD. OPEN THE DOOR.
YOU'VE BROKEN ME, DOOKU. I GIVE UP...

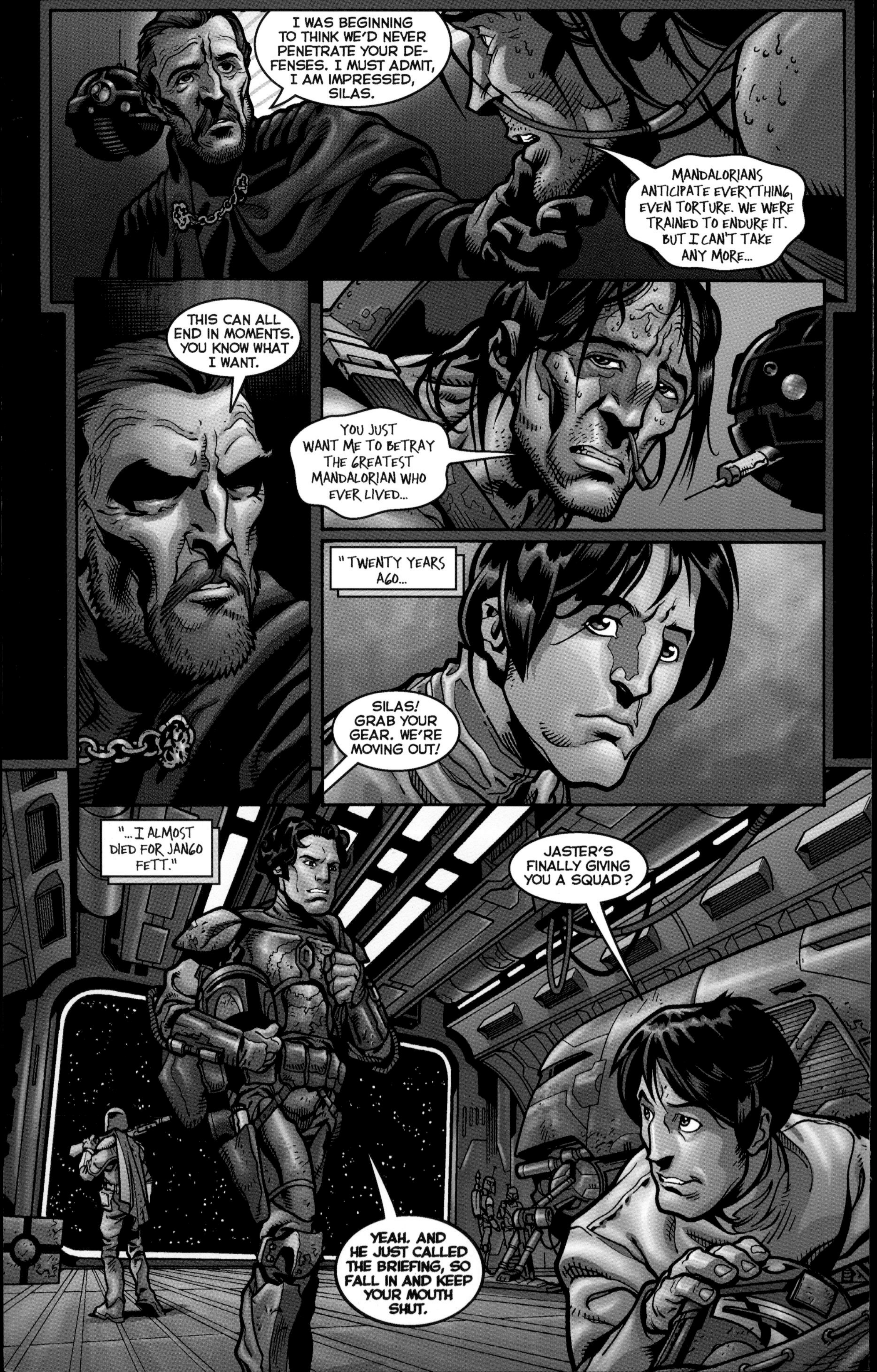
I WAS BEGINNING TO THINK WE'D NEVER PENETRATE YOUR DE-FENSES. I MUST ADMIT, I AM IMPRESSED, SILAS.
MANDALORIANS ANTICIPATE EVERYTHING, EVEN TORTURE. WE WERE TRAINED TO ENDURE IT. BUT I CAN'T TAKE ANY MORE...
THIS CAN ALL END IN MOMENTS. YOU KNOW WHAT I WANT.
YOU JUST WANT ME TO BETRAY THE GREATEST MANDALORIAN WHO EVER LIVED...
"TWENTY YEARS AGO...
SILAS! GRAB YOUR GEAR. WE'RE MOVING OUT!
"...I ALMOST DIED FOR JANGO FETT."
JASTER'S FINALLY GIVING YOU A SQUAD?
YEAH. AND HE JUST CALLED THE BRIEFING, SO FALL IN AND KEEP YOUR MOUTH SHUT.

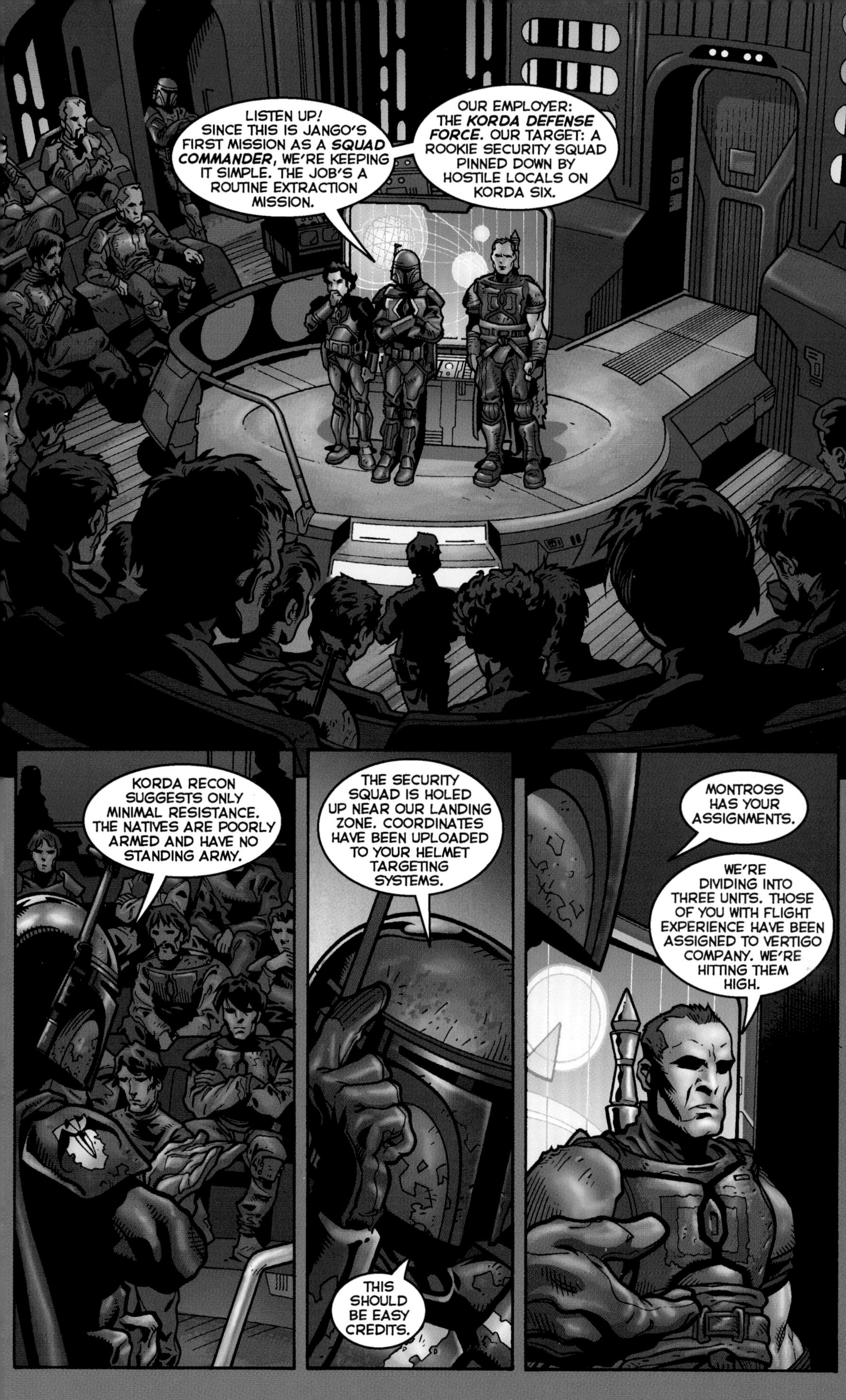
LISTEN UP! SINCE THIS IS JANGO'S FIRST MISSION AS A **SQUAD COMMANDER**, WE'RE KEEPING IT SIMPLE. THE JOB'S A ROUTINE EXTRACTION MISSION.
OUR EMPLOYER: THE **KORDA DEFENSE FORCE**. OUR TARGET: A ROOKIE SECURITY SQUAD PINNED DOWN BY HOSTILE LOCALS ON KORDA SIX.
KORDA RECON SUGGESTS ONLY MINIMAL RESISTANCE. THE NATIVES ARE POORLY ARMED AND HAVE NO STANDING ARMY.
THE SECURITY SQUAD IS HOLED UP NEAR OUR LANDING ZONE. COORDINATES HAVE BEEN UPLOADED TO YOUR HELMET TARGETING SYSTEMS.
THIS SHOULD BE EASY CREDITS.
MONTROSS HAS YOUR ASSIGNMENTS.
WE'RE DIVIDING INTO THREE UNITS. THOSE OF YOU WITH FLIGHT EXPERIENCE HAVE BEEN ASSIGNED TO VERTIGO COMPANY. WE'RE HITTING THEM HIGH.

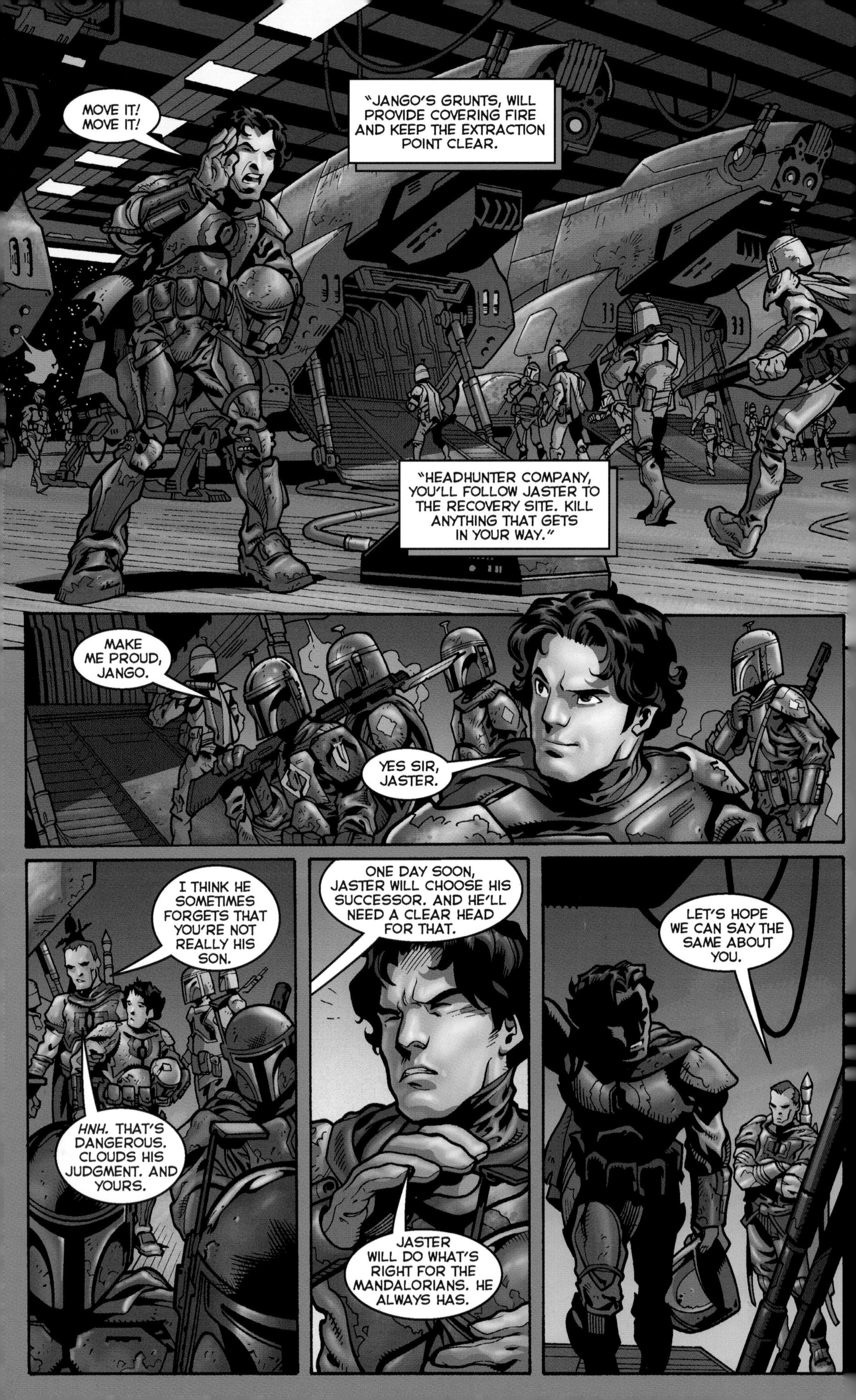
MOVE IT! MOVE IT!
"JANGO'S GRUNTS, WILL PROVIDE COVERING FIRE AND KEEP THE EXTRACTION POINT CLEAR.
"HEADHUNTER COMPANY, YOU'LL FOLLOW JASTER TO THE RECOVERY SITE. KILL ANYTHING THAT GETS IN YOUR WAY."
MAKE ME PROUD, JANGO.
YES SIR, JASTER.
I THINK HE SOMETIMES FORGETS THAT YOU'RE NOT REALLY HIS SON.
HNH. THAT'S DANGEROUS. CLOUDS HIS JUDGMENT. AND YOURS.
ONE DAY SOON, JASTER WILL CHOOSE HIS SUCCESSOR. AND HE'LL NEED A CLEAR HEAD FOR THAT.
JASTER WILL DO WHAT'S RIGHT FOR THE MANDALORIANS. HE ALWAYS HAS.
LET'S HOPE WE CAN SAY THE SAME ABOUT YOU.

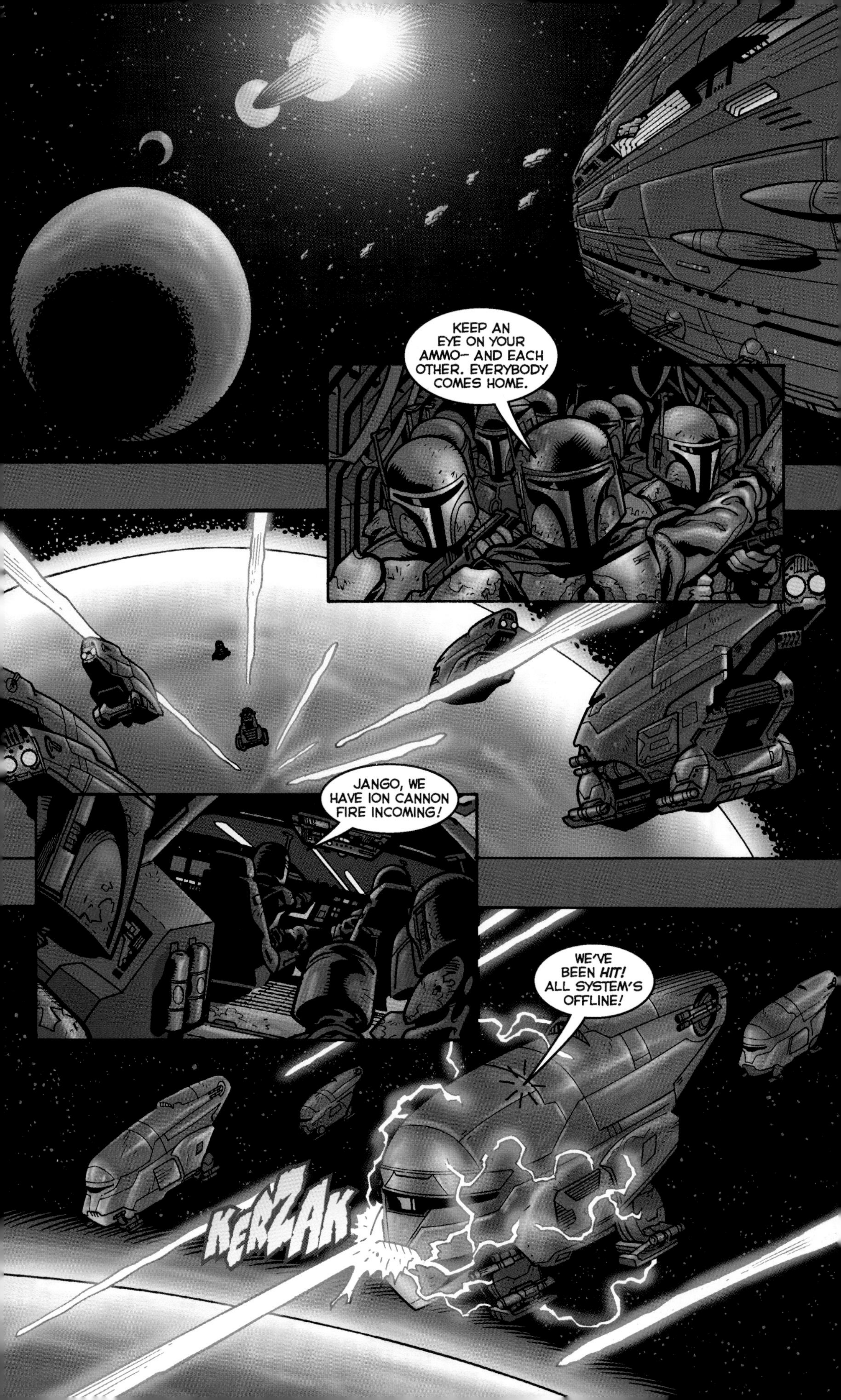
KEEP AN EYE ON YOUR AMMO— AND EACH OTHER. EVERYBODY COMES HOME.
JANGO, WE HAVE ION CANNON FIRE INCOMING!
WE'VE BEEN HIT! ALL SYSTEM'S OFFLINE!
KERZAK

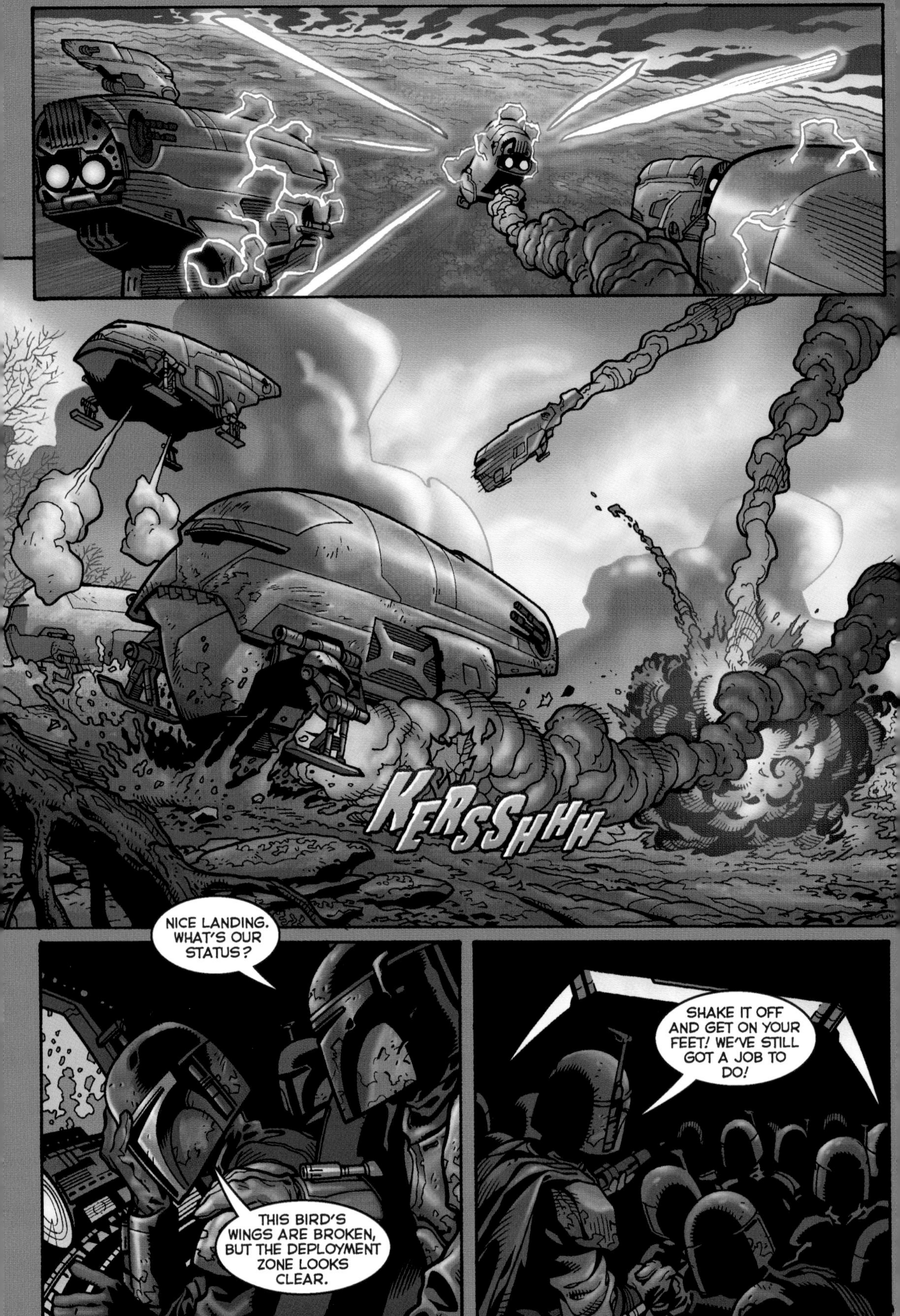
KERSSHHH
NICE LANDING. WHAT'S OUR STATUS?
THIS BIRD'S WINGS ARE BROKEN, BUT THE DEPLOYMENT ZONE LOOKS CLEAR.
SHAKE IT OFF AND GET ON YOUR FEET! WE'VE STILL GOT A JOB TO DO!

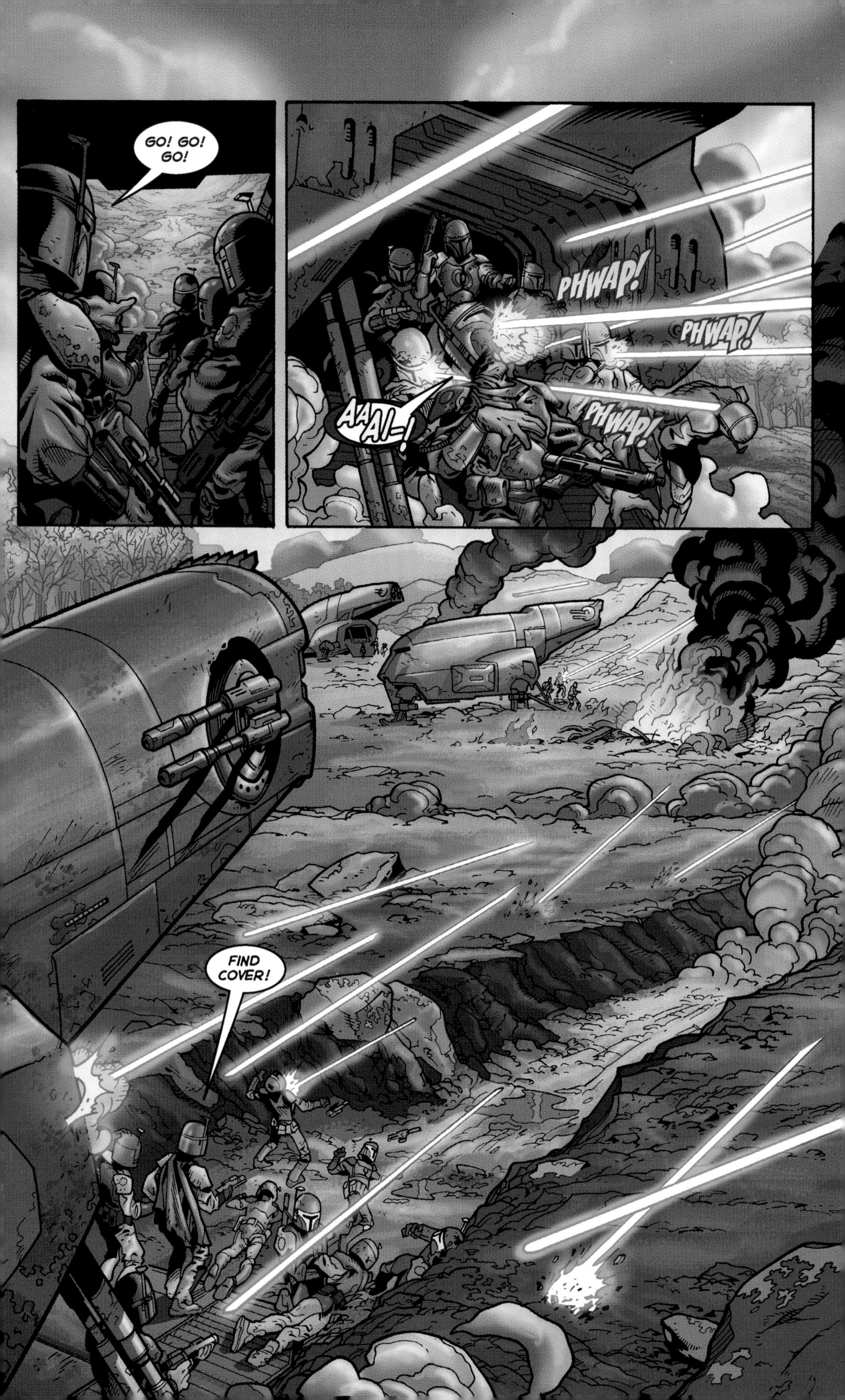
GO! GO! GO!
PHWAP!
PHWAP!
AAAI--!
PHWAP!
FIND COVER!

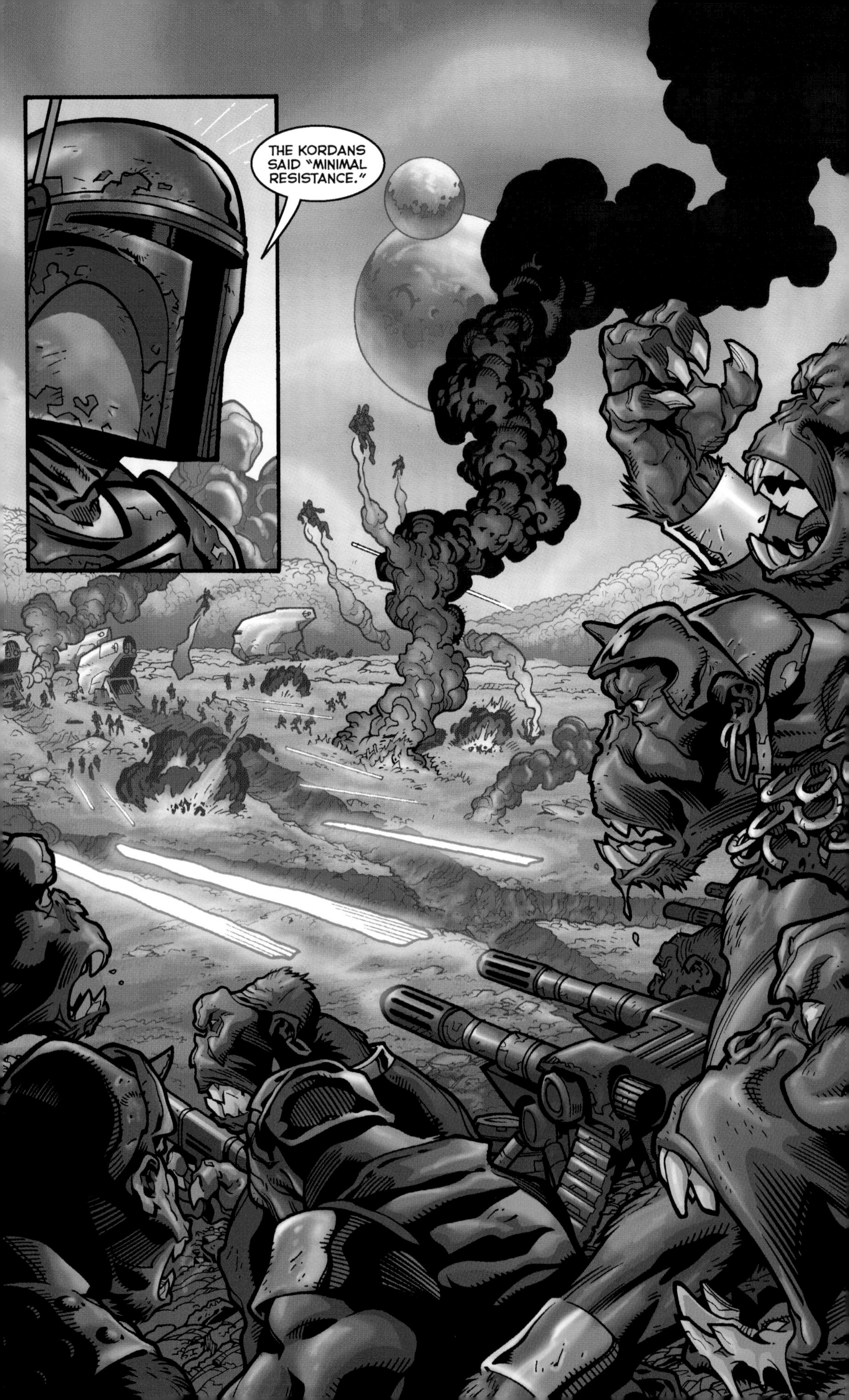
THE KORDANS SAID "MINIMAL RESISTANCE."

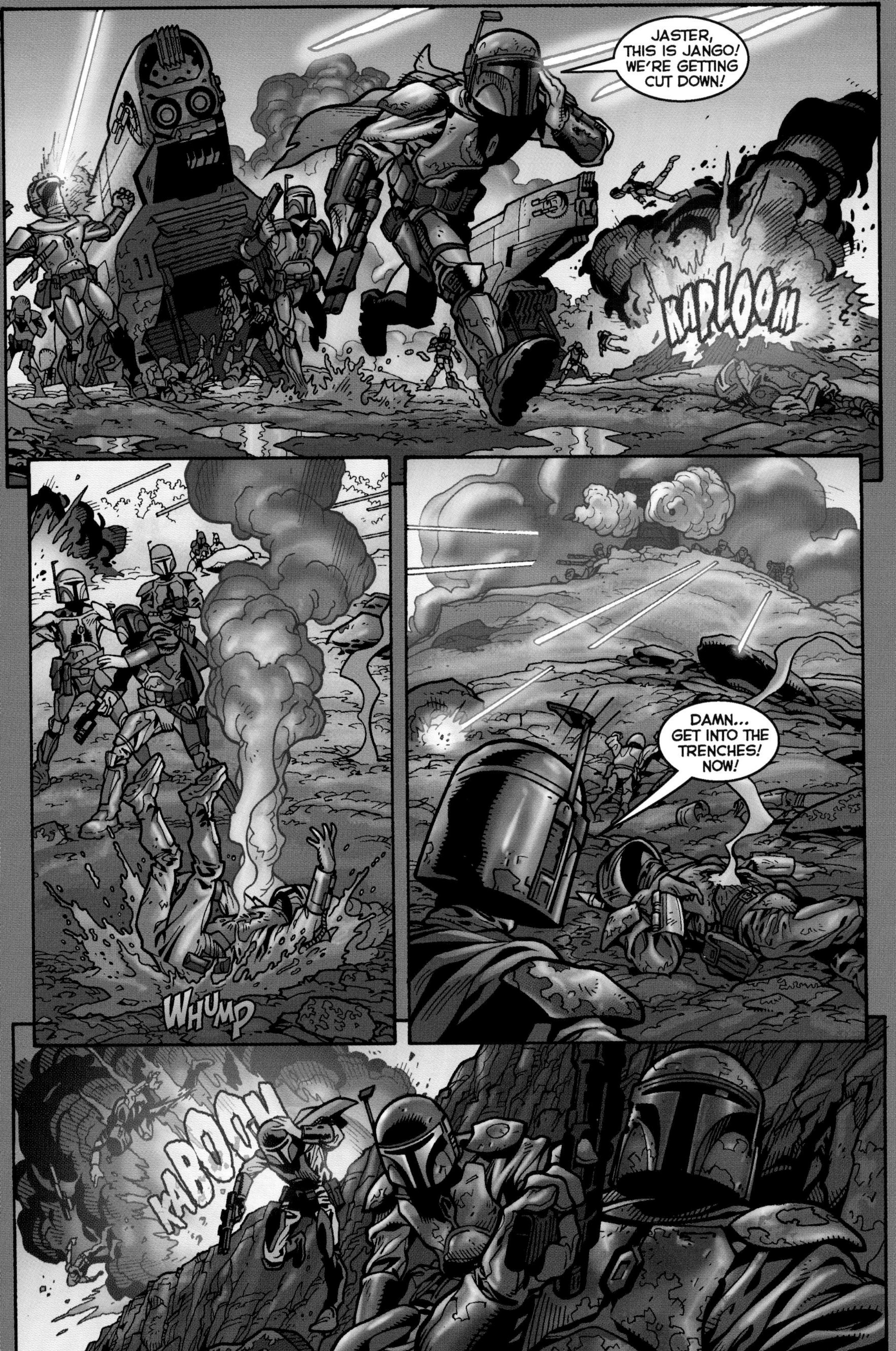
JASTER, THIS IS JANGO! WE'RE GETTING CUT DOWN!
KAPLOOM
WHUMP
DAMN... GET INTO THE TRENCHES! NOW!
KABOOM

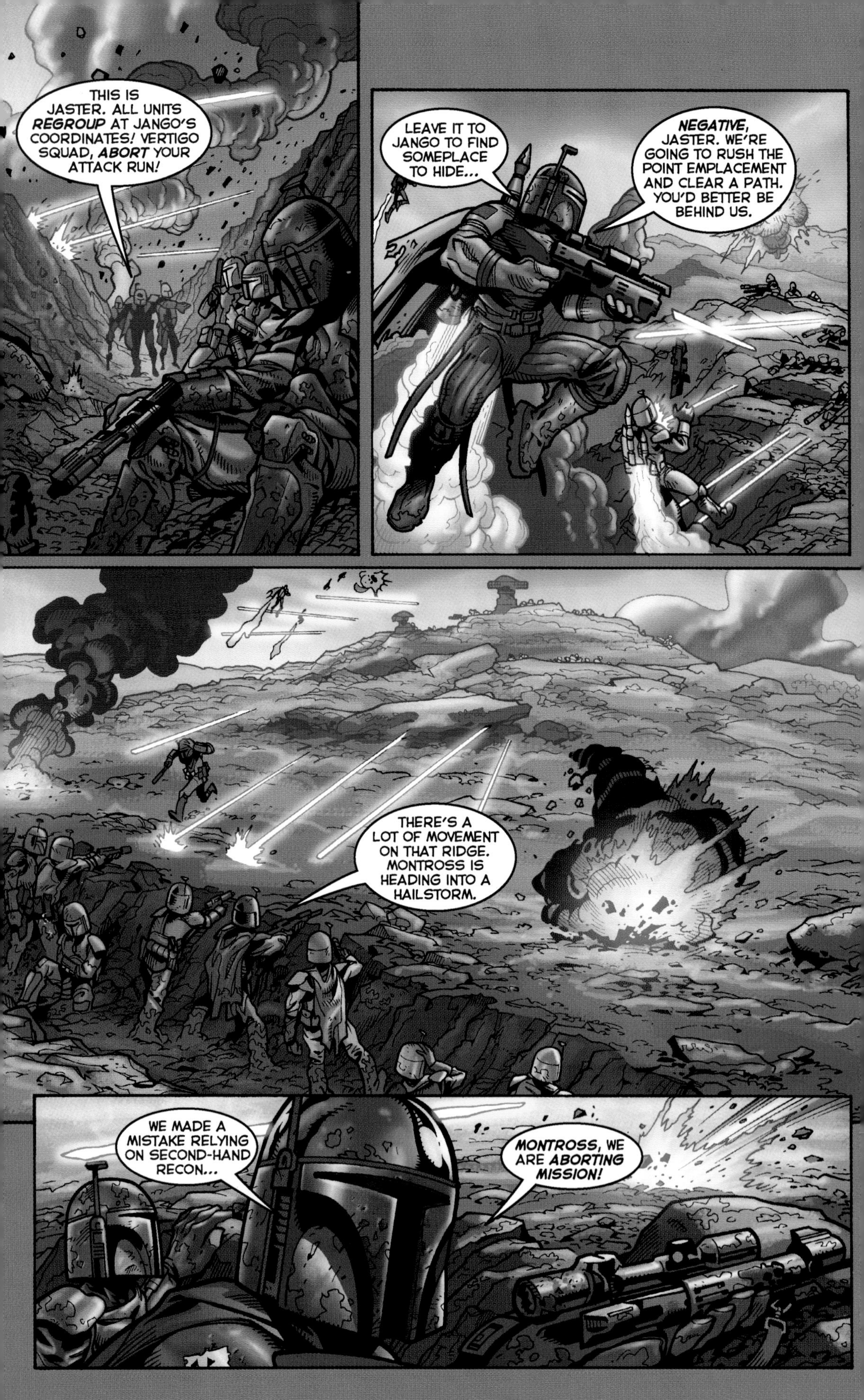
THIS IS JASTER. ALL UNITS *REGROUP* AT JANGO'S COORDINATES! VERTIGO SQUAD, *ABORT* YOUR ATTACK RUN!
LEAVE IT TO JANGO TO FIND SOMEPLACE TO HIDE...
NEGATIVE, JASTER. WE'RE GOING TO RUSH THE POINT EMPLACEMENT AND CLEAR A PATH. YOU'D BETTER BE BEHIND US.
THERE'S A LOT OF MOVEMENT ON THAT RIDGE. MONTROSS IS HEADING INTO A HAILSTORM.
WE MADE A MISTAKE RELYING ON SECOND-HAND RECON...
MONTROSS, WE ARE *ABORTING MISSION!*

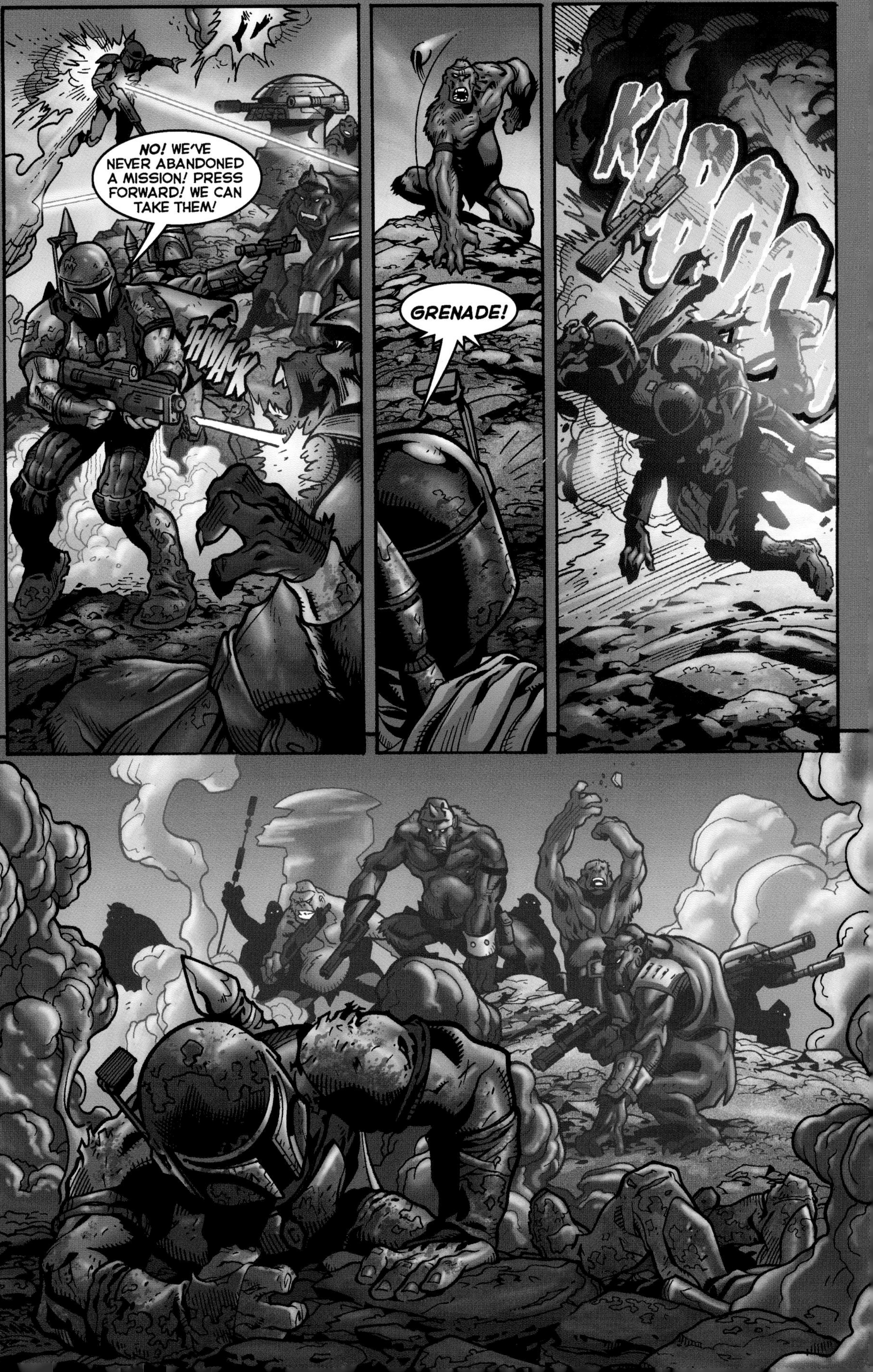
NO! WE'VE NEVER ABANDONED A MISSION! PRESS FORWARD! WE CAN TAKE THEM!
THWACK
GRENADE!
KABOO

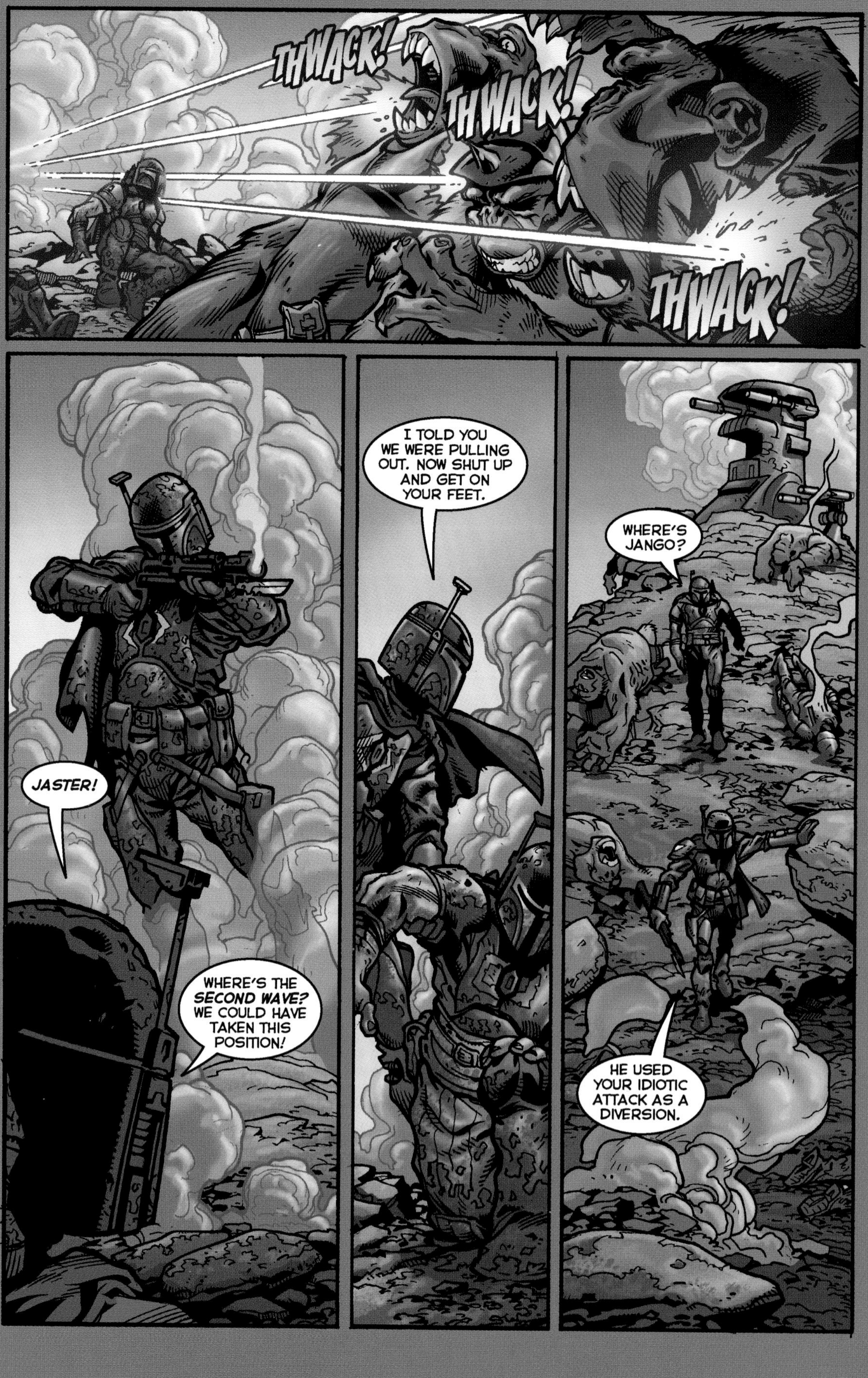
THWACK!
THWACK!
THWACK!
JASTER!
WHERE'S THE SECOND WAVE? WE COULD HAVE TAKEN THIS POSITION!
I TOLD YOU WE WERE PULLING OUT. NOW SHUT UP AND GET ON YOUR FEET.
WHERE'S JANGO?
HE USED YOUR IDIOTIC ATTACK AS A DIVERSION.

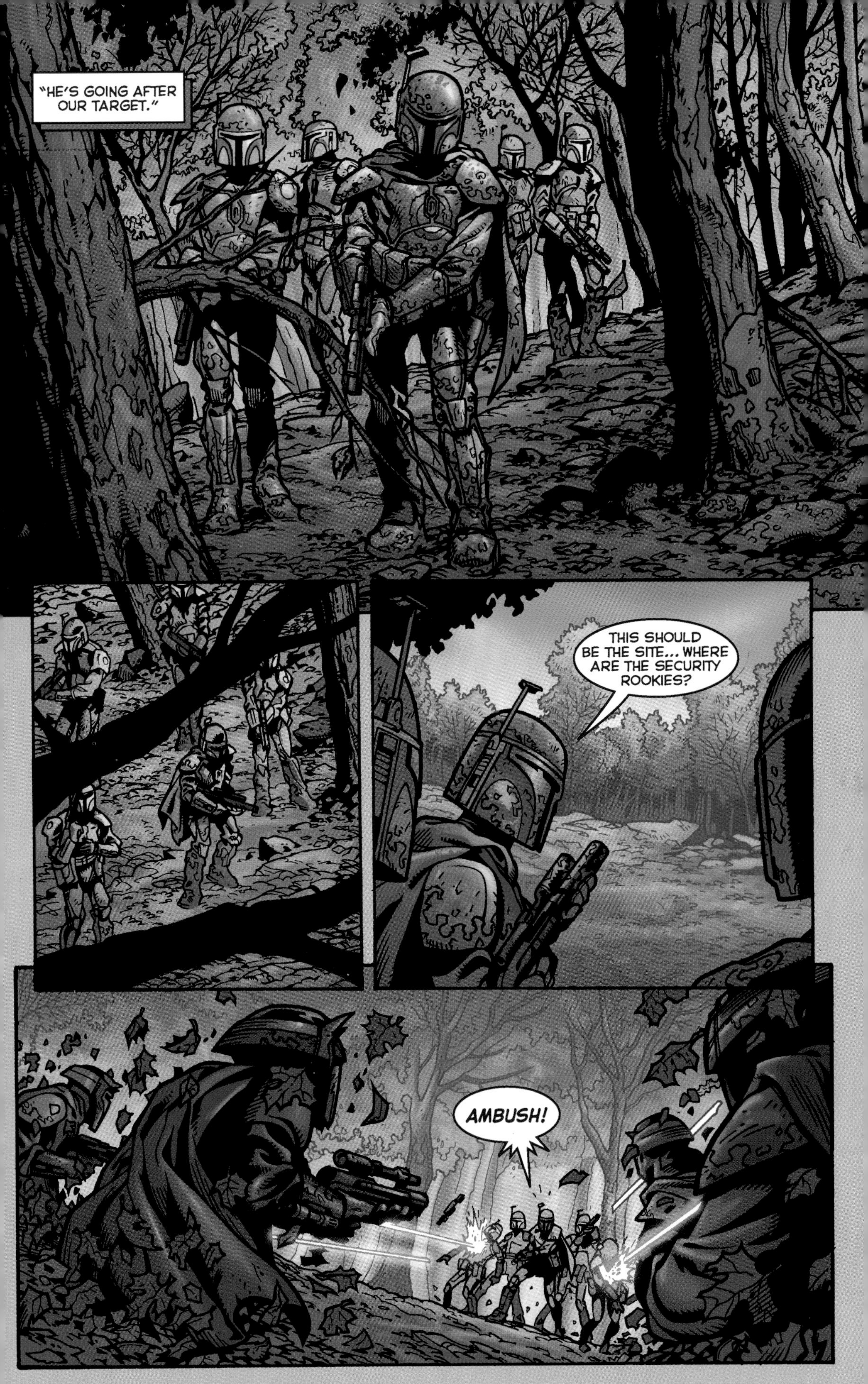
"HE'S GOING AFTER OUR TARGET."
THIS SHOULD BE THE SITE... WHERE ARE THE SECURITY ROOKIES?
AMBUSH!

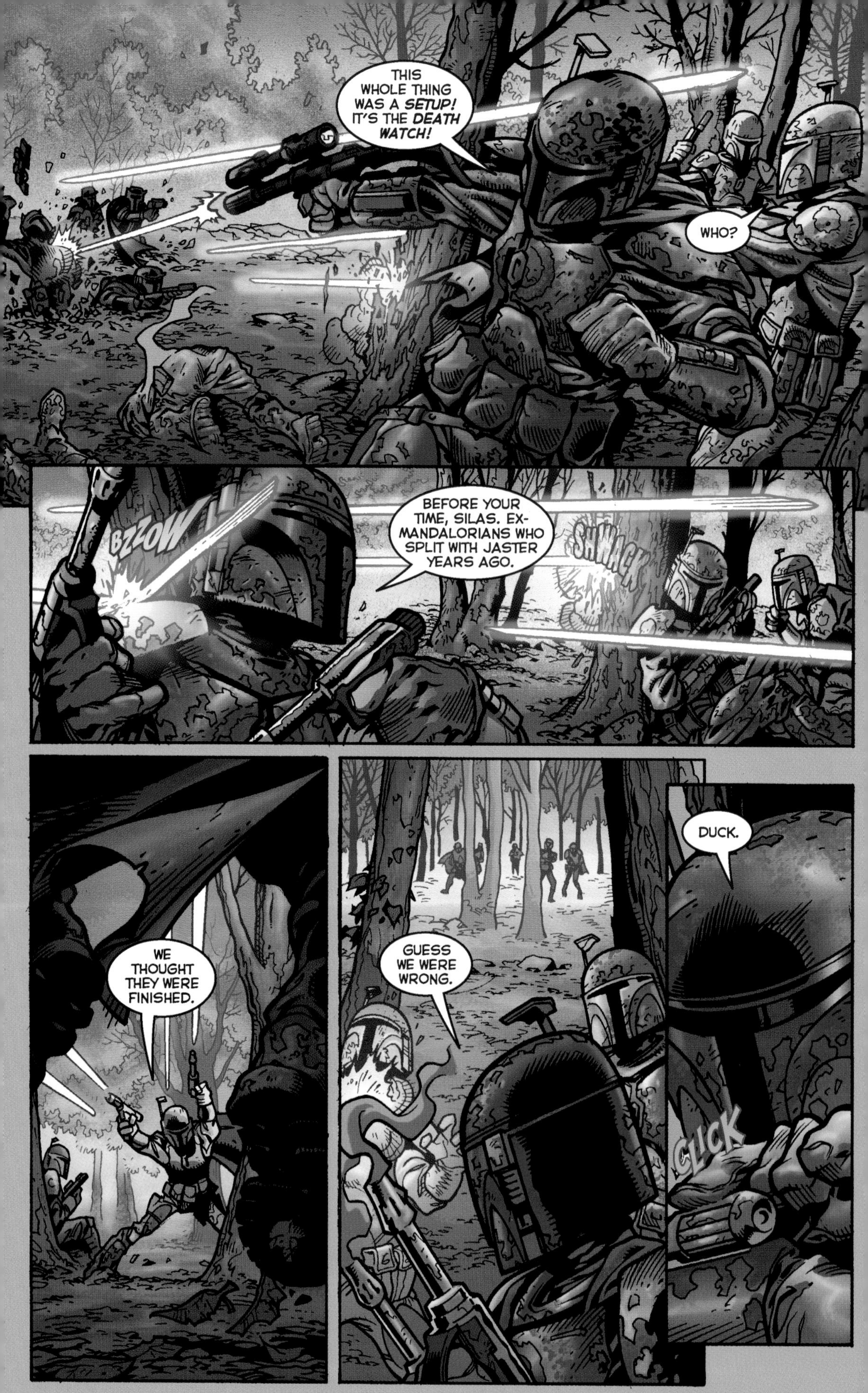
THIS WHOLE THING WAS A *SETUP!* IT'S THE *DEATH WATCH!*
WHO?
BZZOW
BEFORE YOUR TIME, SILAS. EX-MANDALORIANS WHO SPLIT WITH JASTER YEARS AGO.
SHWACK
WE THOUGHT THEY WERE FINISHED.
GUESS WE WERE WRONG.
DUCK.
CLICK

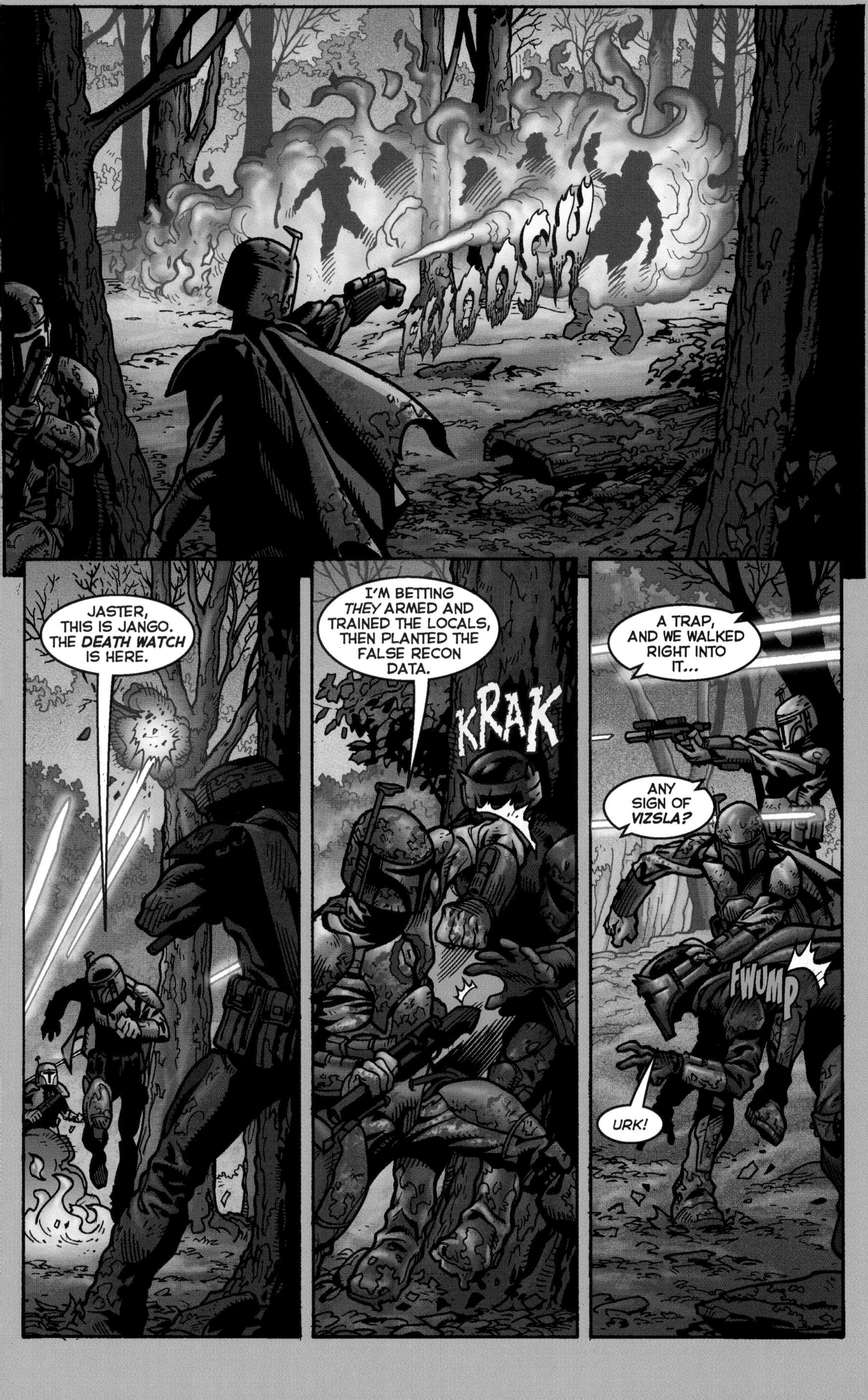
FWOOSH!
JASTER, THIS IS JANGO. THE DEATH WATCH IS HERE.
I'M BETTING THEY ARMED AND TRAINED THE LOCALS, THEN PLANTED THE FALSE RECON DATA.
KRAK
A TRAP, AND WE WALKED RIGHT INTO IT...
ANY SIGN OF VIZSLA?
FWUMP
URK!

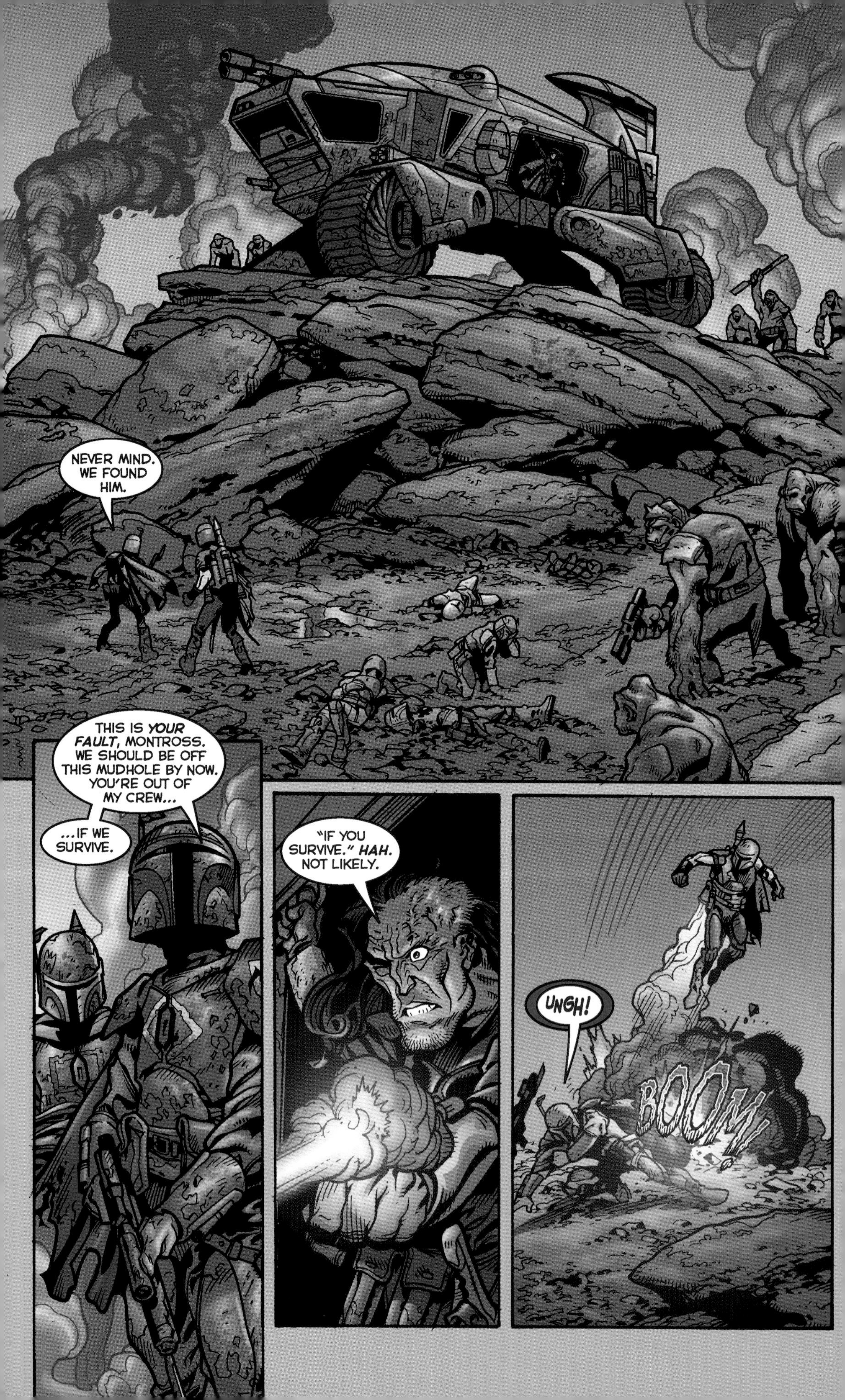
NEVER MIND. WE FOUND HIM.
THIS IS *YOUR FAULT*, MONTROSS. WE SHOULD BE OFF THIS MUDHOLE BY NOW. YOU'RE OUT OF MY CREW...
...IF WE SURVIVE.
"IF YOU SURVIVE." *HAH.* NOT LIKELY.
UNGH!
BOOM!

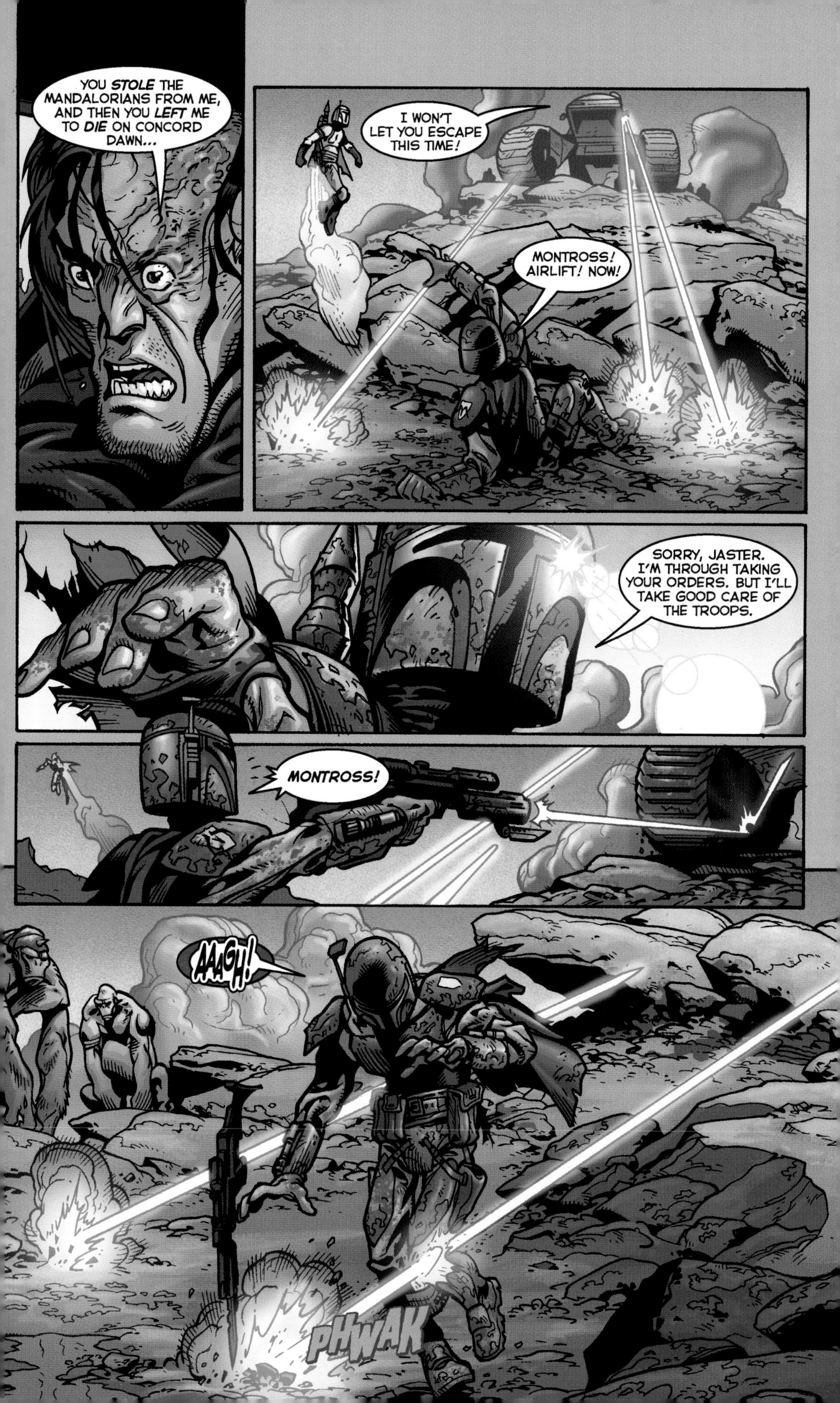

YOU STOLE THE MANDALORIANS FROM ME, AND THEN YOU LEFT ME TO DIE ON CONCORD DAWN...
I WON'T LET YOU ESCAPE THIS TIME!
MONTROSS! AIRLIFT! NOW!
SORRY, JASTER. I'M THROUGH TAKING YOUR ORDERS. BUT I'LL TAKE GOOD CARE OF THE TROOPS.
MONTROSS!
AAAGH!
PHWAK

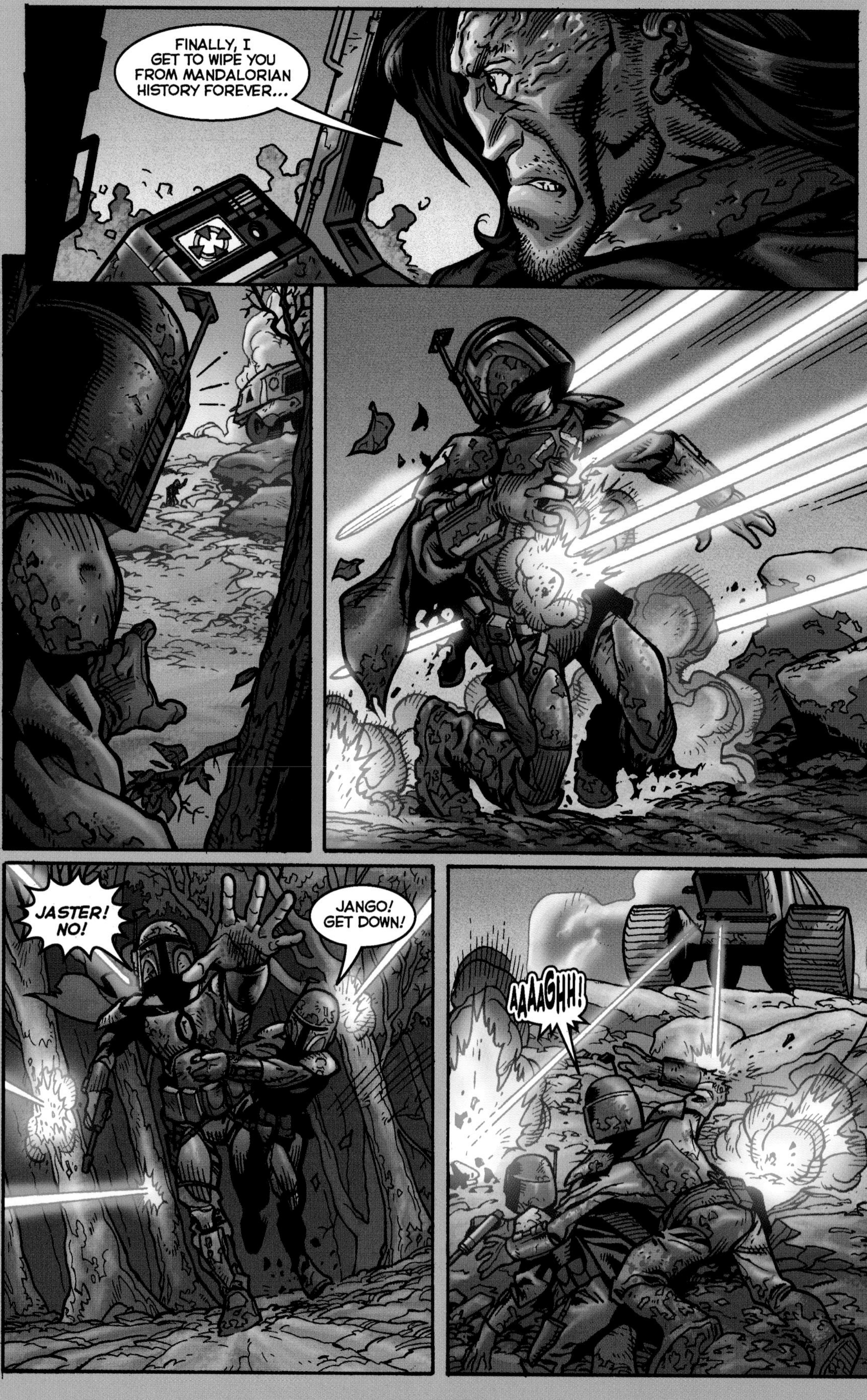
FINALLY, I GET TO WIPE YOU FROM MANDALORIAN HISTORY FOREVER...
JASTER! NO!
JANGO! GET DOWN!
AAAAGHH!

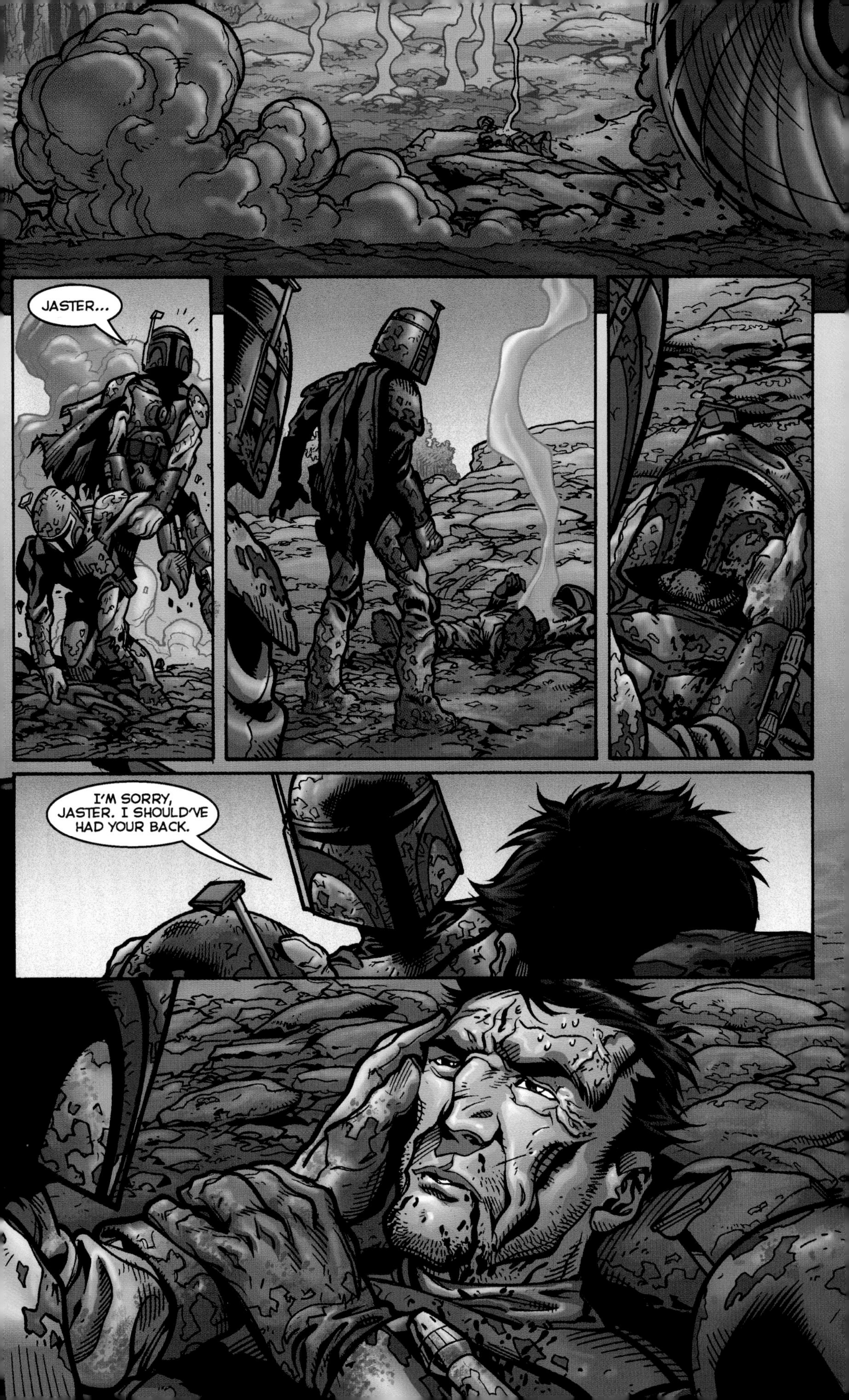
JASTER...
I'M SORRY, JASTER. I SHOULD'VE HAD YOUR BACK.

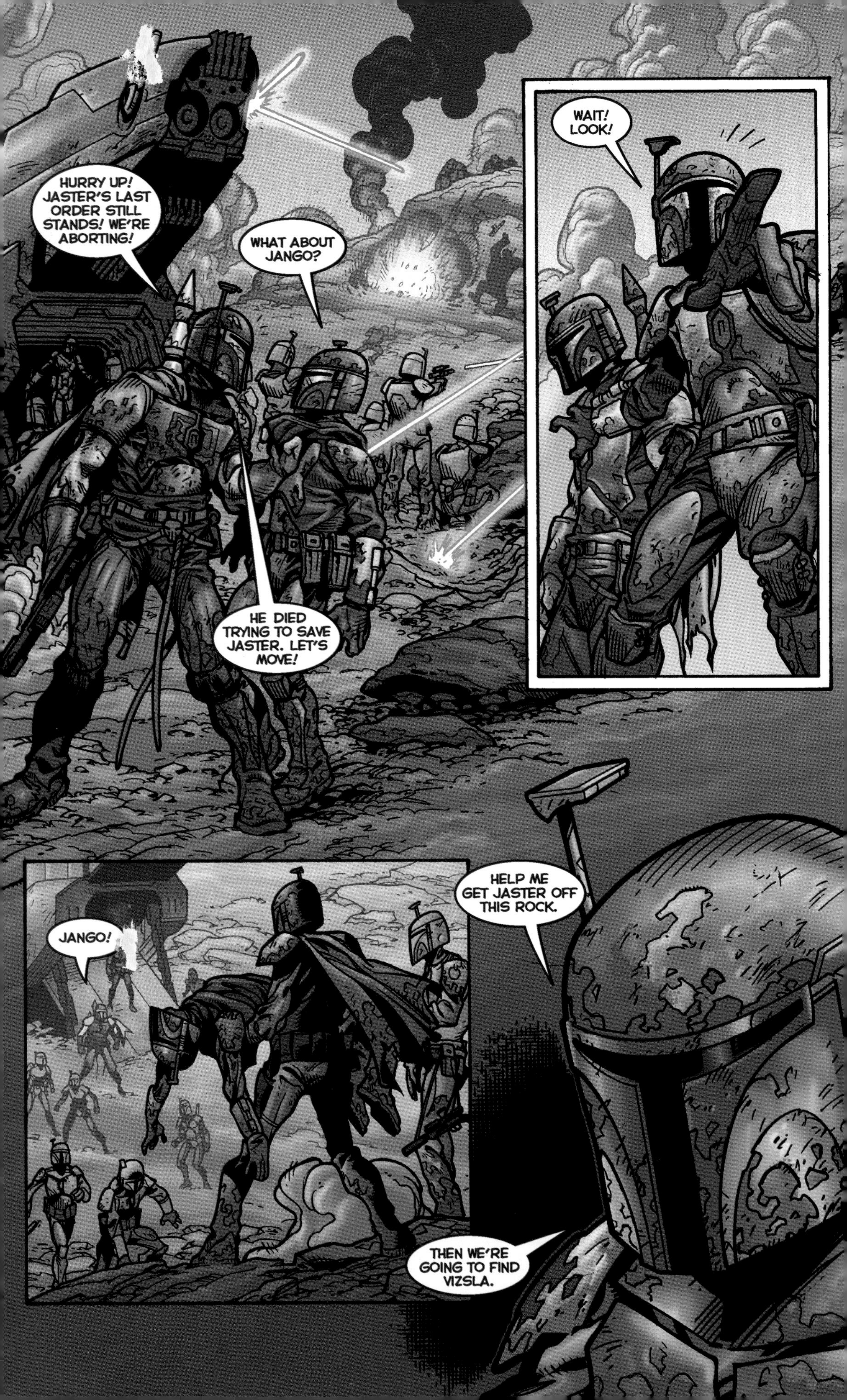
HURRY UP! JASTER'S LAST ORDER STILL STANDS! WE'RE ABORTING!
WHAT ABOUT JANGO?
HE DIED TRYING TO SAVE JASTER. LET'S MOVE!
WAIT! LOOK!
JANGO!
HELP ME GET JASTER OFF THIS ROCK.
THEN WE'RE GOING TO FIND VIZSLA.

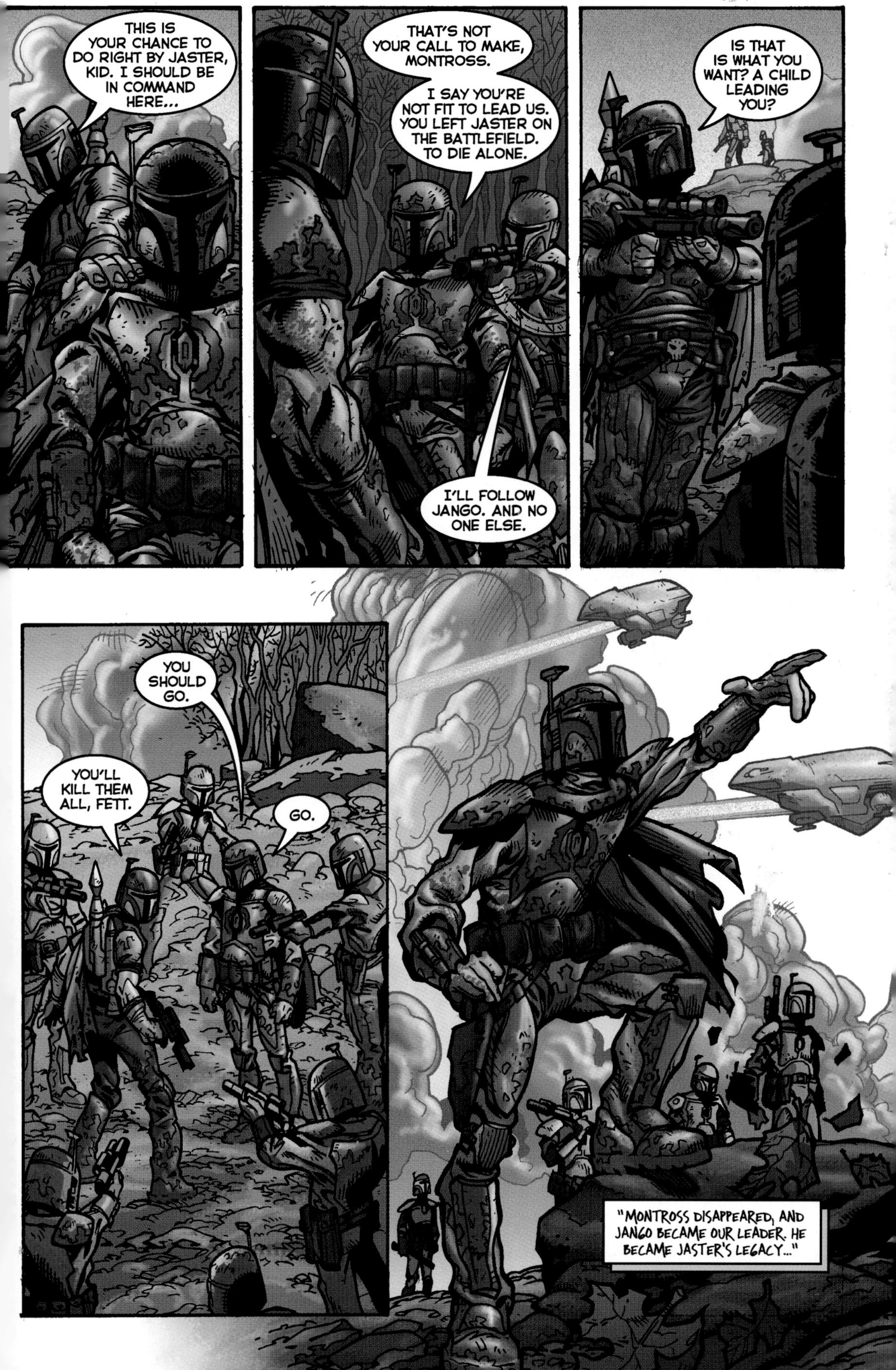
THIS IS YOUR CHANCE TO DO RIGHT BY JASTER, KID. I SHOULD BE IN COMMAND HERE...
THAT'S NOT YOUR CALL TO MAKE, MONTROSS.
I SAY YOU'RE NOT FIT TO LEAD US. YOU LEFT JASTER ON THE BATTLEFIELD. TO DIE ALONE.
I'LL FOLLOW JANGO. AND NO ONE ELSE.
IS THAT IS WHAT YOU WANT? A CHILD LEADING YOU?
YOU'LL KILL THEM ALL, FETT.
YOU SHOULD GO.
GO.
"MONTROSS DISAPPEARED, AND JANGO BECAME OUR LEADER. HE BECAME JASTER'S LEGACY..."

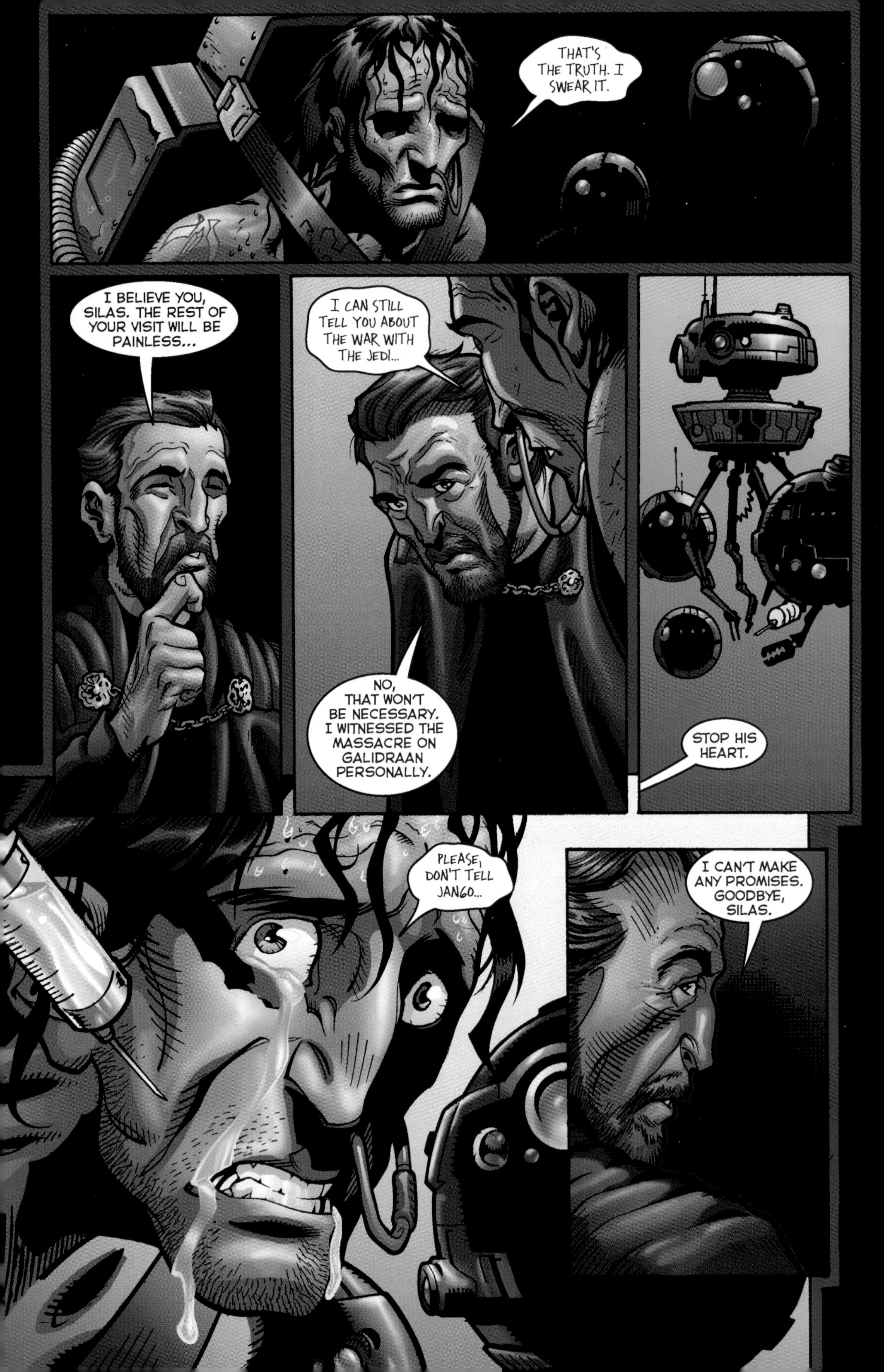
THAT'S THE TRUTH. I SWEAR IT.
I BELIEVE YOU, SILAS. THE REST OF YOUR VISIT WILL BE PAINLESS...
I CAN STILL TELL YOU ABOUT THE WAR WITH THE JEDI...
NO, THAT WON'T BE NECESSARY. I WITNESSED THE MASSACRE ON GALIDRAAN PERSONALLY.
STOP HIS HEART.
PLEASE, DON'T TELL JANGO...
I CAN'T MAKE ANY PROMISES. GOODBYE, SILAS.

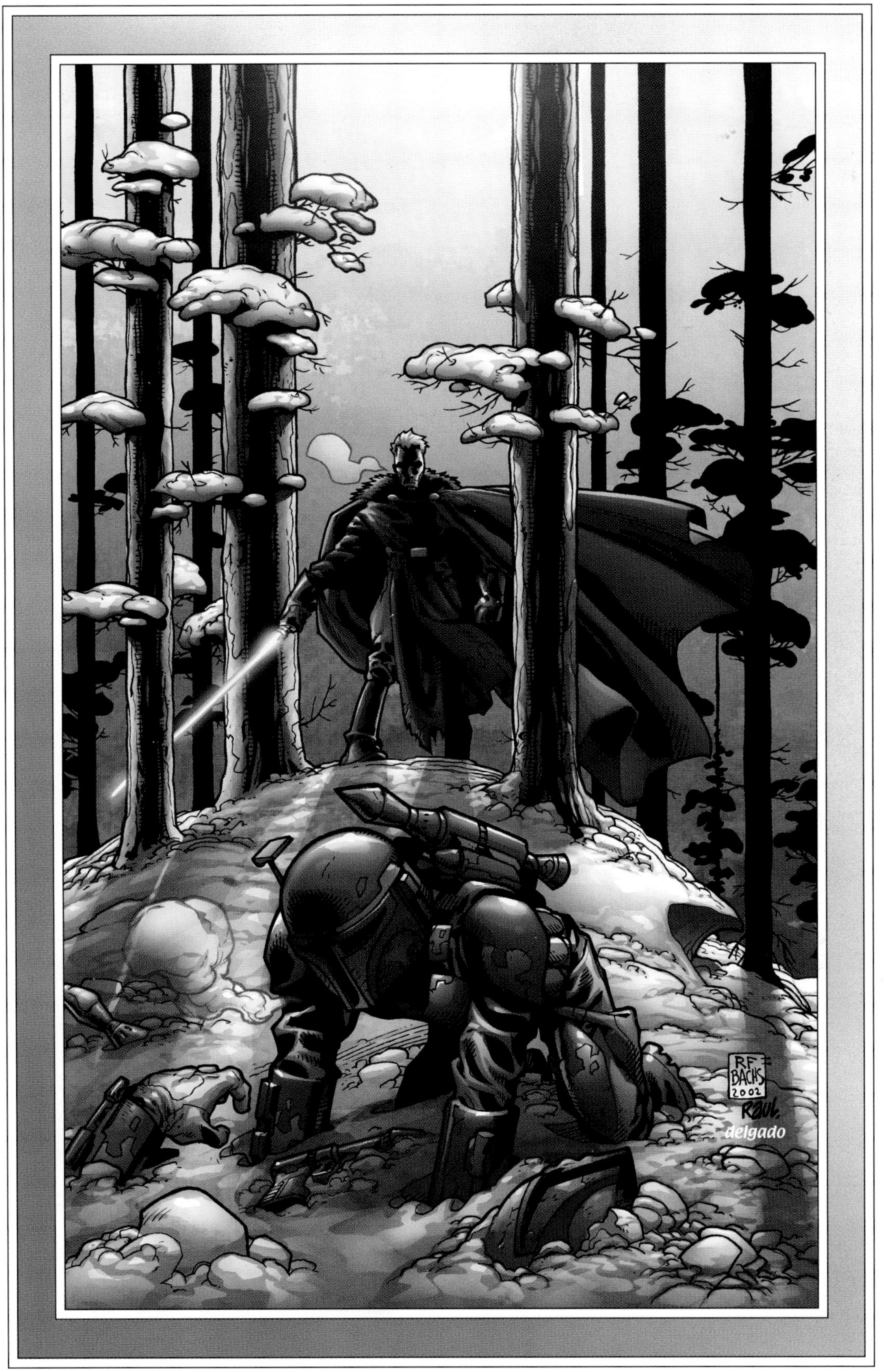
RF BACHS 2002
RAUL delgado

W I N T E R

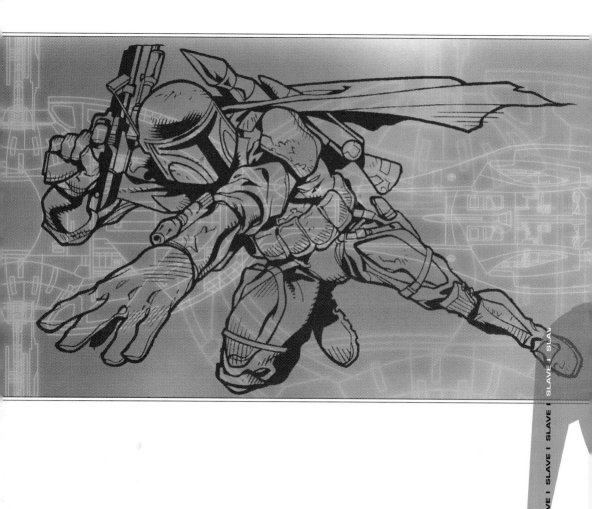

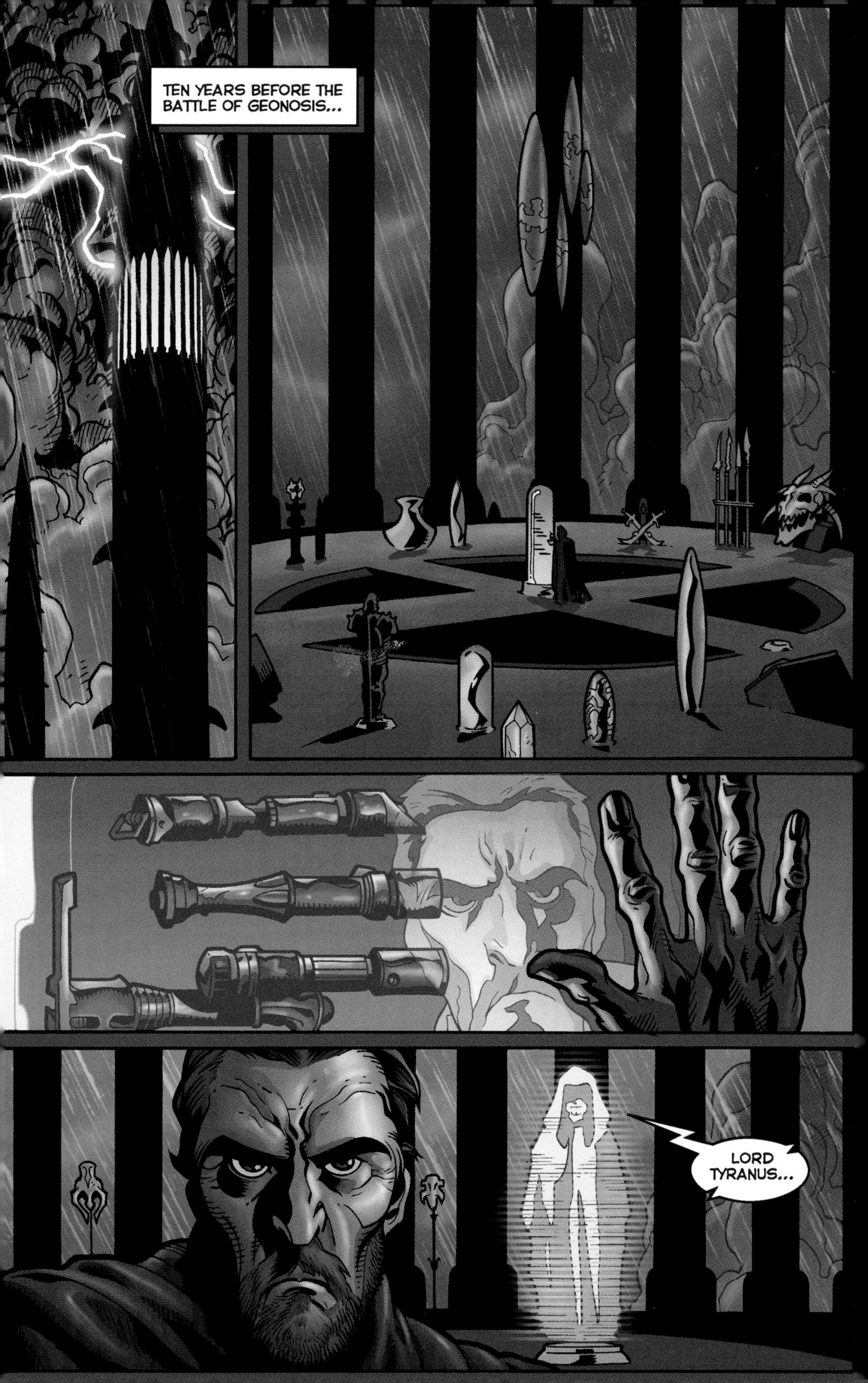
TEN YEARS BEFORE THE BATTLE OF GEONOSIS...
LORD TYRANUS...

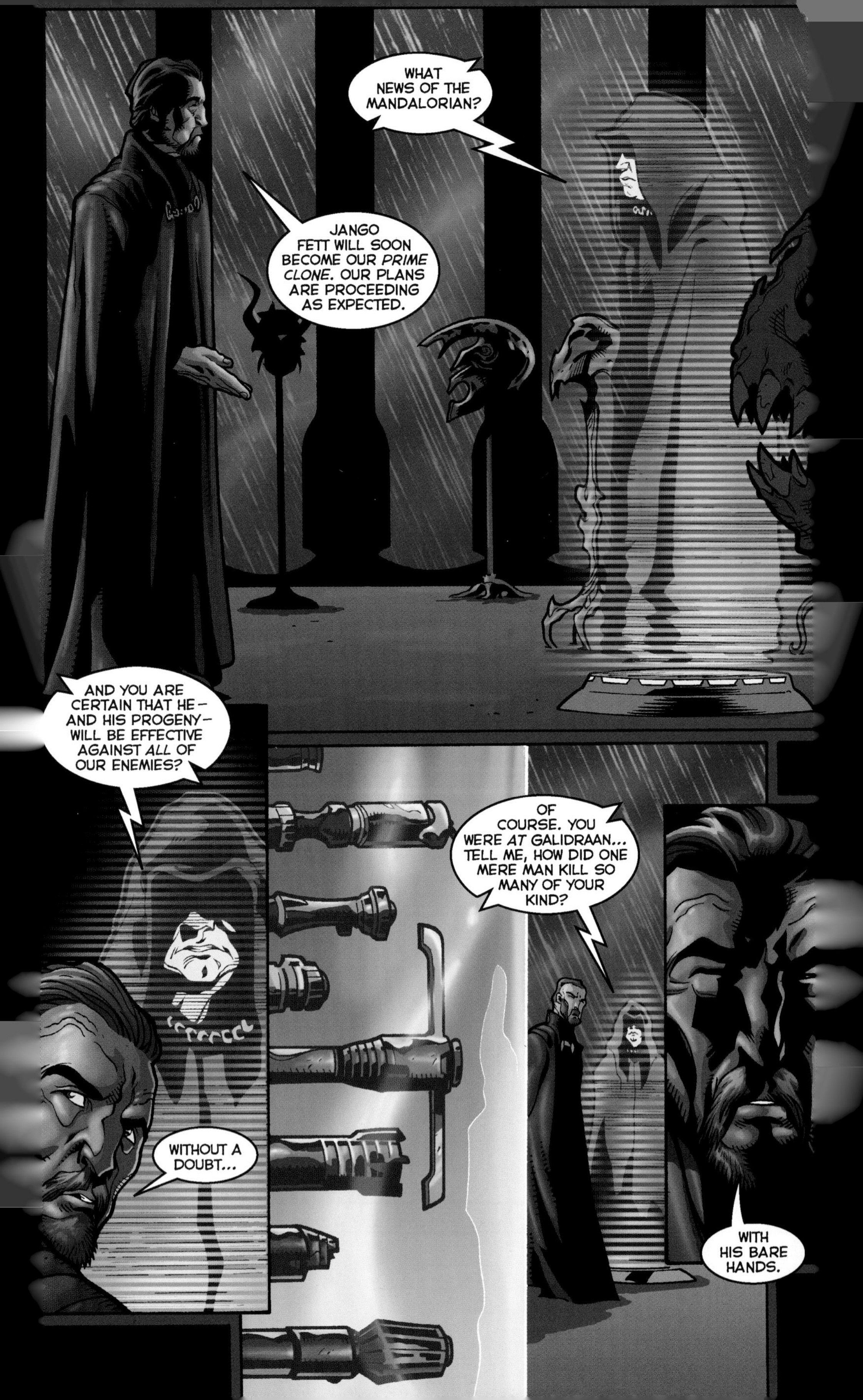
WHAT NEWS OF THE MANDALORIAN?
JANGO FETT WILL SOON BECOME OUR *PRIME CLONE*. OUR PLANS ARE PROCEEDING AS EXPECTED.
AND YOU ARE CERTAIN THAT HE— AND HIS PROGENY— WILL BE EFFECTIVE AGAINST *ALL* OF OUR ENEMIES?
WITHOUT A DOUBT...
OF COURSE. YOU WERE *AT* GALIDRAAN... TELL ME, HOW DID ONE MERE MAN KILL SO MANY OF YOUR KIND?
WITH HIS BARE HANDS.

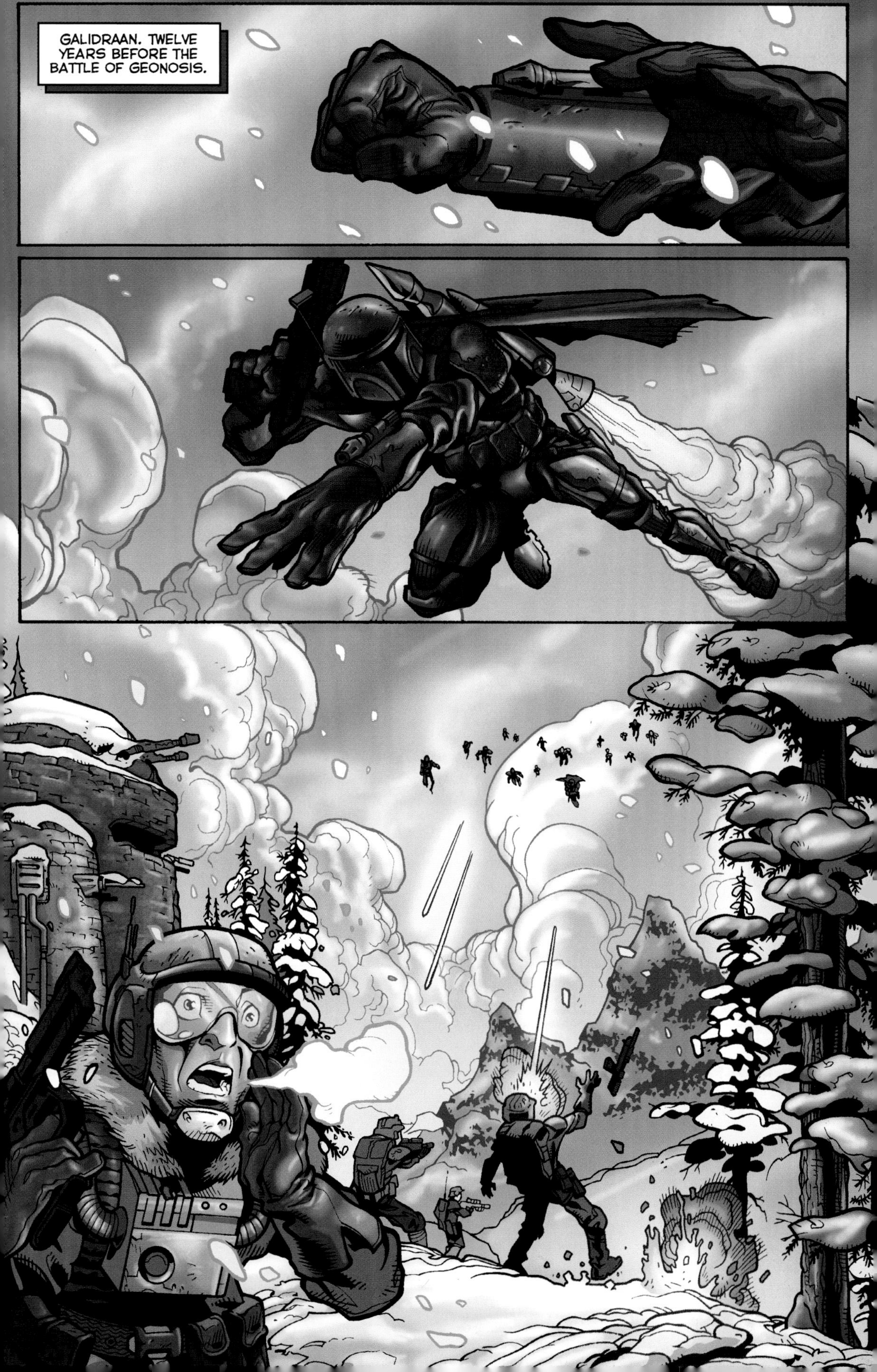
GALIDRAAN. TWELVE YEARS BEFORE THE BATTLE OF GEONOSIS.

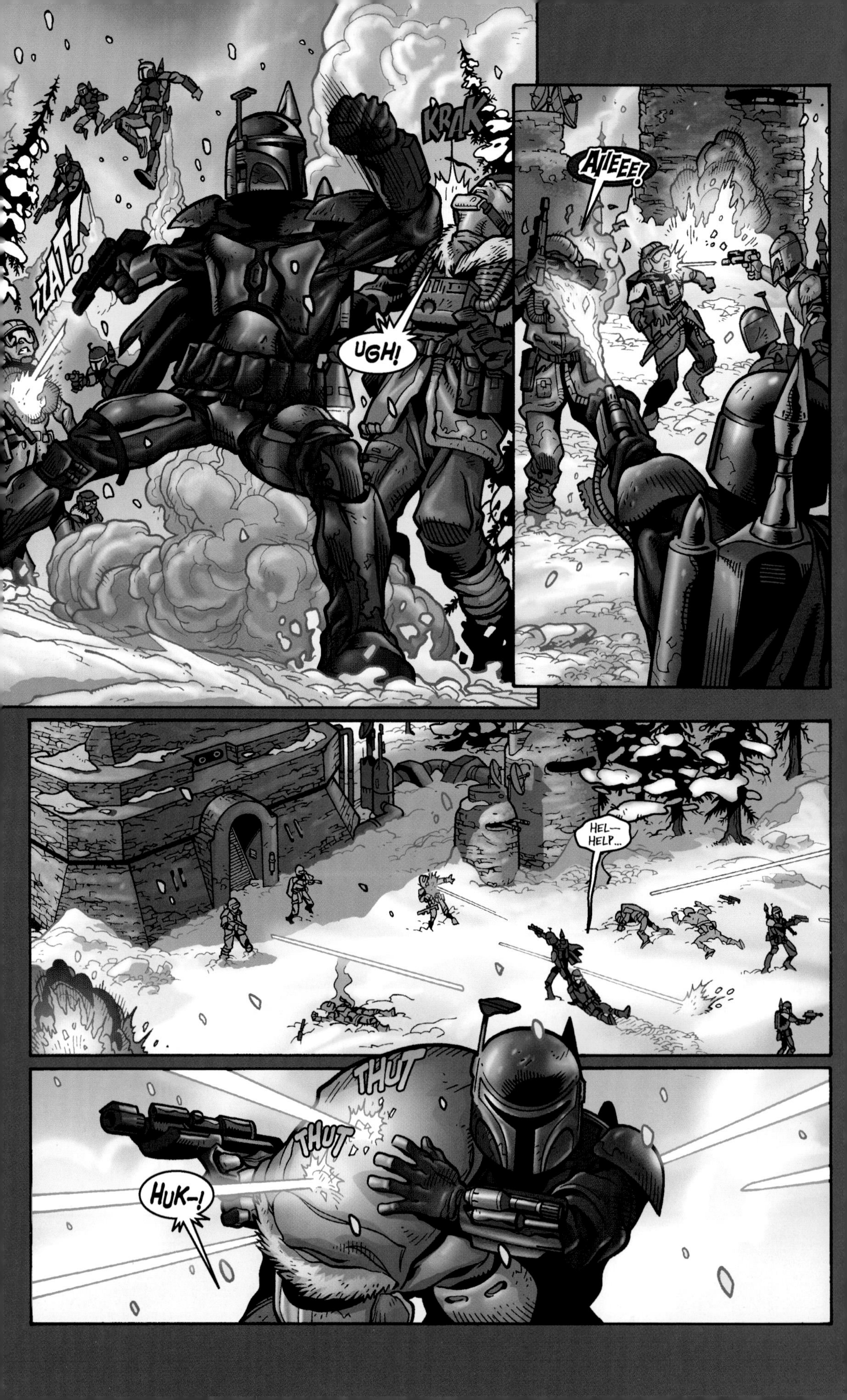
ZZAT!
KRAK
UGH!
AIIEEE!
HEL—
HELP...
THUT
THUT
HUK-!

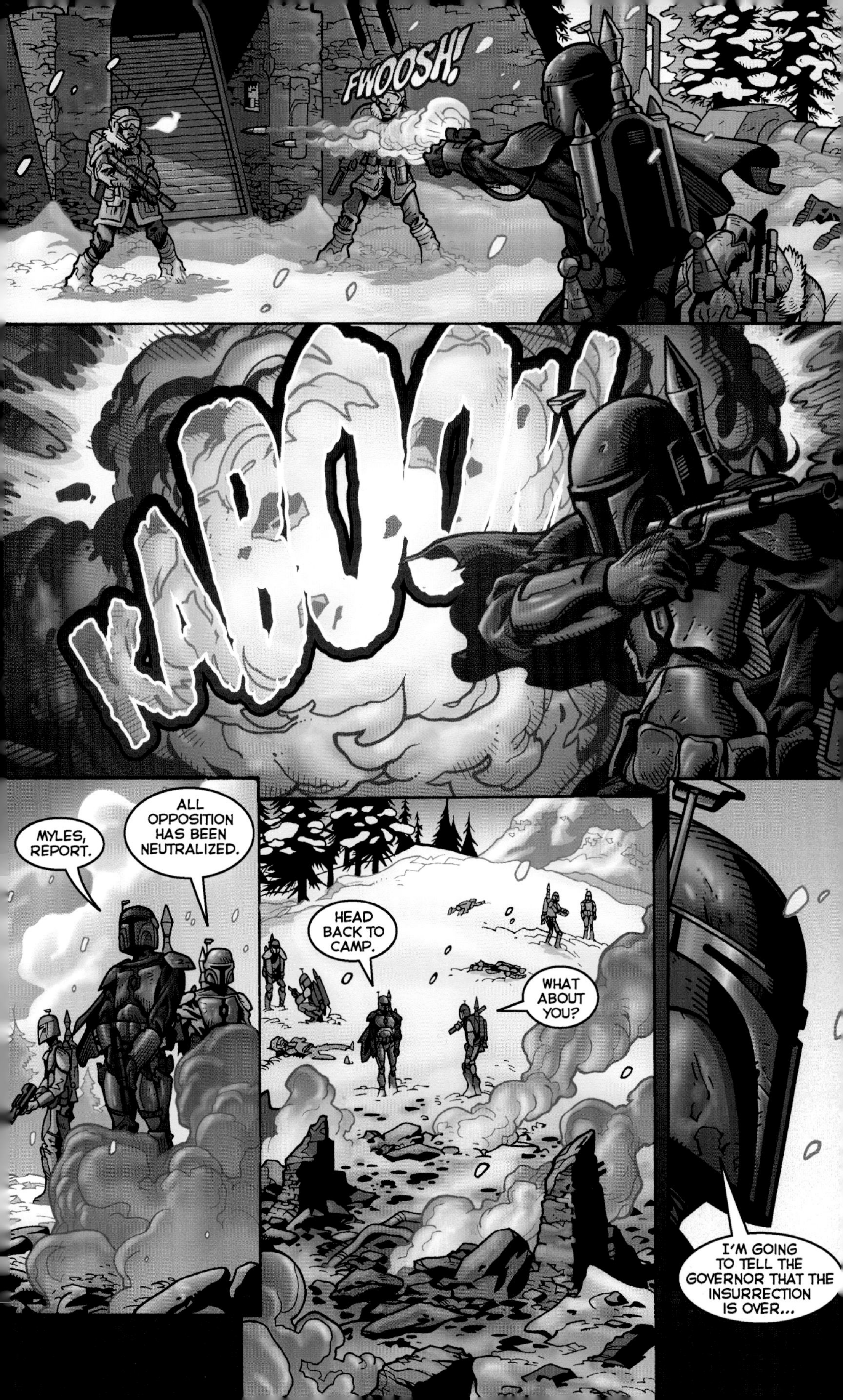
FWOOSH!
KABOOM!
MYLES, REPORT.
ALL OPPOSITION HAS BEEN NEUTRALIZED.
HEAD BACK TO CAMP.
WHAT ABOUT YOU?
I'M GOING TO TELL THE GOVERNOR THAT THE INSURRECTION IS OVER...

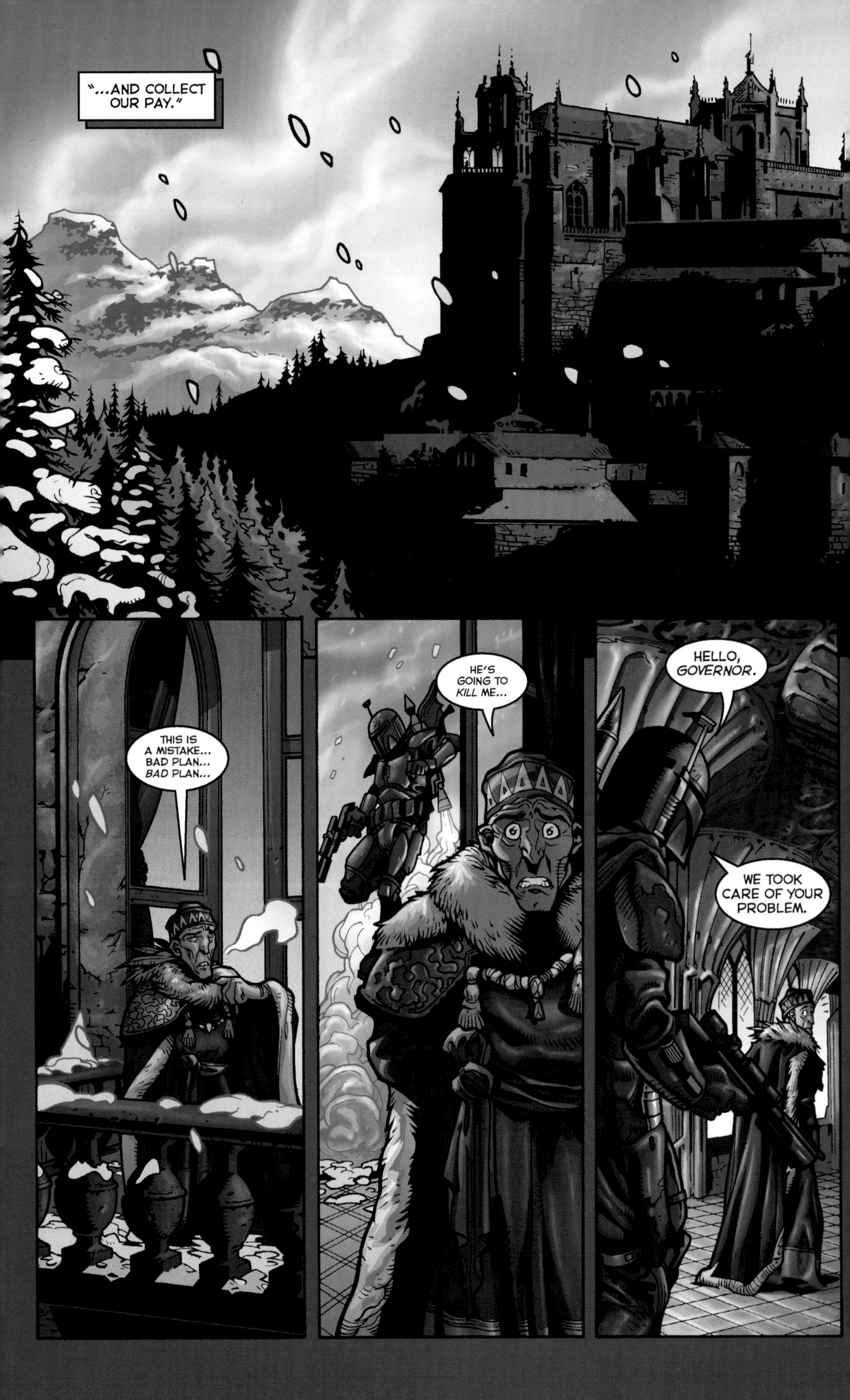
"...AND COLLECT OUR PAY."
THIS IS A MISTAKE... BAD PLAN... BAD PLAN...
HE'S GOING TO KILL ME...
HELLO, GOVERNOR.
WE TOOK CARE OF YOUR PROBLEM.

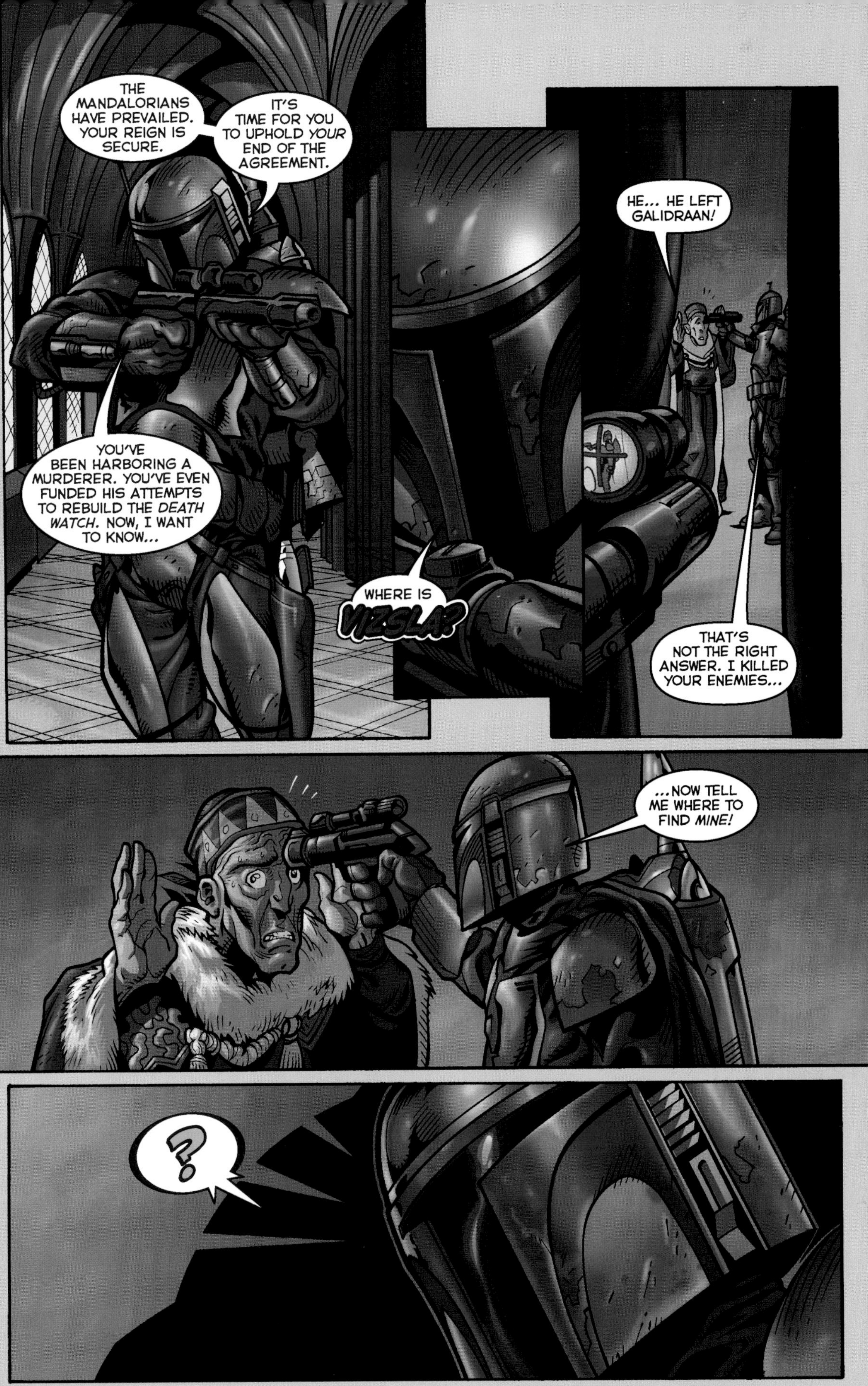
THE MANDALORIANS HAVE PREVAILED. YOUR REIGN IS SECURE.
IT'S TIME FOR YOU TO UPHOLD *YOUR* END OF THE AGREEMENT.
HE... HE LEFT GALIDRAAN!
YOU'VE BEEN HARBORING A MURDERER. YOU'VE EVEN FUNDED HIS ATTEMPTS TO REBUILD THE *DEATH WATCH*. NOW, I WANT TO KNOW...
WHERE IS VIZSLA?
THAT'S NOT THE RIGHT ANSWER. I KILLED YOUR ENEMIES...
...NOW TELL ME WHERE TO FIND *MINE!*
?

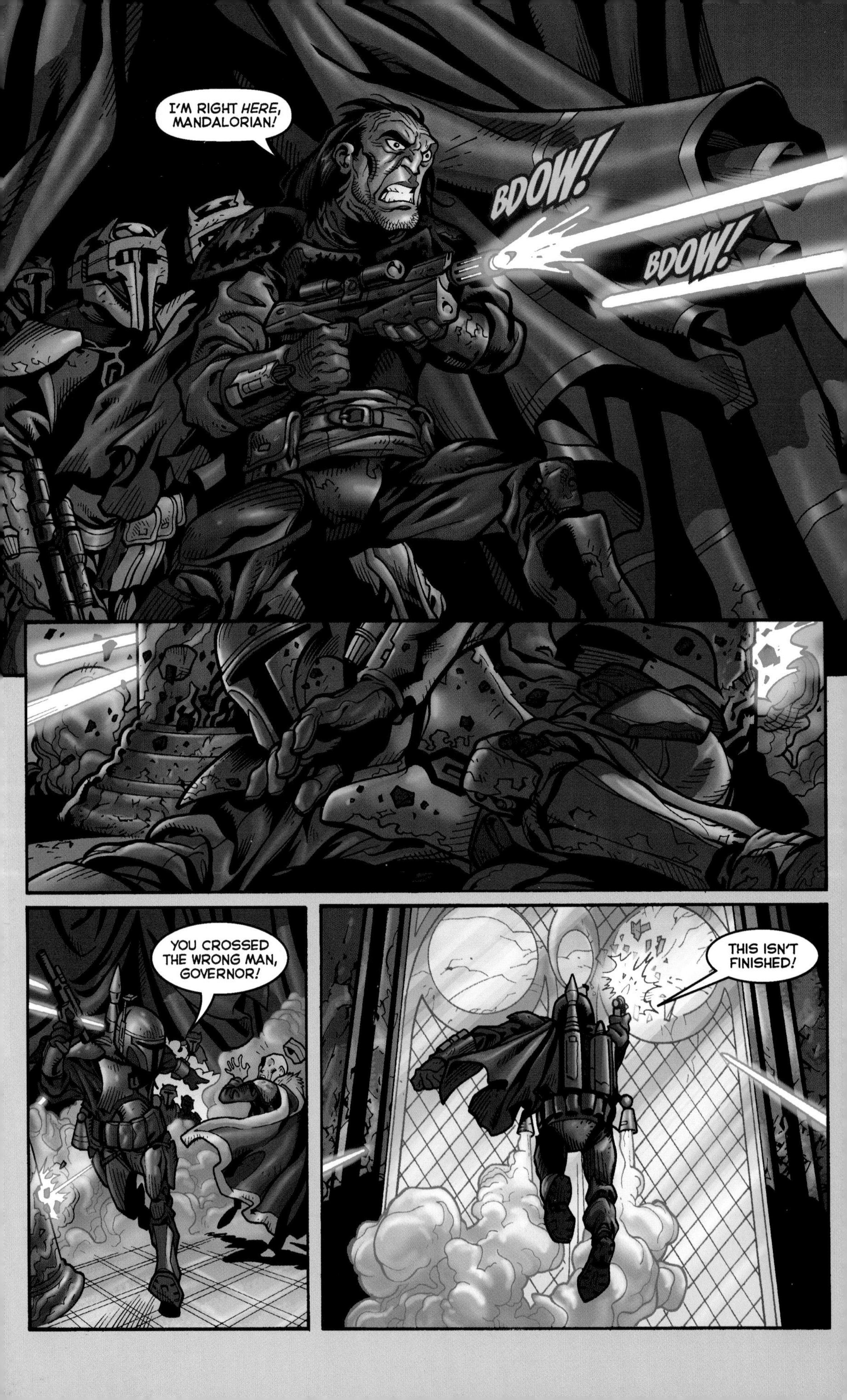
I'M RIGHT *HERE*, MANDALORIAN!
BDOW!
BDOW!
YOU CROSSED THE WRONG MAN, GOVERNOR!
THIS ISN'T FINISHED!

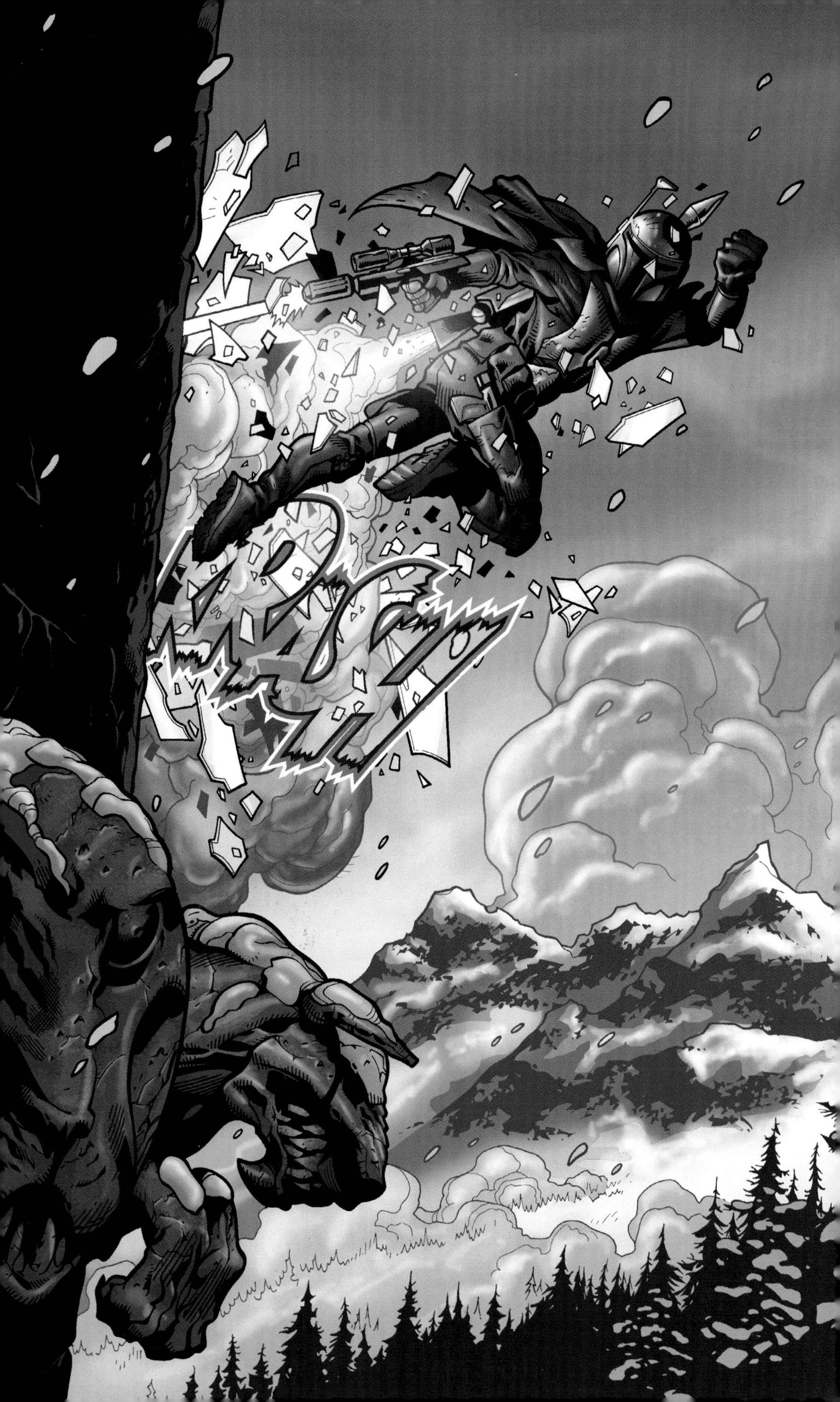

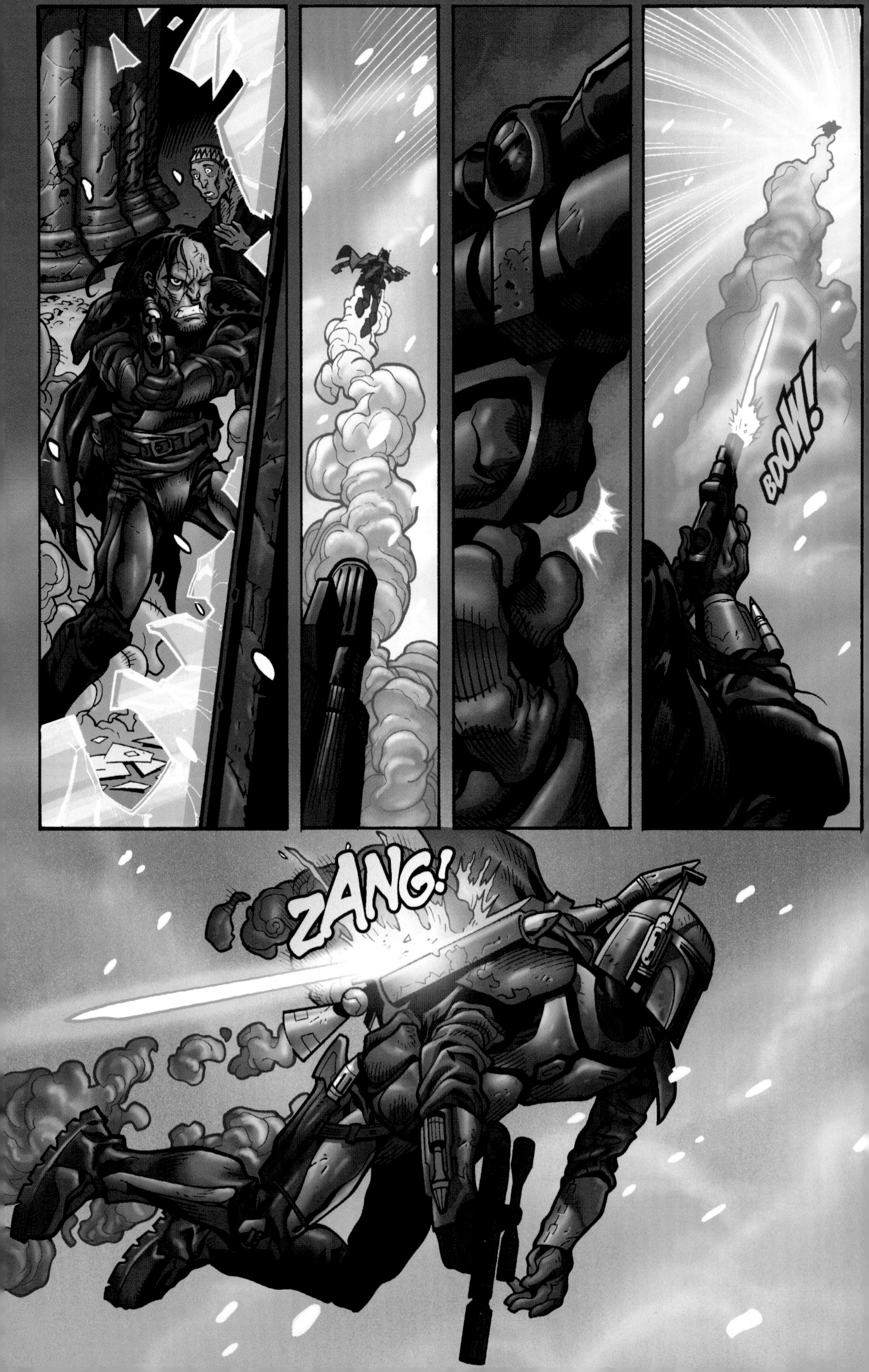
BDOW!
ZANG!

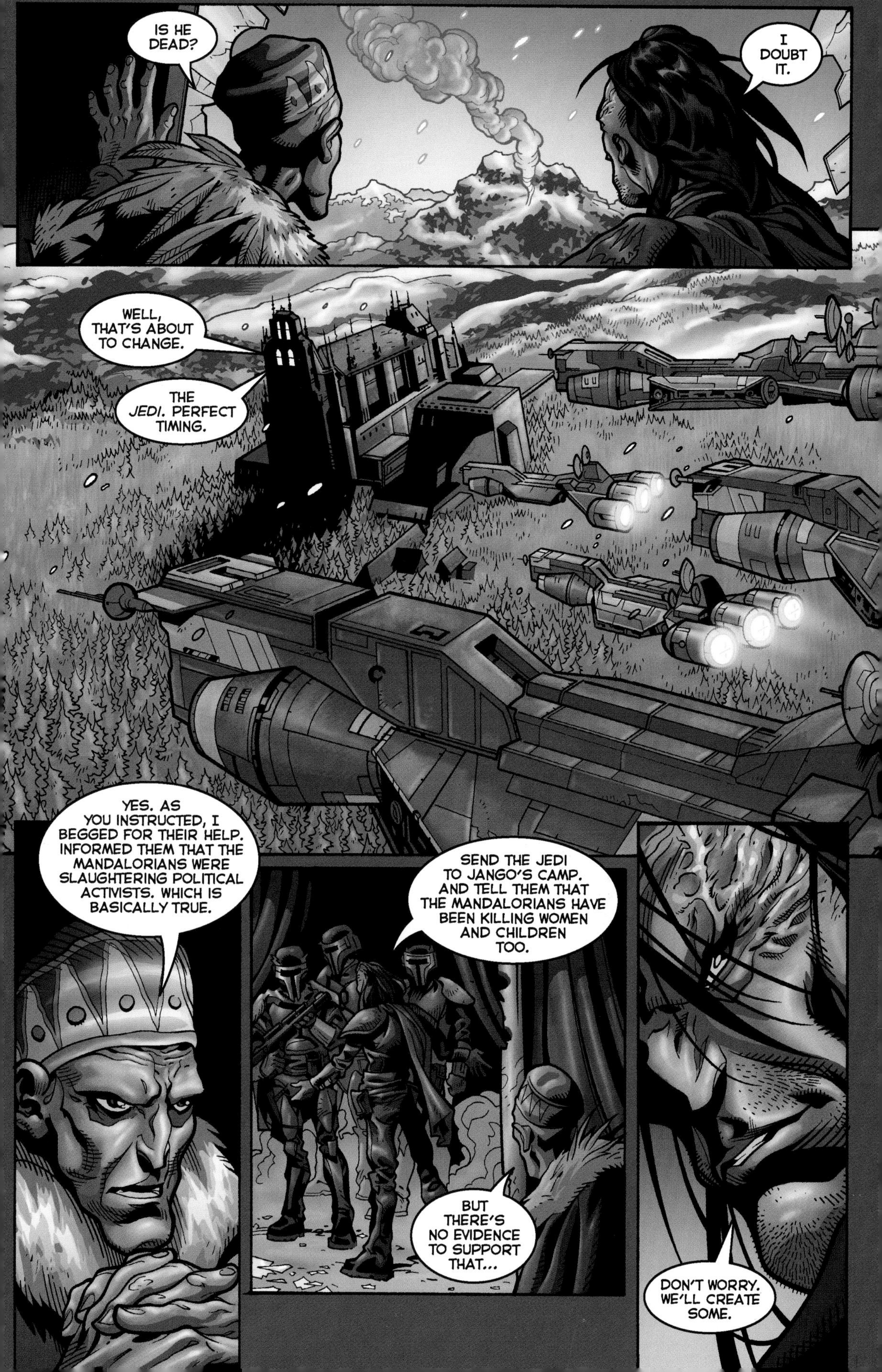

IS HE DEAD?
I DOUBT IT.
WELL, THAT'S ABOUT TO CHANGE.
THE *JEDI*. PERFECT TIMING.
YES. AS YOU INSTRUCTED, I BEGGED FOR THEIR HELP. INFORMED THEM THAT THE MANDALORIANS WERE SLAUGHTERING POLITICAL ACTIVISTS. WHICH IS BASICALLY TRUE.
SEND THE JEDI TO JANGO'S CAMP. AND TELL THEM THAT THE MANDALORIANS HAVE BEEN KILLING WOMEN AND CHILDREN TOO.
BUT THERE'S NO EVIDENCE TO SUPPORT THAT...
DON'T WORRY. WE'LL CREATE SOME.

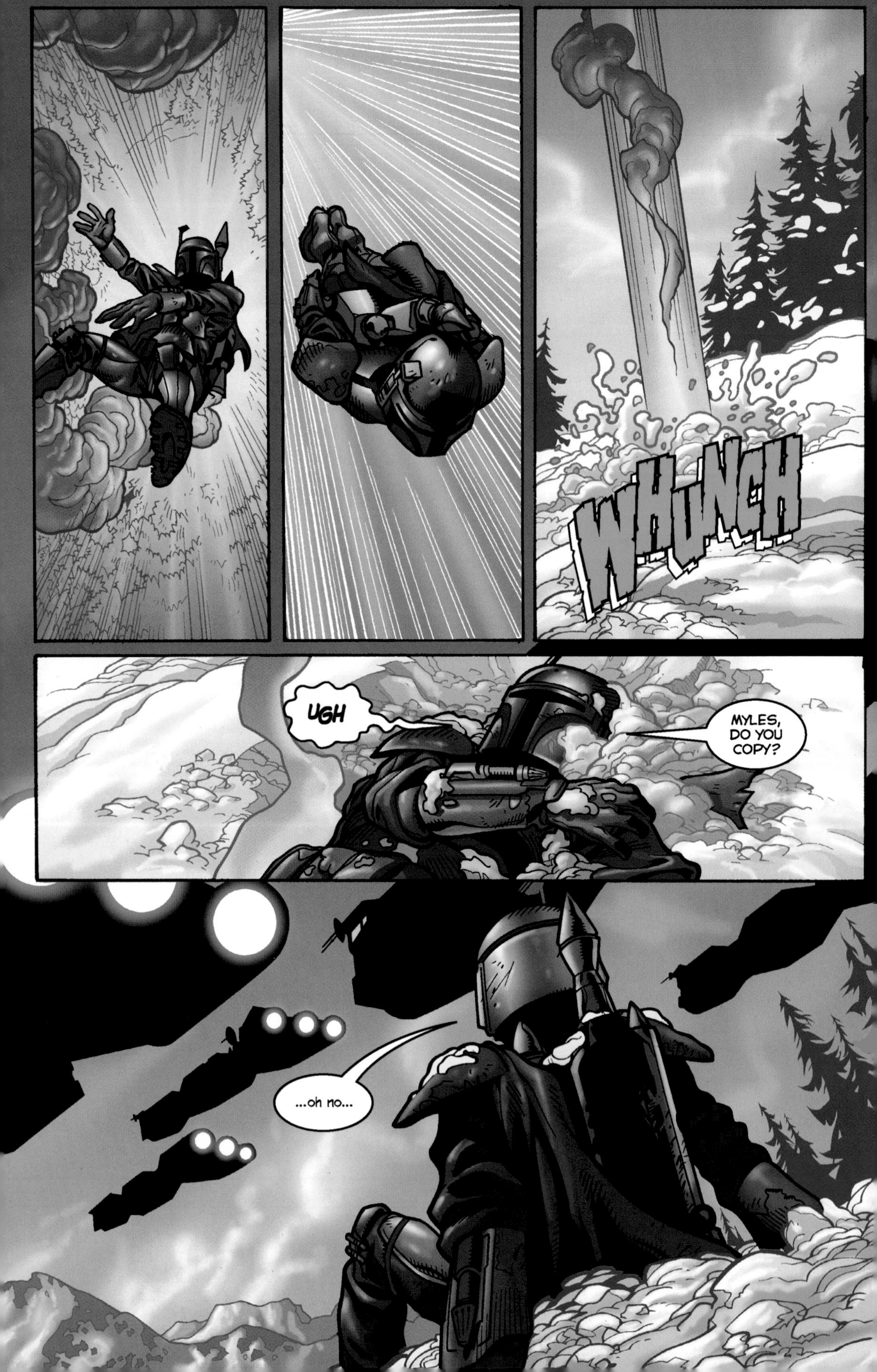
WHUNCH
UGH
MYLES, DO YOU COPY?
...oh no...

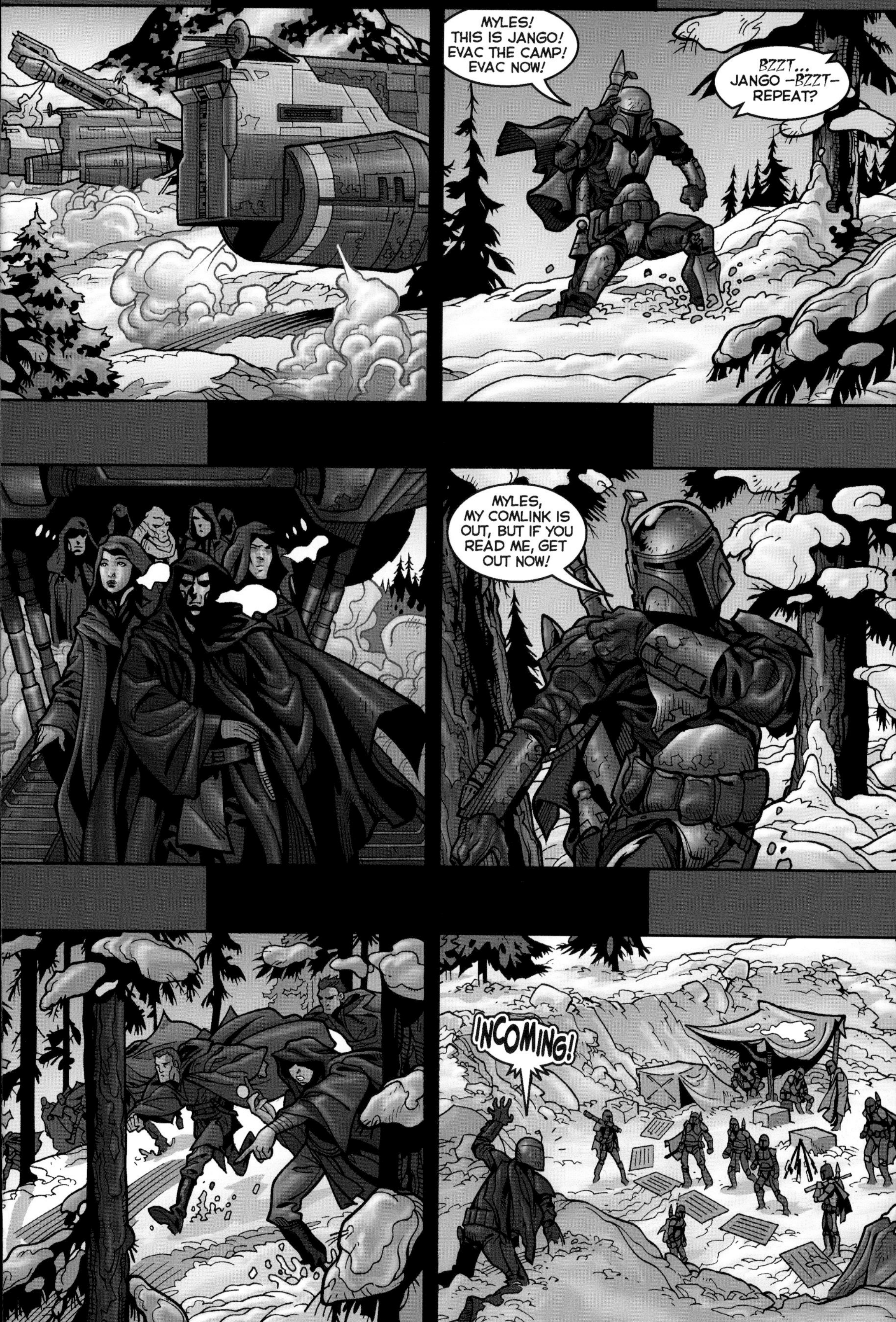
MYLES!
THIS IS JANGO!
EVAC THE CAMP!
EVAC NOW!
BZZT... JANGO -BZZT- REPEAT?
MYLES, MY COMLINK IS OUT, BUT IF YOU READ ME, GET OUT NOW!
INCOMING!

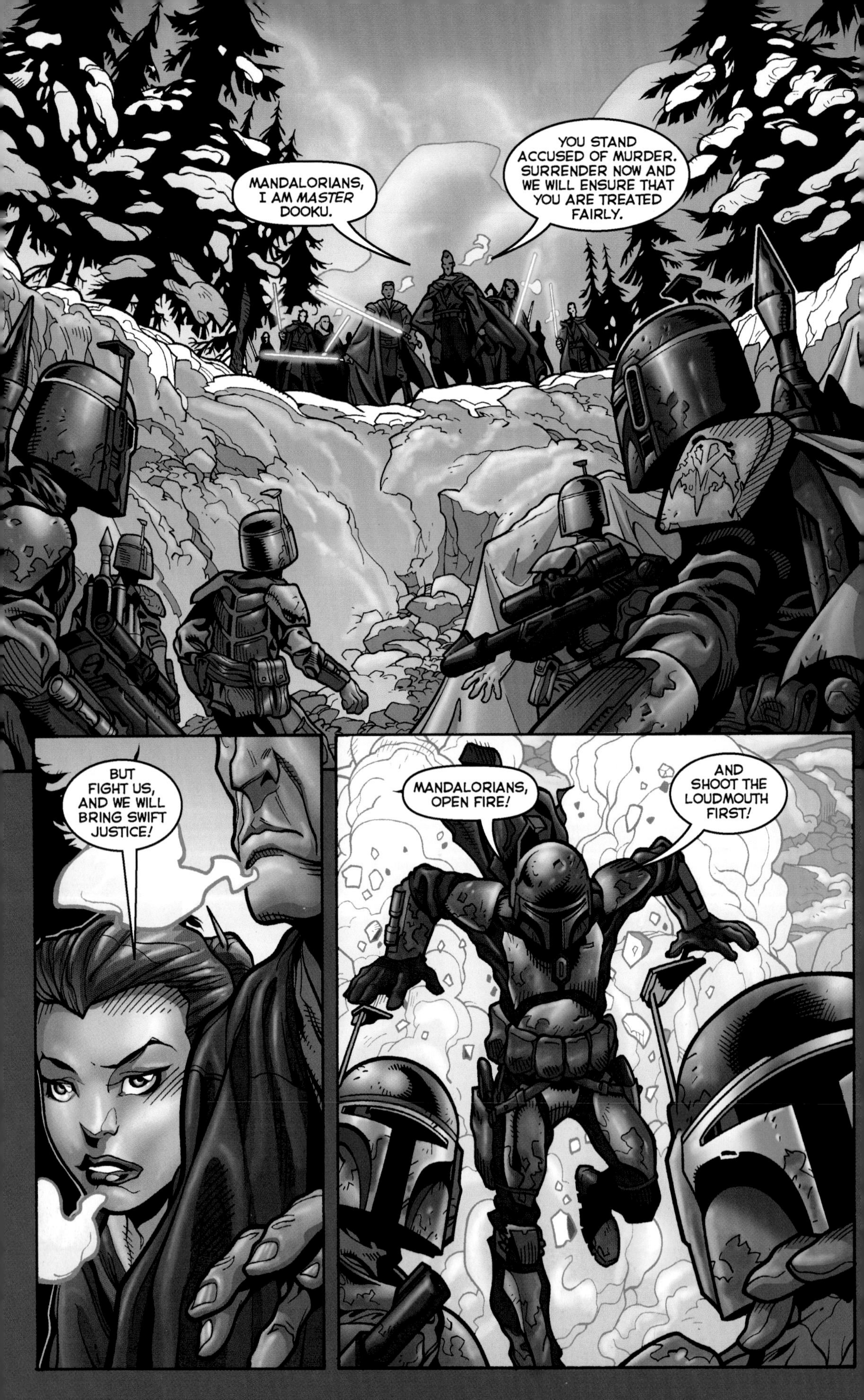

MANDALORIANS, I AM *MASTER* DOOKU.
YOU STAND ACCUSED OF MURDER. SURRENDER NOW AND WE WILL ENSURE THAT YOU ARE TREATED FAIRLY.
BUT FIGHT US, AND WE WILL BRING SWIFT JUSTICE!
MANDALORIANS, OPEN FIRE!
AND SHOOT THE LOUDMOUTH FIRST!

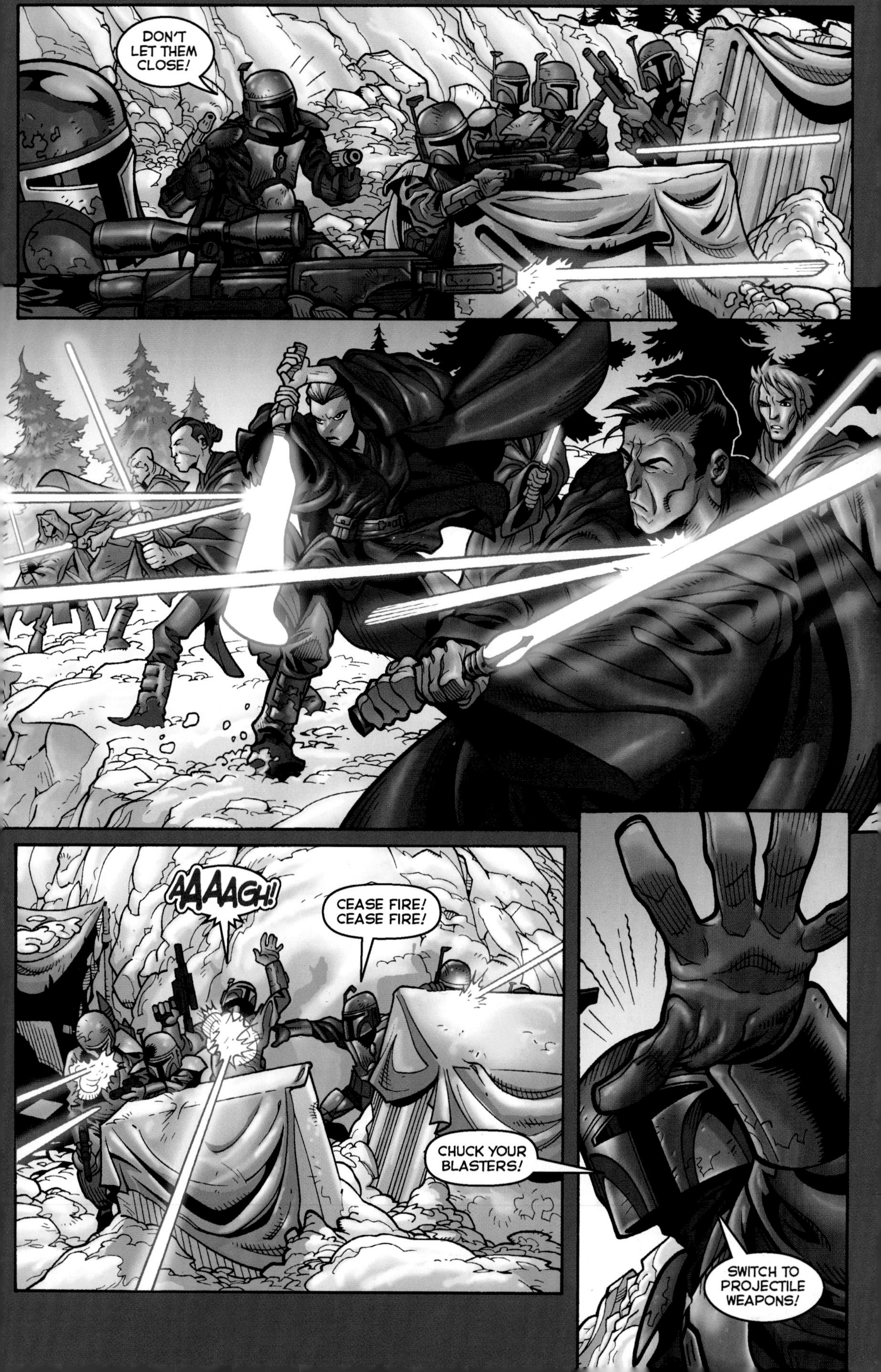
DON'T LET THEM CLOSE!
AAAAGH!
CEASE FIRE! CEASE FIRE!
CHUCK YOUR BLASTERS!
SWITCH TO PROJECTILE WEAPONS!

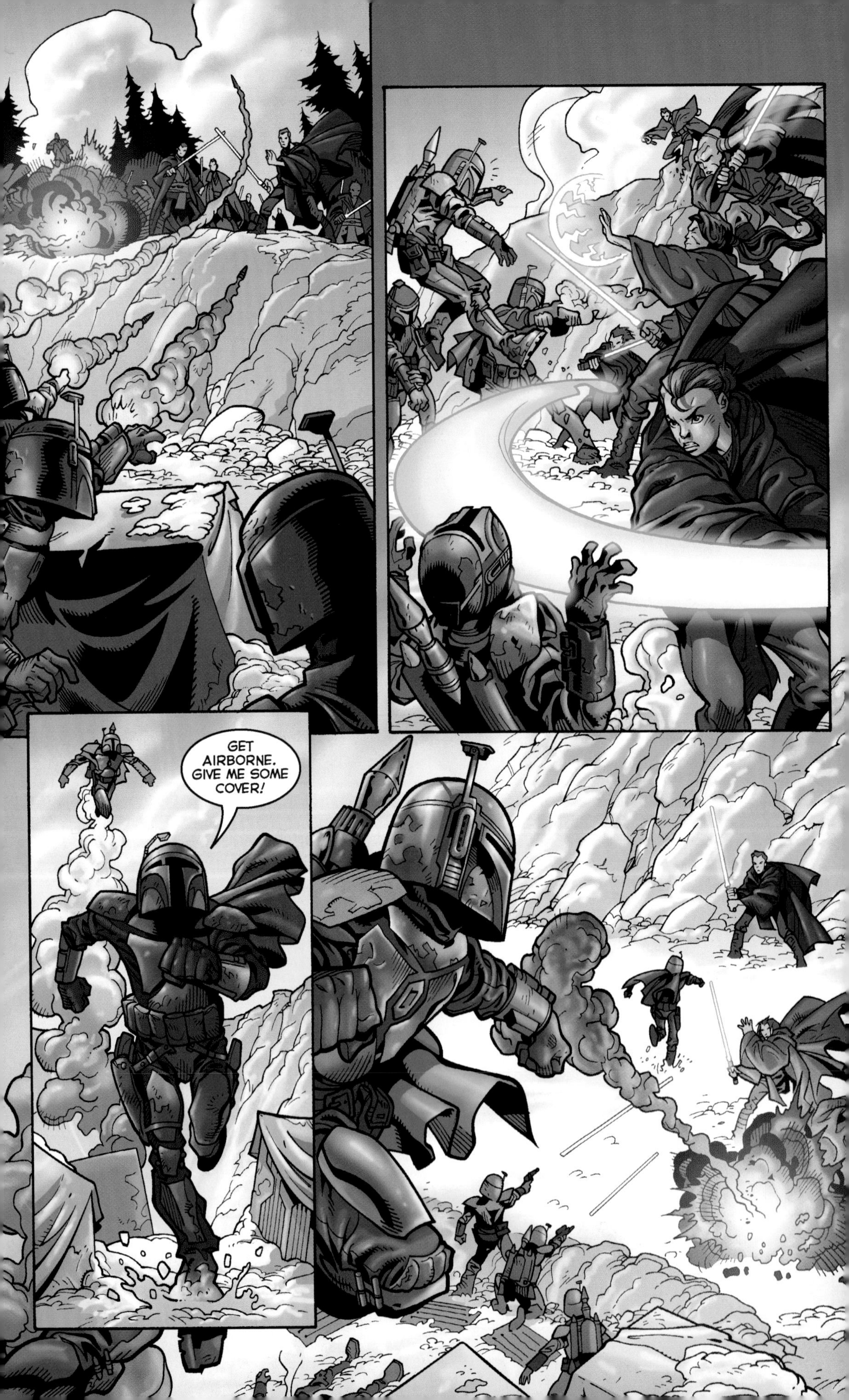
GET AIRBORNE. GIVE ME SOME COVER!

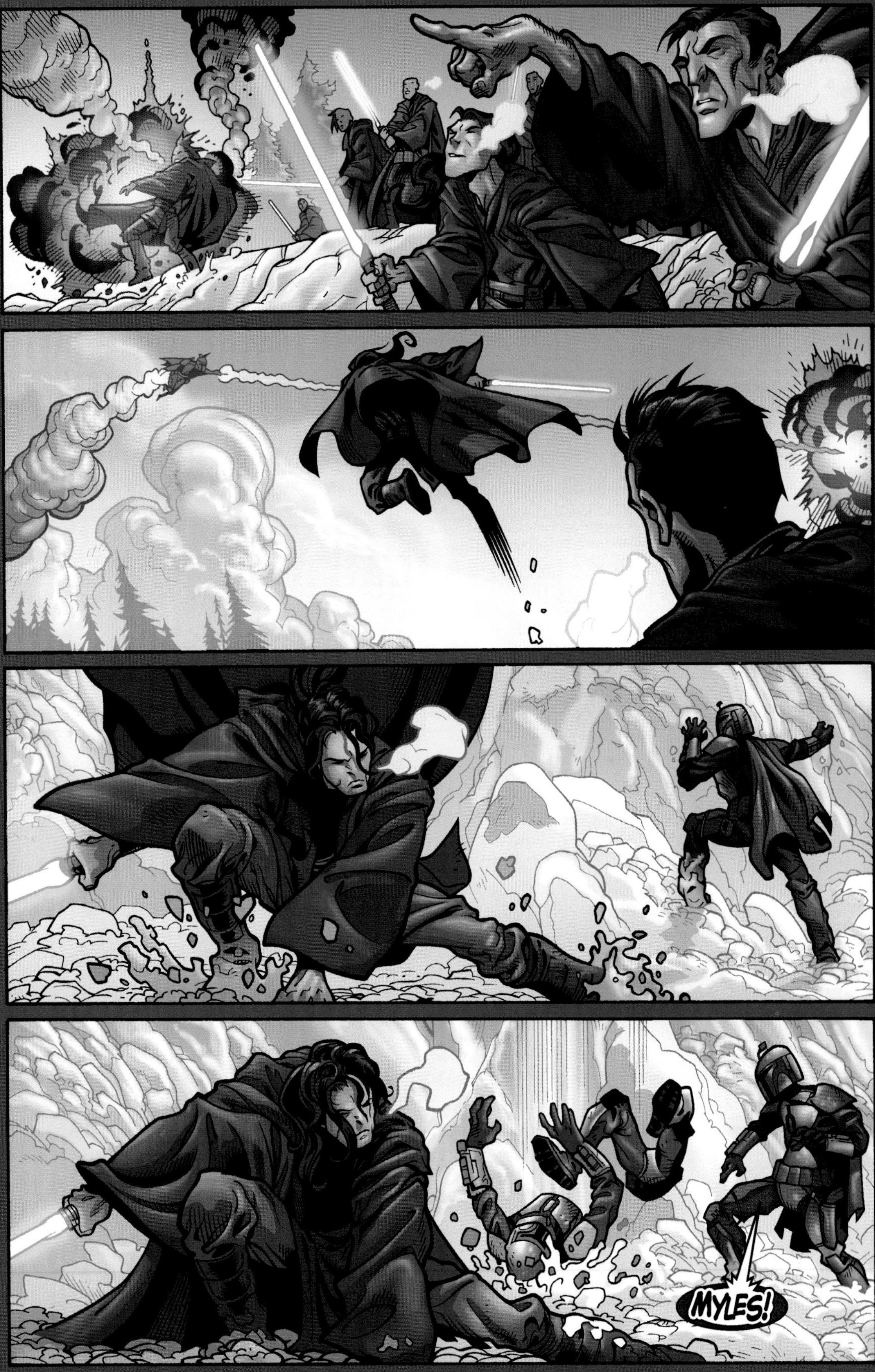
MYLES!

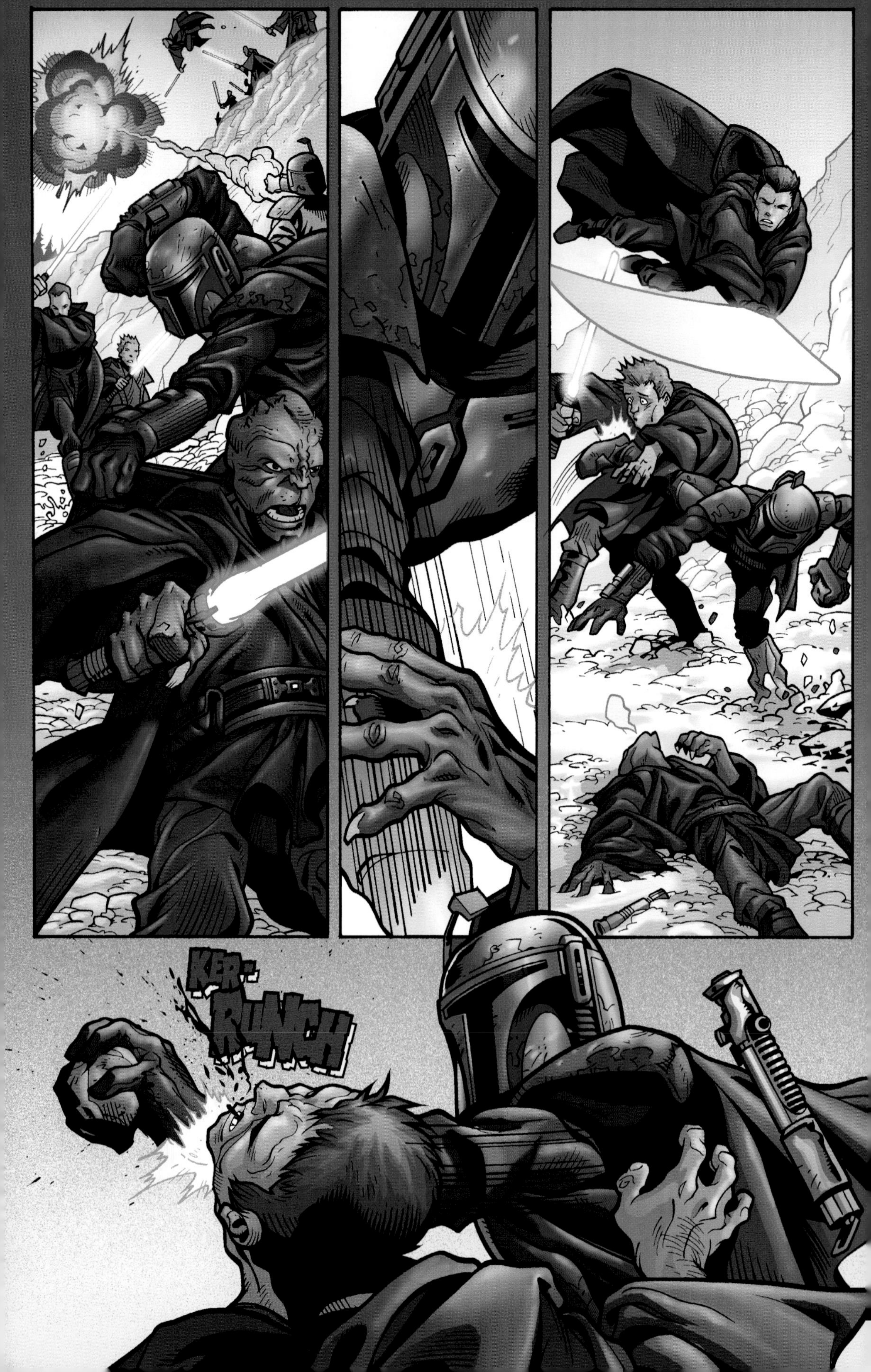
KER-RUNCH

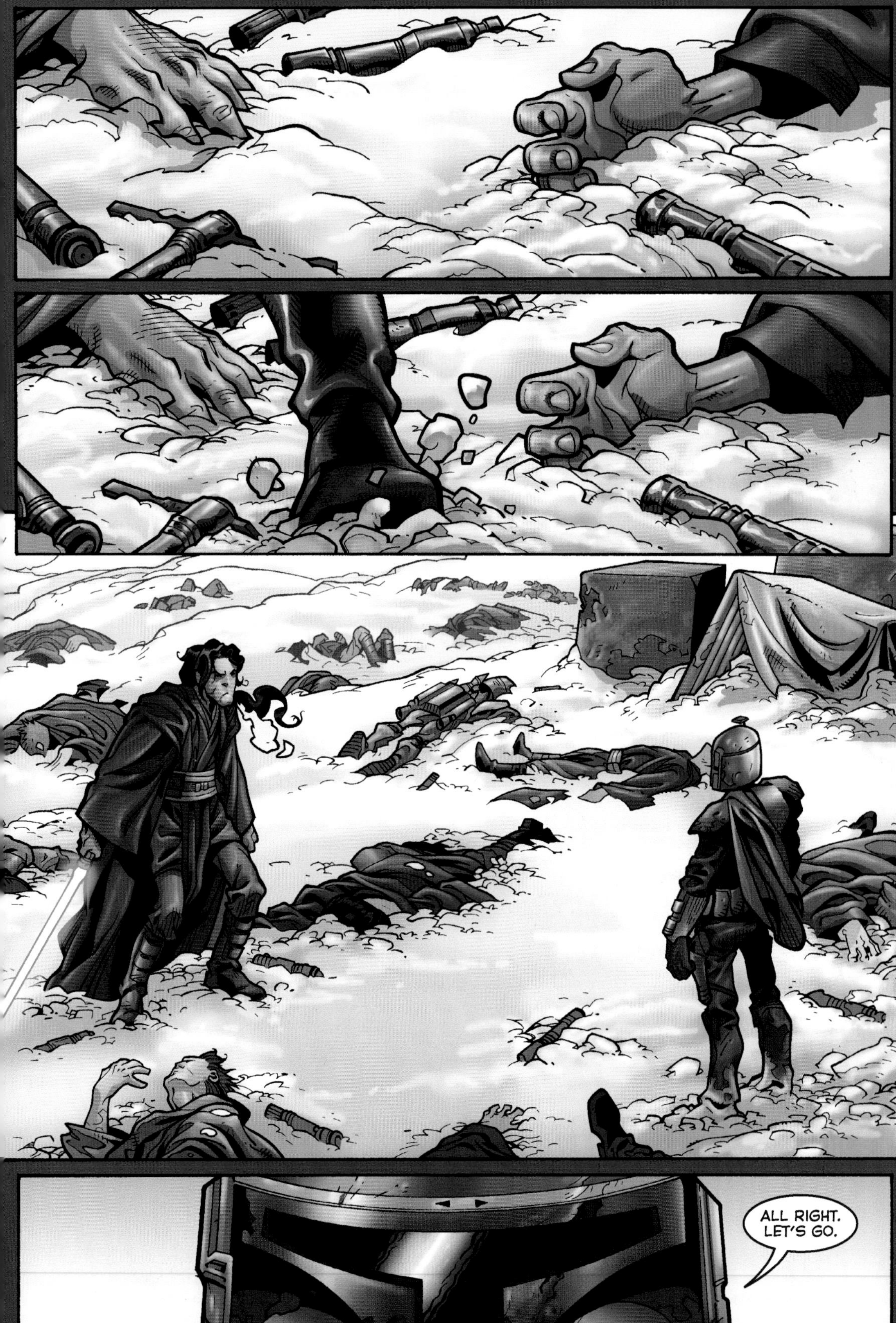
ALL RIGHT. LET'S GO.

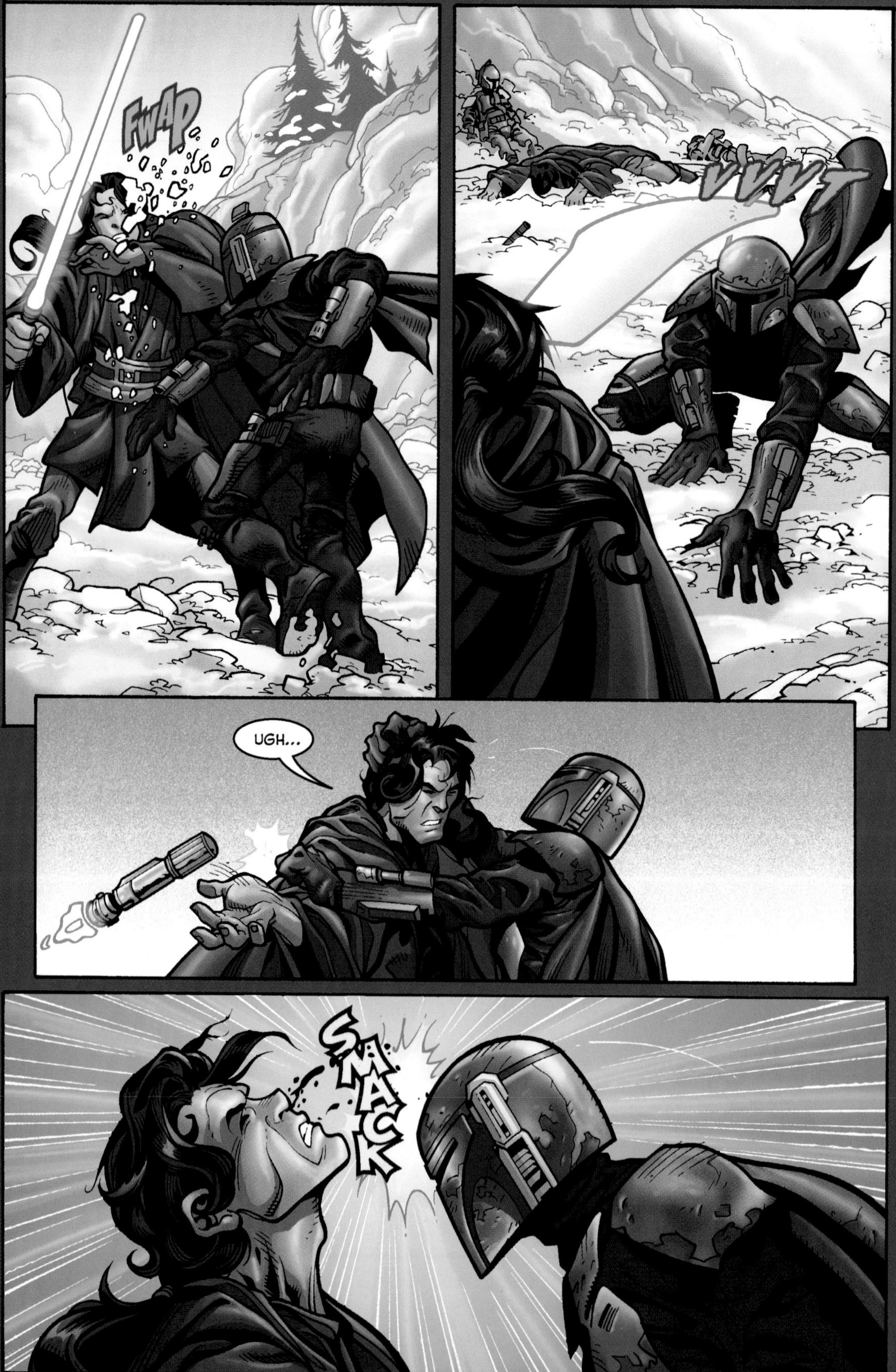
FWAP
VVVT
UGH...
SMACK

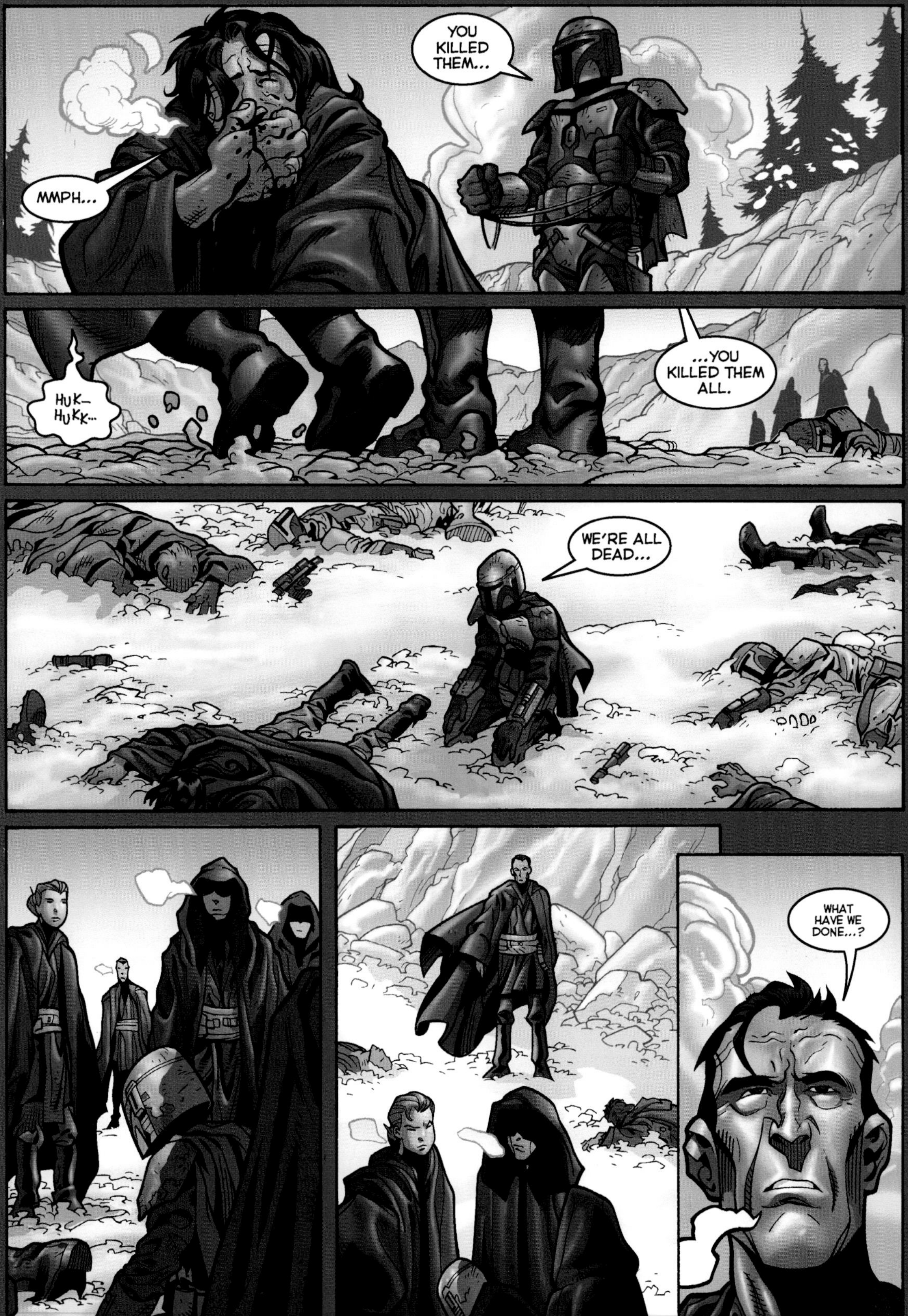
YOU KILLED THEM...
MMPH...
HUK-HUKK...
...YOU KILLED THEM ALL.
WE'RE ALL DEAD...
WHAT HAVE WE DONE...?

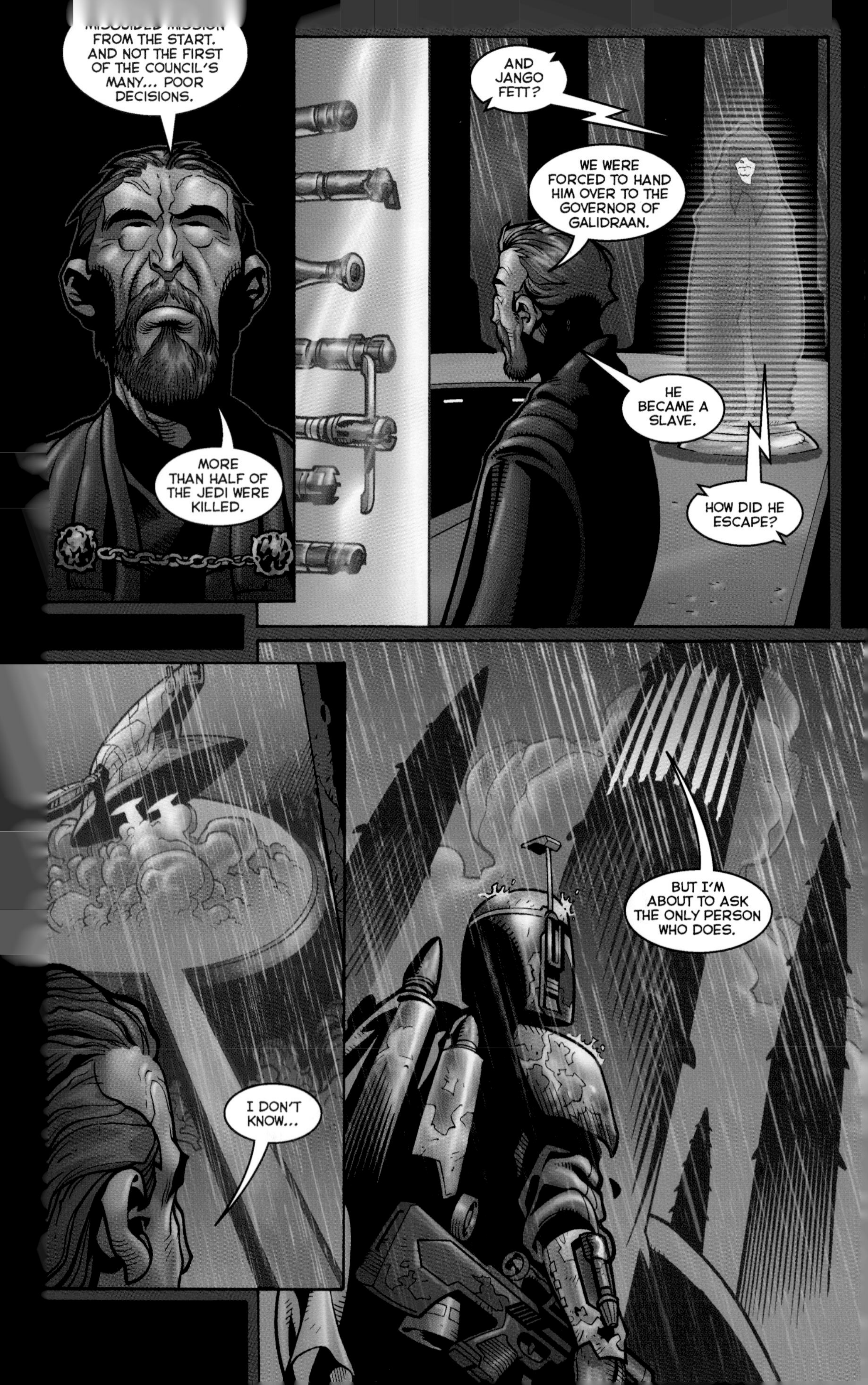
FROM THE START. AND NOT THE FIRST OF THE COUNCIL'S MANY... POOR DECISIONS.
MORE THAN HALF OF THE JEDI WERE KILLED.
AND JANGO FETT?
WE WERE FORCED TO HAND HIM OVER TO THE GOVERNOR OF GALIDRAAN.
HE BECAME A SLAVE.
HOW DID HE ESCAPE?
I DON'T KNOW...
BUT I'M ABOUT TO ASK THE ONLY PERSON WHO DOES.

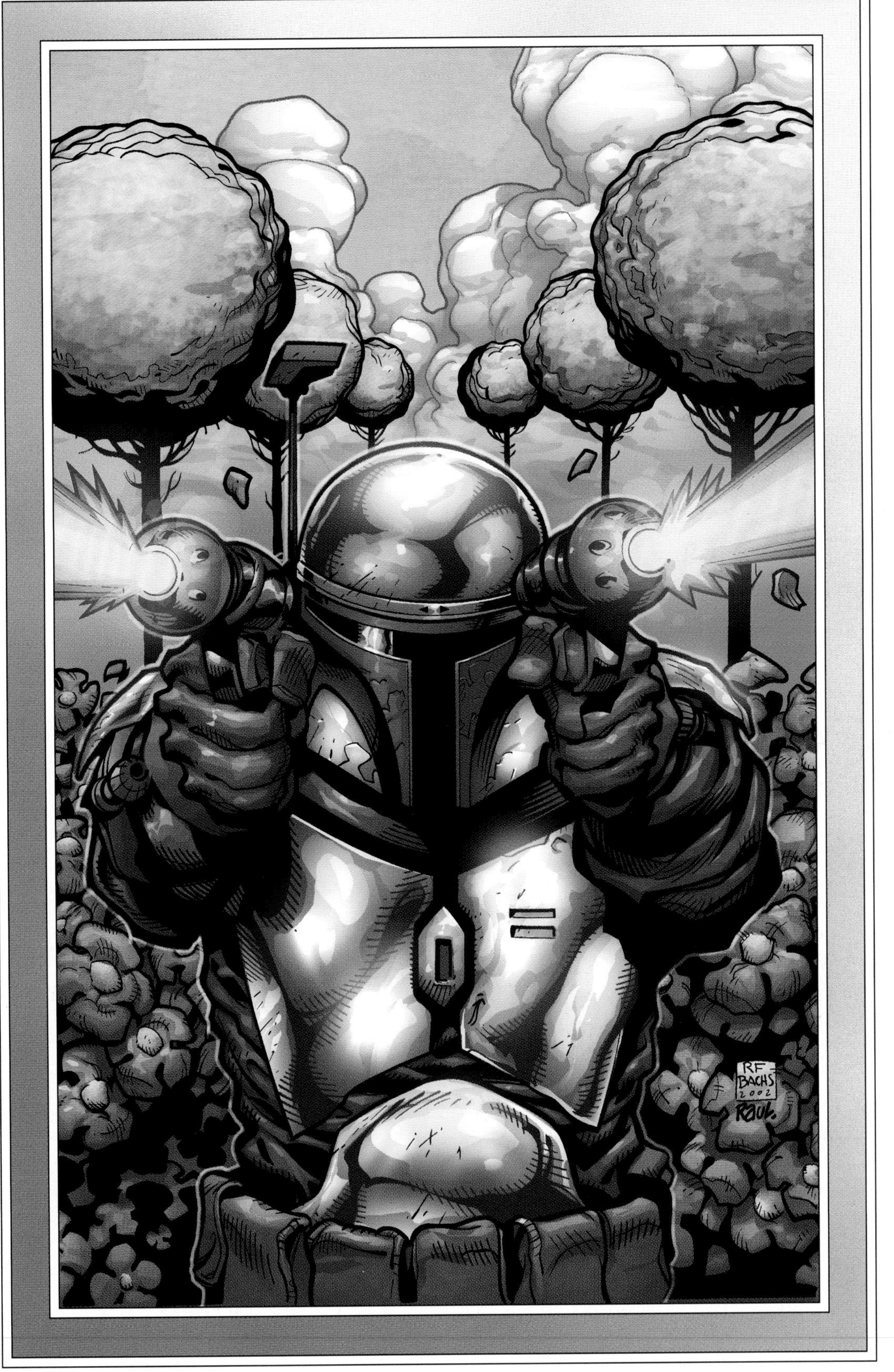
RF BACHS 2002
RAUL.

S P R I N G

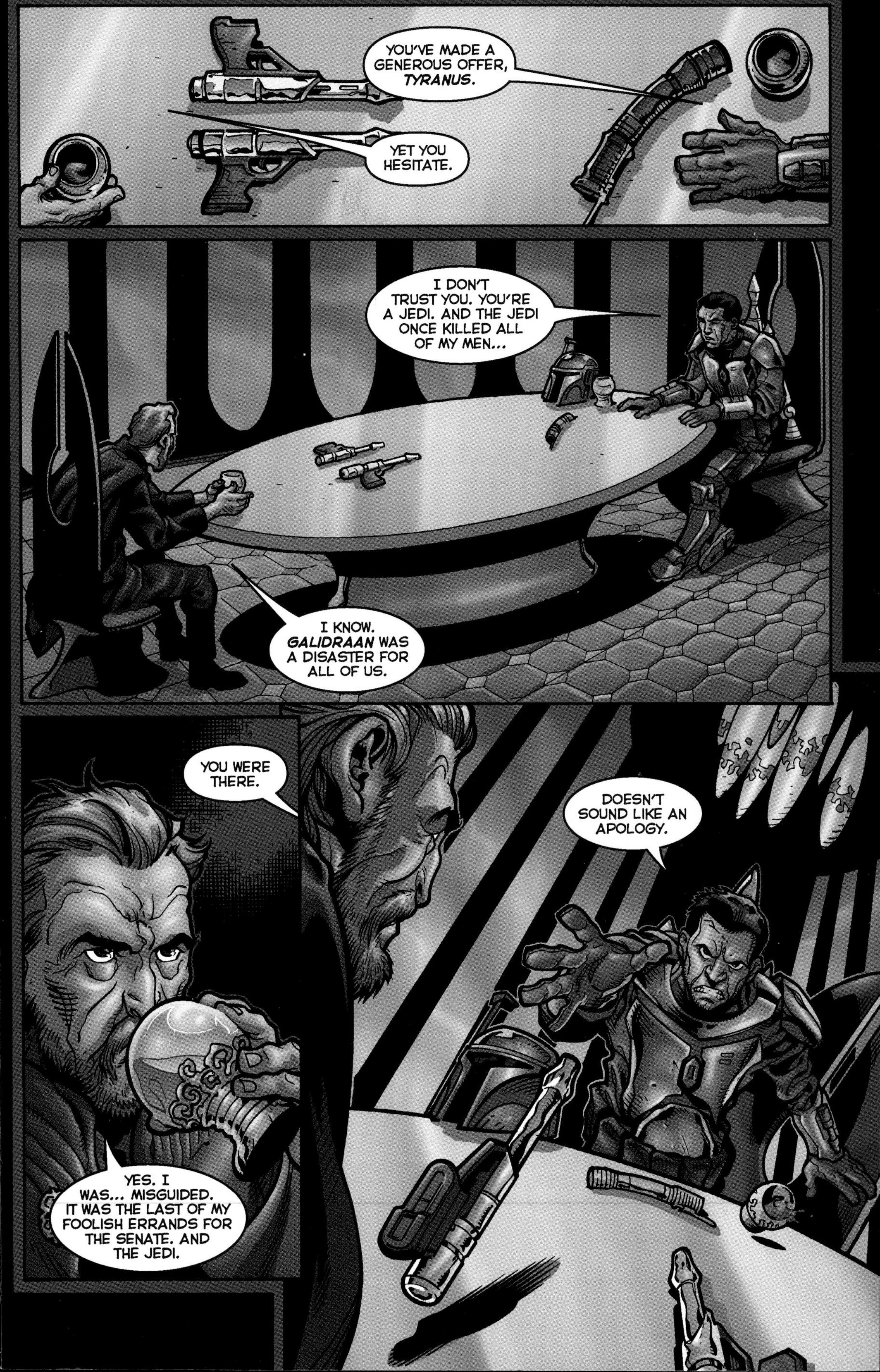
YOU'VE MADE A GENEROUS OFFER, TYRANUS.
YET YOU HESITATE.
I DON'T TRUST YOU. YOU'RE A JEDI. AND THE JEDI ONCE KILLED ALL OF MY MEN...
I KNOW. GALIDRAAN WAS A DISASTER FOR ALL OF US.
YOU WERE THERE.
DOESN'T SOUND LIKE AN APOLOGY.
YES. I WAS... MISGUIDED. IT WAS THE LAST OF MY FOOLISH ERRANDS FOR THE SENATE. AND THE JEDI.

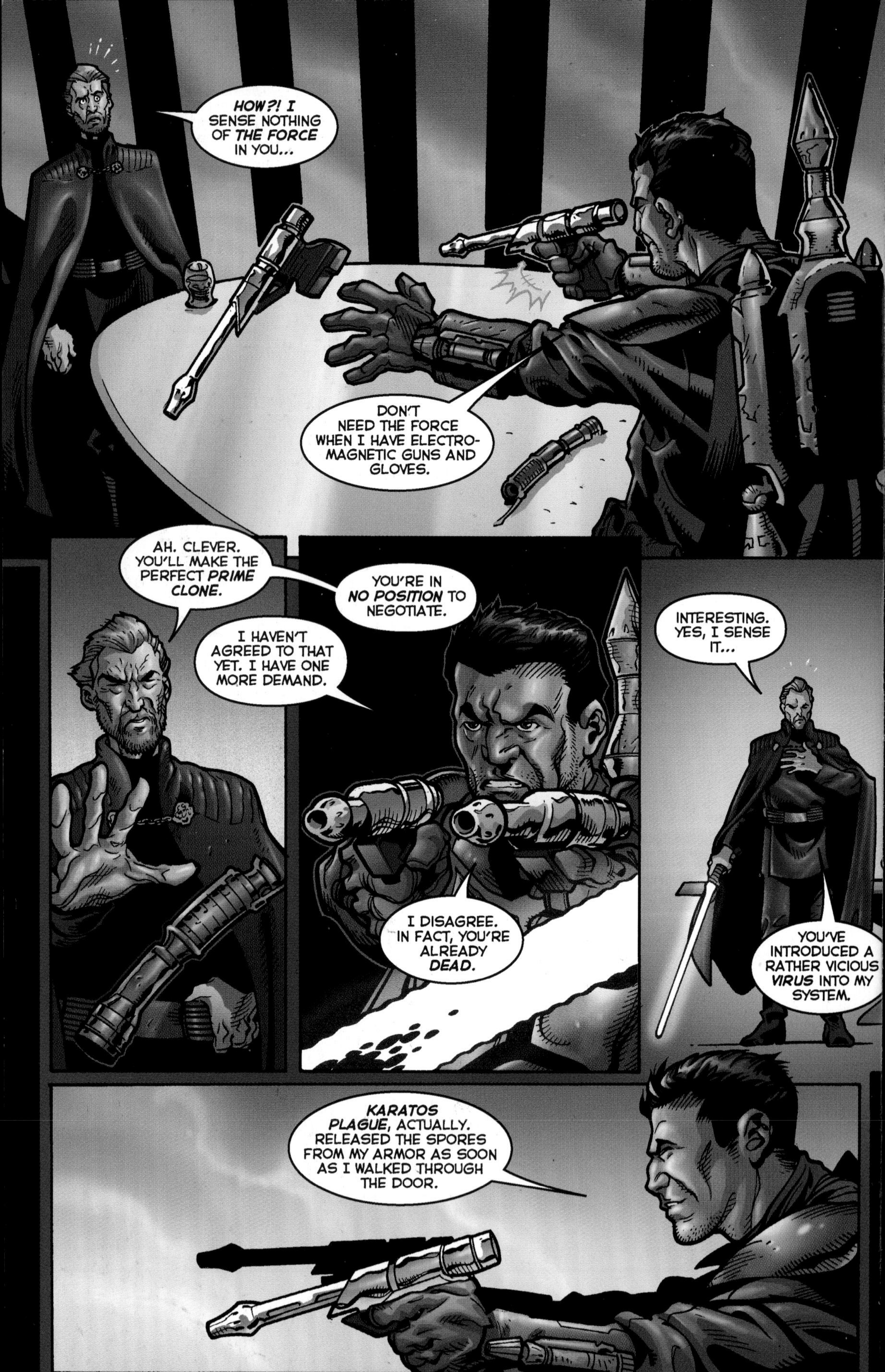
HOW?! I SENSE NOTHING OF THE FORCE IN YOU...
DON'T NEED THE FORCE WHEN I HAVE ELECTRO-MAGNETIC GUNS AND GLOVES.
AH. CLEVER. YOU'LL MAKE THE PERFECT PRIME CLONE.
I HAVEN'T AGREED TO THAT YET. I HAVE ONE MORE DEMAND.
YOU'RE IN NO POSITION TO NEGOTIATE.
I DISAGREE. IN FACT, YOU'RE ALREADY DEAD.
INTERESTING. YES, I SENSE IT...
YOU'VE INTRODUCED A RATHER VICIOUS VIRUS INTO MY SYSTEM.
KARATOS PLAGUE, ACTUALLY. RELEASED THE SPORES FROM MY ARMOR AS SOON AS I WALKED THROUGH THE DOOR.

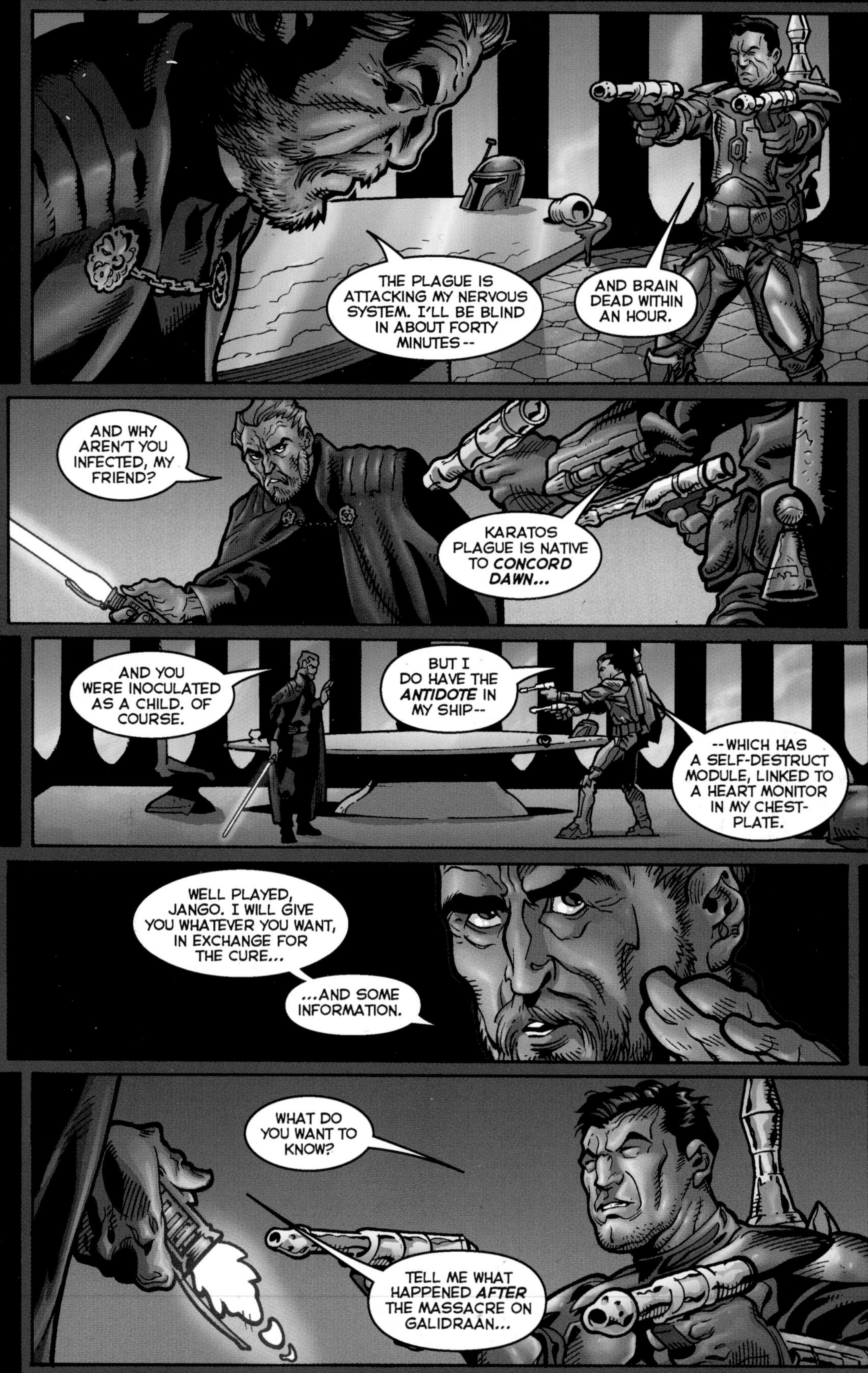
THE PLAGUE IS ATTACKING MY NERVOUS SYSTEM. I'LL BE BLIND IN ABOUT FORTY MINUTES--
AND BRAIN DEAD WITHIN AN HOUR.
AND WHY AREN'T YOU INFECTED, MY FRIEND?
KARATOS PLAGUE IS NATIVE TO *CONCORD DAWN...*
AND YOU WERE INOCULATED AS A CHILD. OF COURSE.
BUT I DO HAVE THE *ANTIDOTE* IN MY SHIP--
--WHICH HAS A SELF-DESTRUCT MODULE, LINKED TO A HEART MONITOR IN MY CHEST-PLATE.
WELL PLAYED, JANGO. I WILL GIVE YOU WHATEVER YOU WANT, IN EXCHANGE FOR THE CURE...
...AND SOME INFORMATION.
WHAT DO YOU WANT TO KNOW?
TELL ME WHAT HAPPENED *AFTER* THE MASSACRE ON GALIDRAAN...

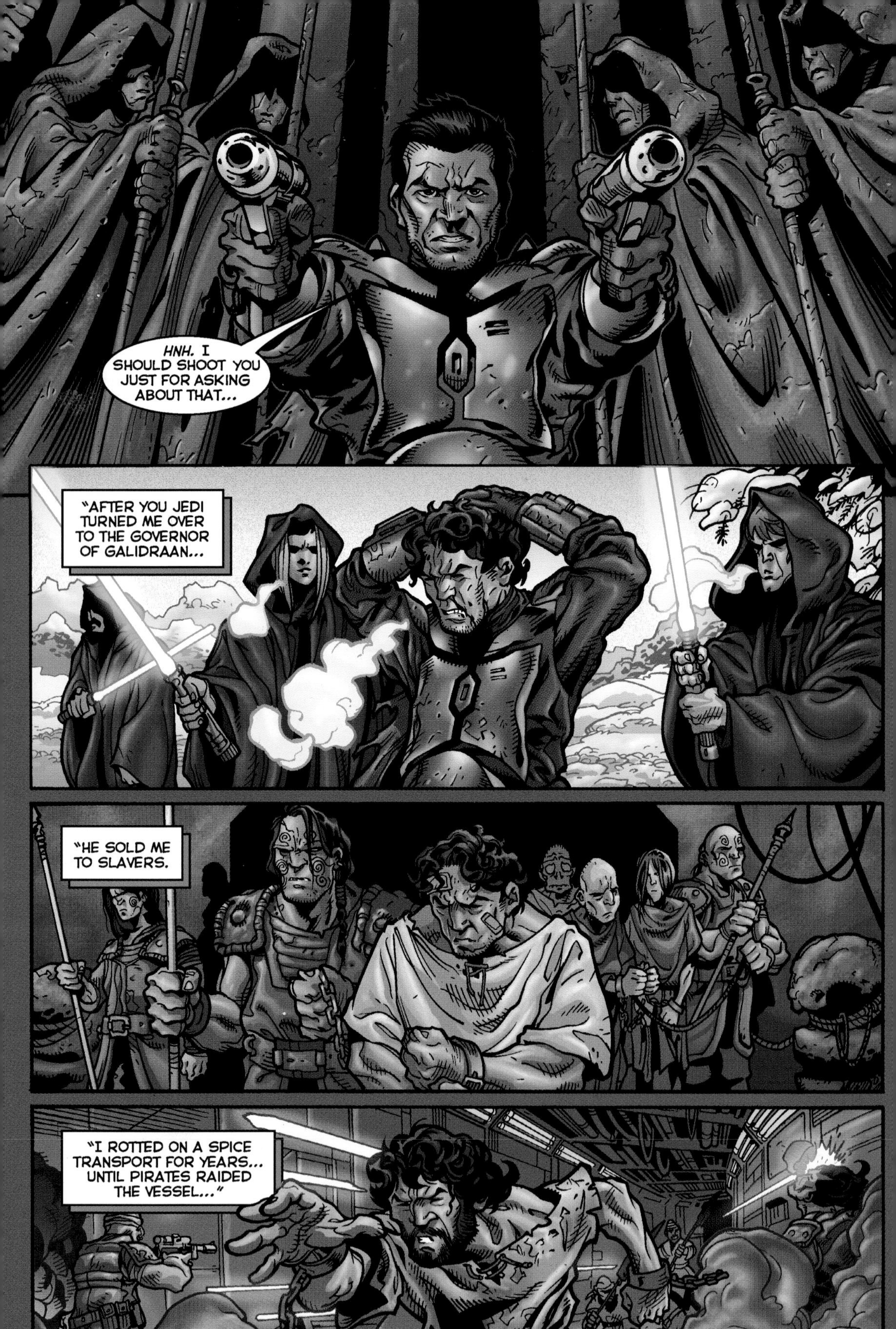
HNH. I SHOULD SHOOT YOU JUST FOR ASKING ABOUT THAT...
"AFTER YOU JEDI TURNED ME OVER TO THE GOVERNOR OF GALIDRAAN...
"HE SOLD ME TO SLAVERS.
"I ROTTED ON A SPICE TRANSPORT FOR YEARS... UNTIL PIRATES RAIDED THE VESSEL..."

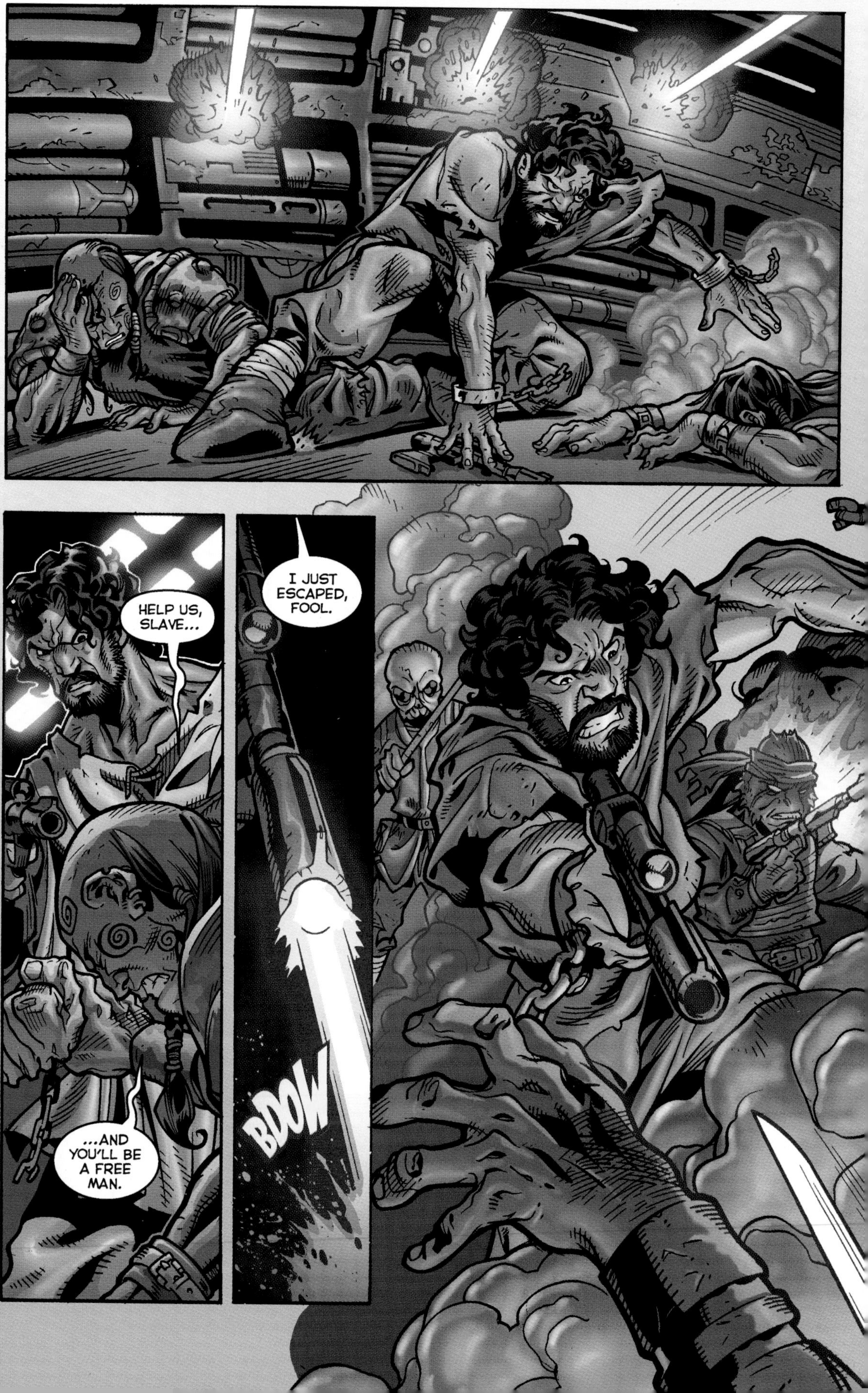

HELP US, SLAVE...
...AND YOU'LL BE A FREE MAN.
I JUST ESCAPED, FOOL.
BDOW

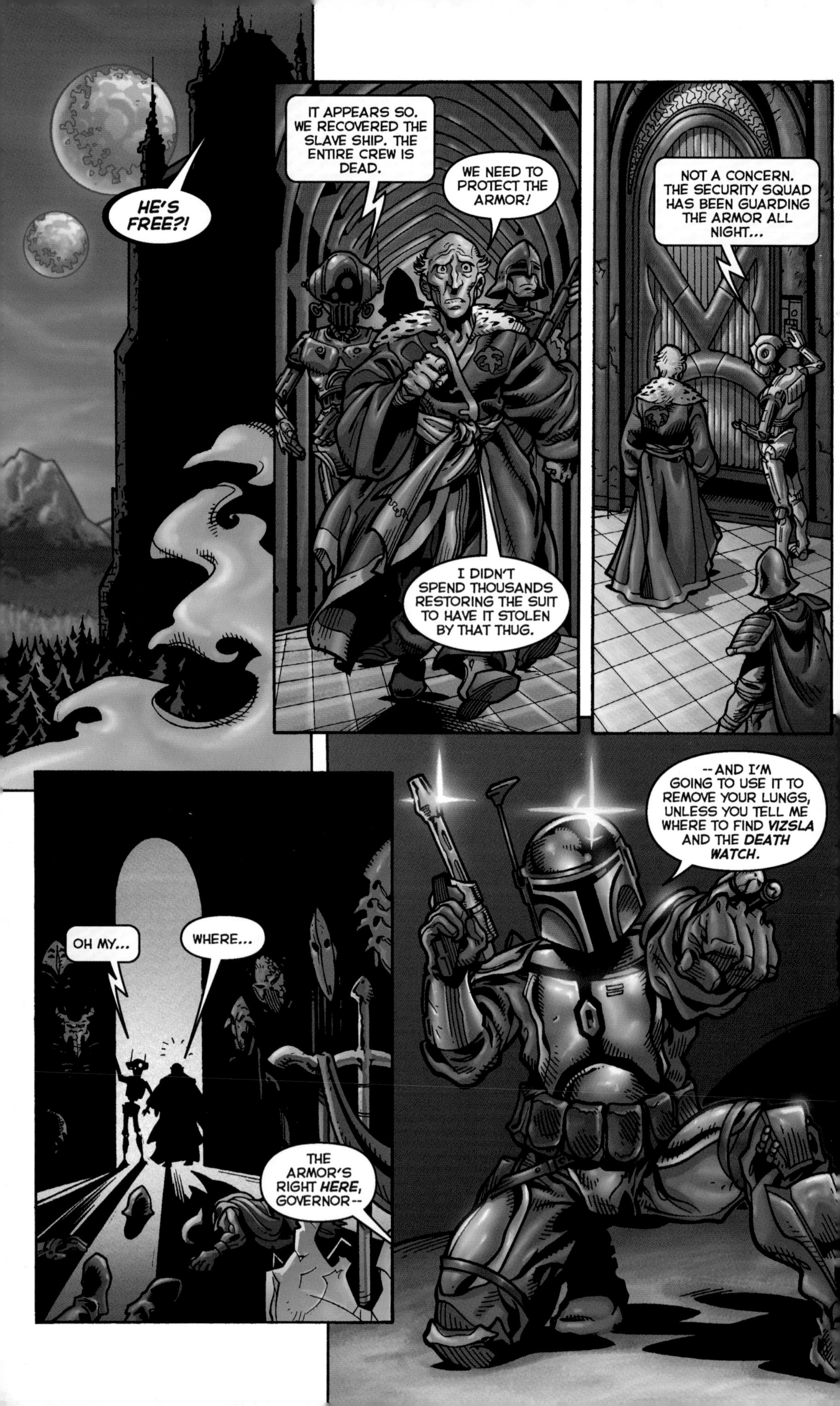
HE'S FREE?!
IT APPEARS SO. WE RECOVERED THE SLAVE SHIP. THE ENTIRE CREW IS DEAD.
WE NEED TO PROTECT THE ARMOR!
I DIDN'T SPEND THOUSANDS RESTORING THE SUIT TO HAVE IT STOLEN BY THAT THUG.
NOT A CONCERN. THE SECURITY SQUAD HAS BEEN GUARDING THE ARMOR ALL NIGHT...
OH MY...
WHERE...
THE ARMOR'S RIGHT HERE, GOVERNOR--
--AND I'M GOING TO USE IT TO REMOVE YOUR LUNGS, UNLESS YOU TELL ME WHERE TO FIND VIZSLA AND THE DEATH WATCH.

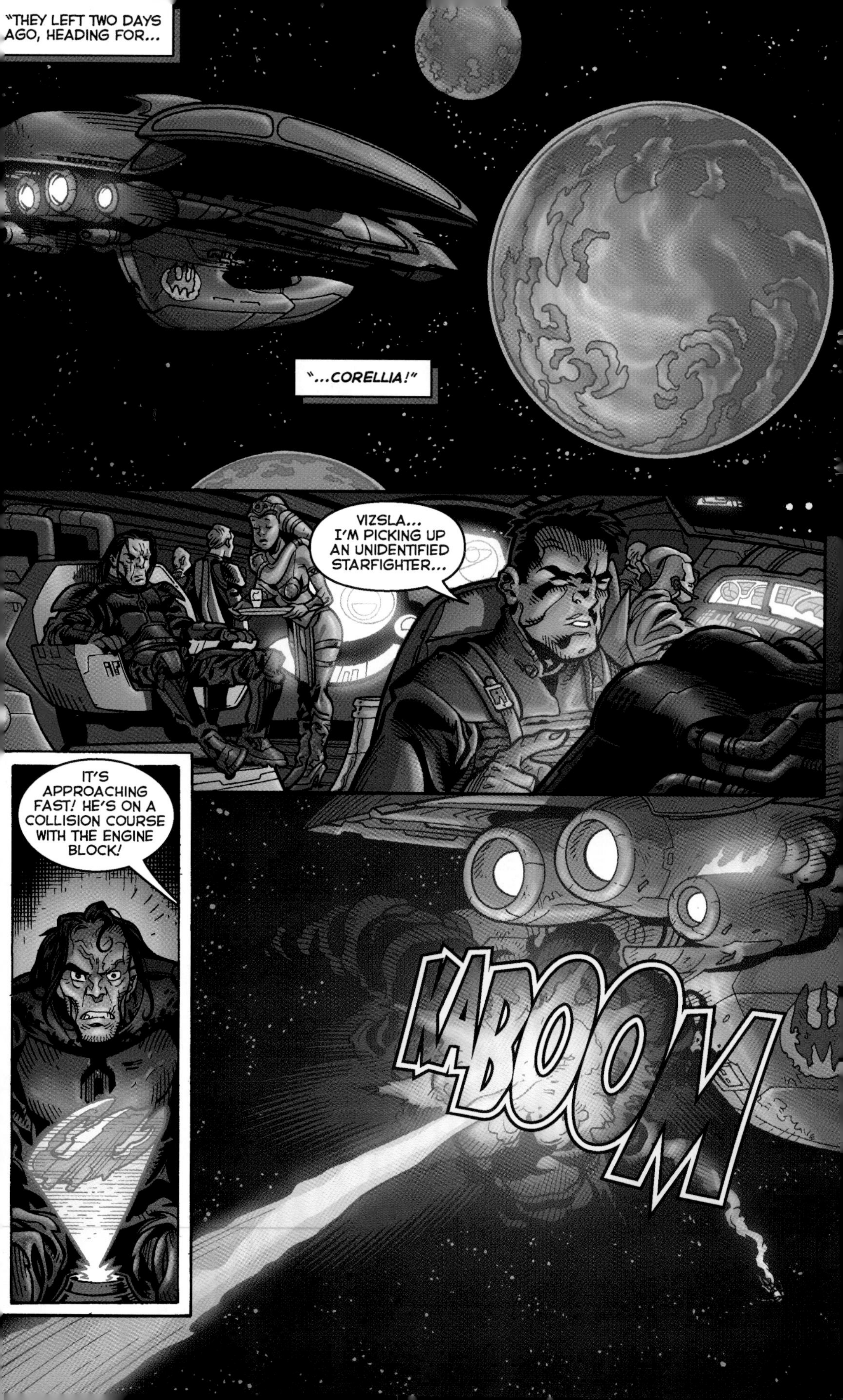
"THEY LEFT TWO DAYS AGO, HEADING FOR...
"...CORELLIA!"
VIZSLA... I'M PICKING UP AN UNIDENTIFIED STARFIGHTER...
IT'S APPROACHING FAST! HE'S ON A COLLISION COURSE WITH THE ENGINE BLOCK!
KABOOM

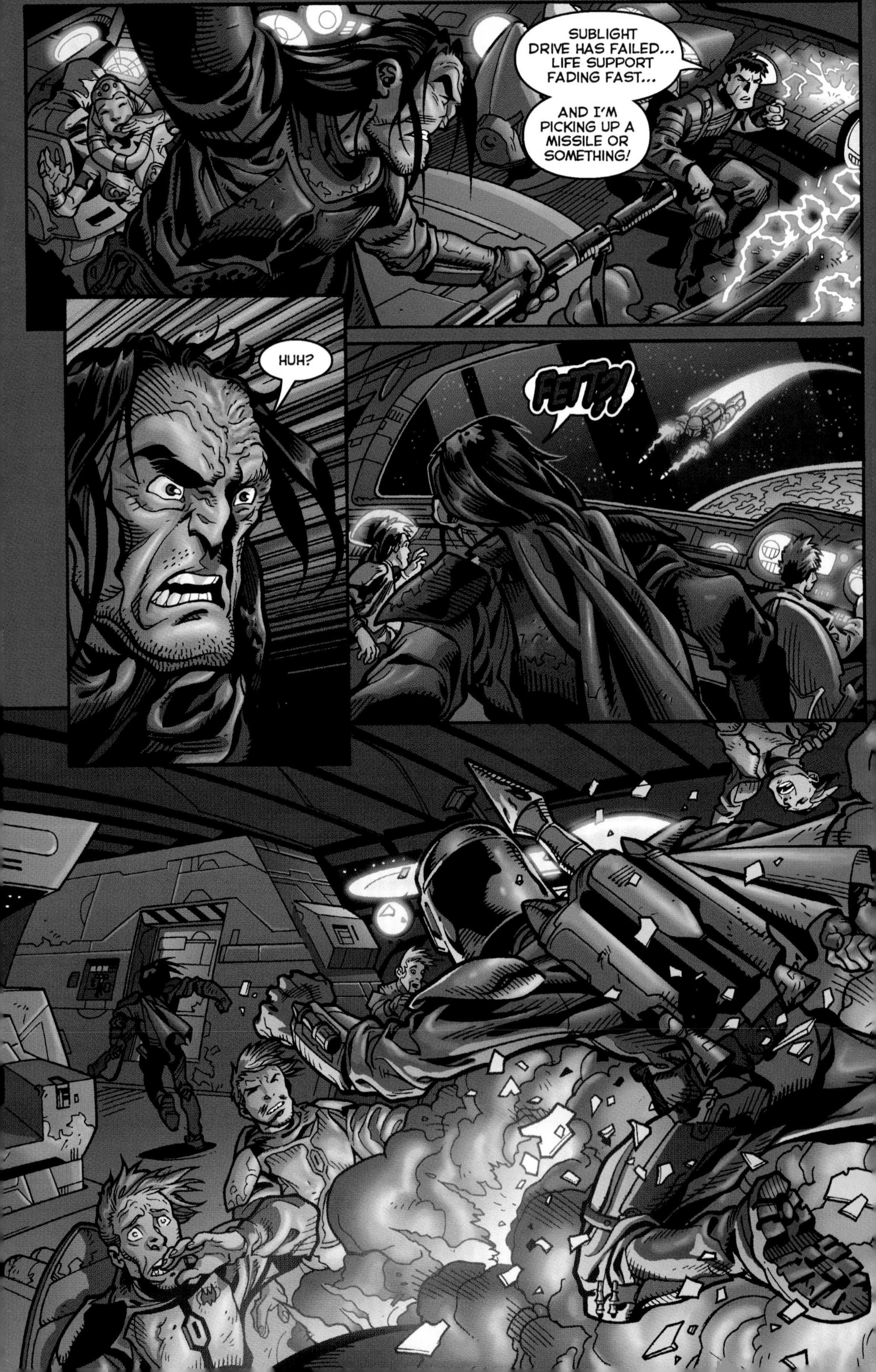
SUBLIGHT DRIVE HAS FAILED... LIFE SUPPORT FADING FAST...
AND I'M PICKING UP A MISSILE OR SOMETHING!
HUH?
FETT?!

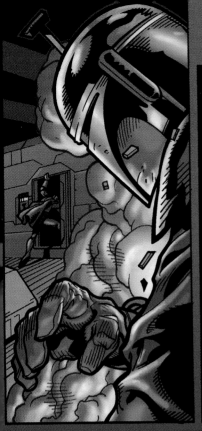

THE BLAST DOORS ARE CLOSING!

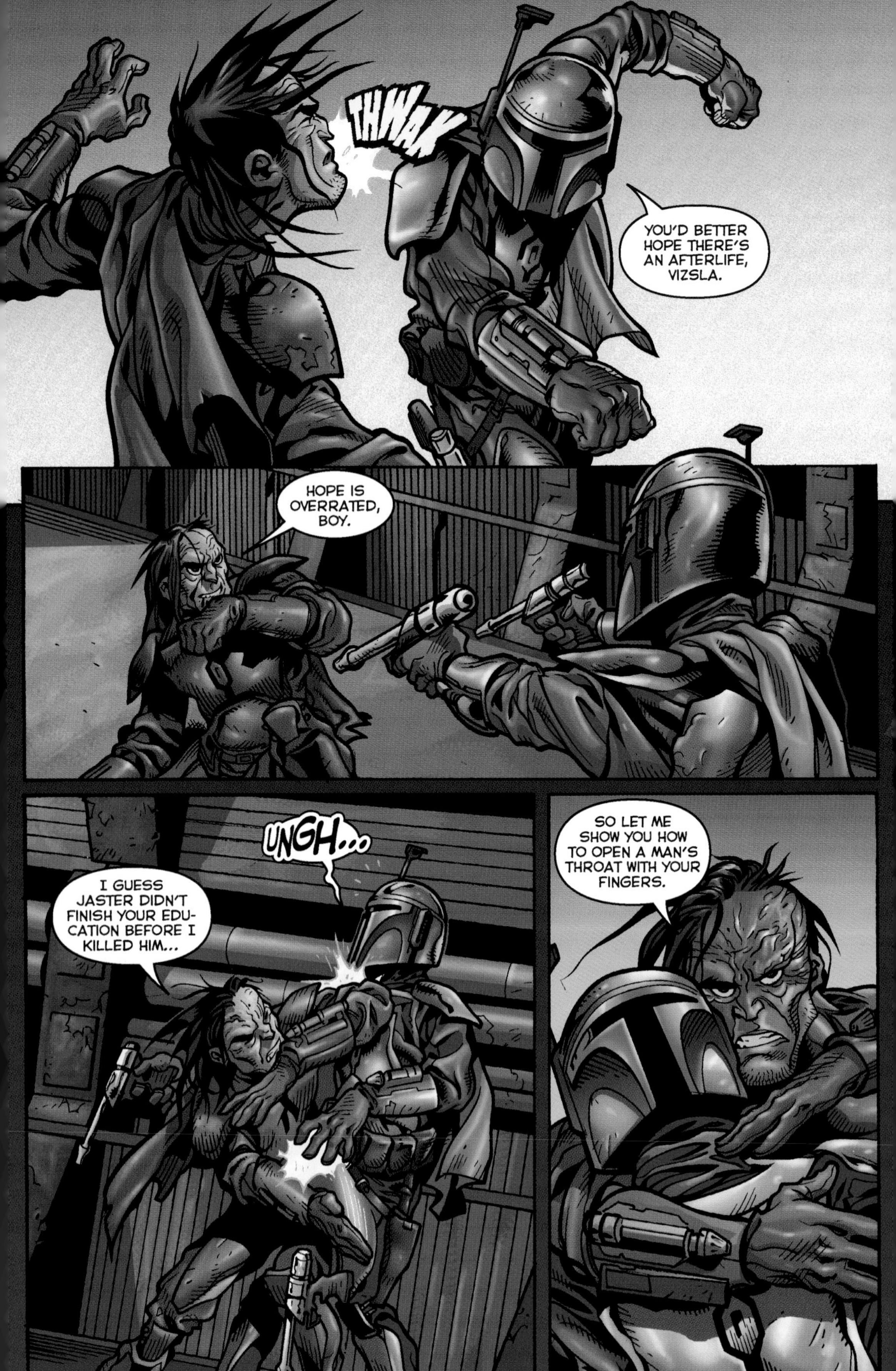
THWAK
YOU'D BETTER HOPE THERE'S AN AFTERLIFE, VIZSLA.
HOPE IS OVERRATED, BOY.
UNGH...
I GUESS JASTER DIDN'T FINISH YOUR EDU-CATION BEFORE I KILLED HIM...
SO LET ME SHOW YOU HOW TO OPEN A MAN'S THROAT WITH YOUR FINGERS.

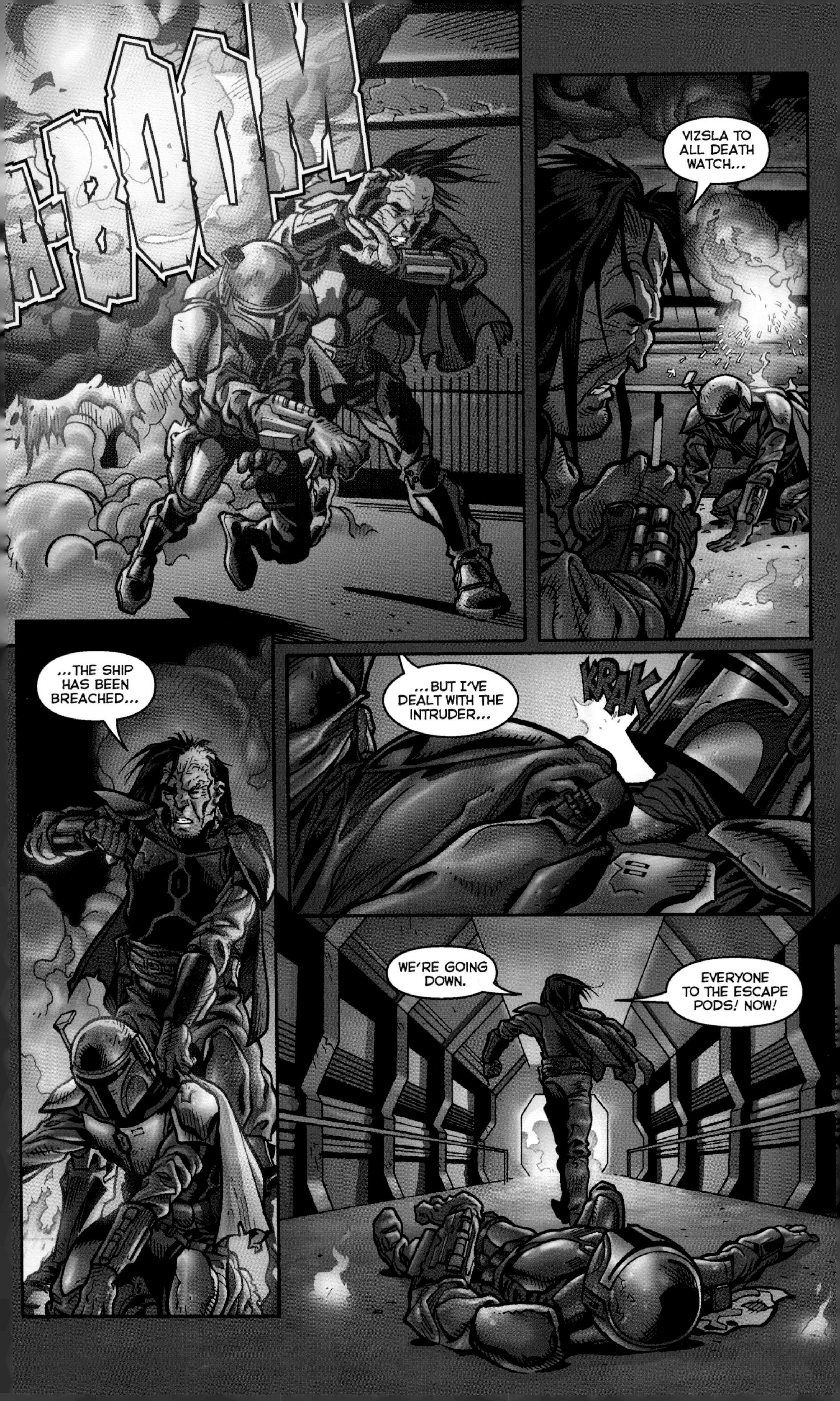

KA-BOOM
VIZSLA TO ALL DEATH WATCH...
...THE SHIP HAS BEEN BREACHED...
...BUT I'VE DEALT WITH THE INTRUDER...
KRAK
WE'RE GOING DOWN.
EVERYONE TO THE ESCAPE PODS! NOW!

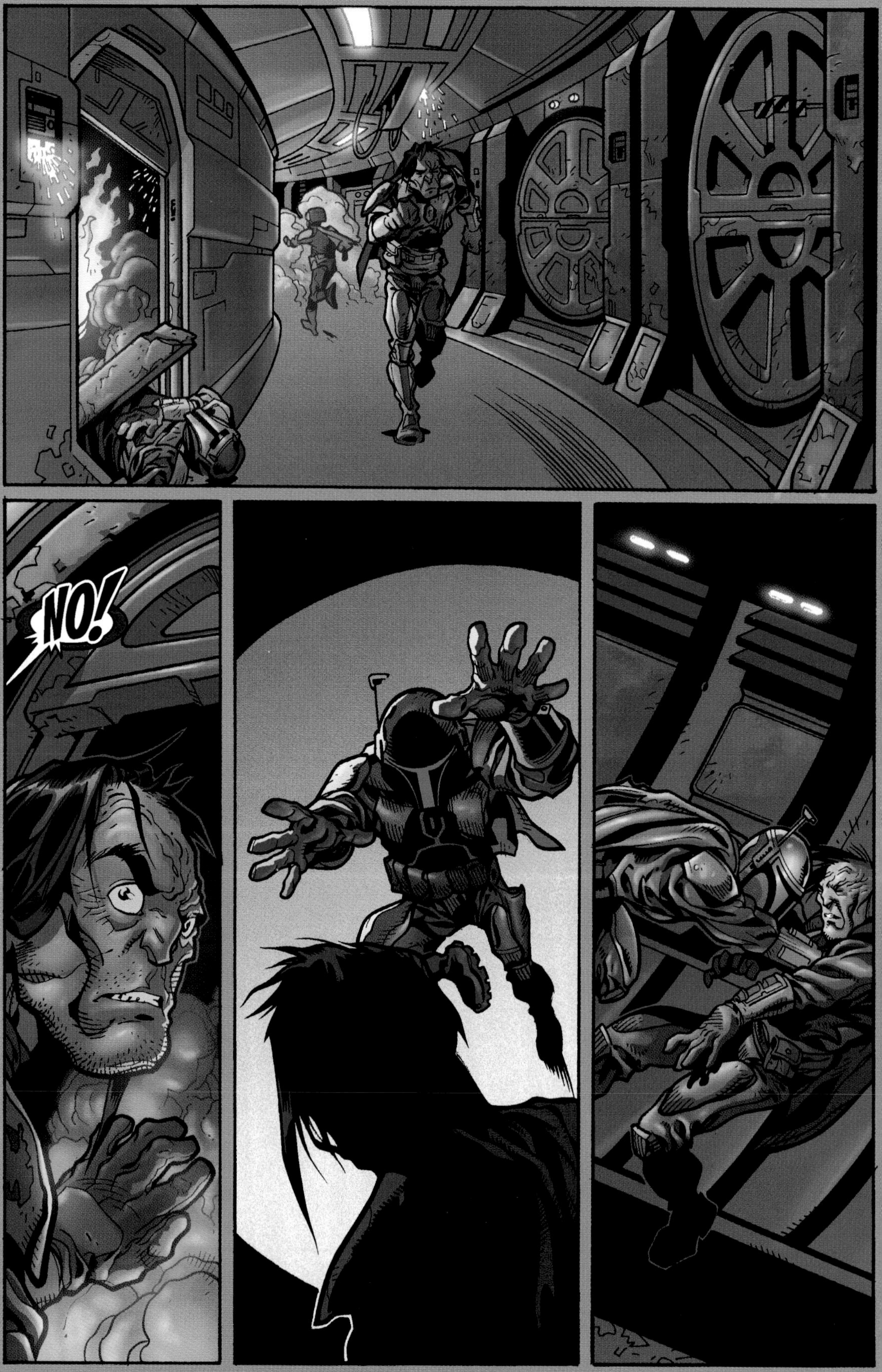
NO!

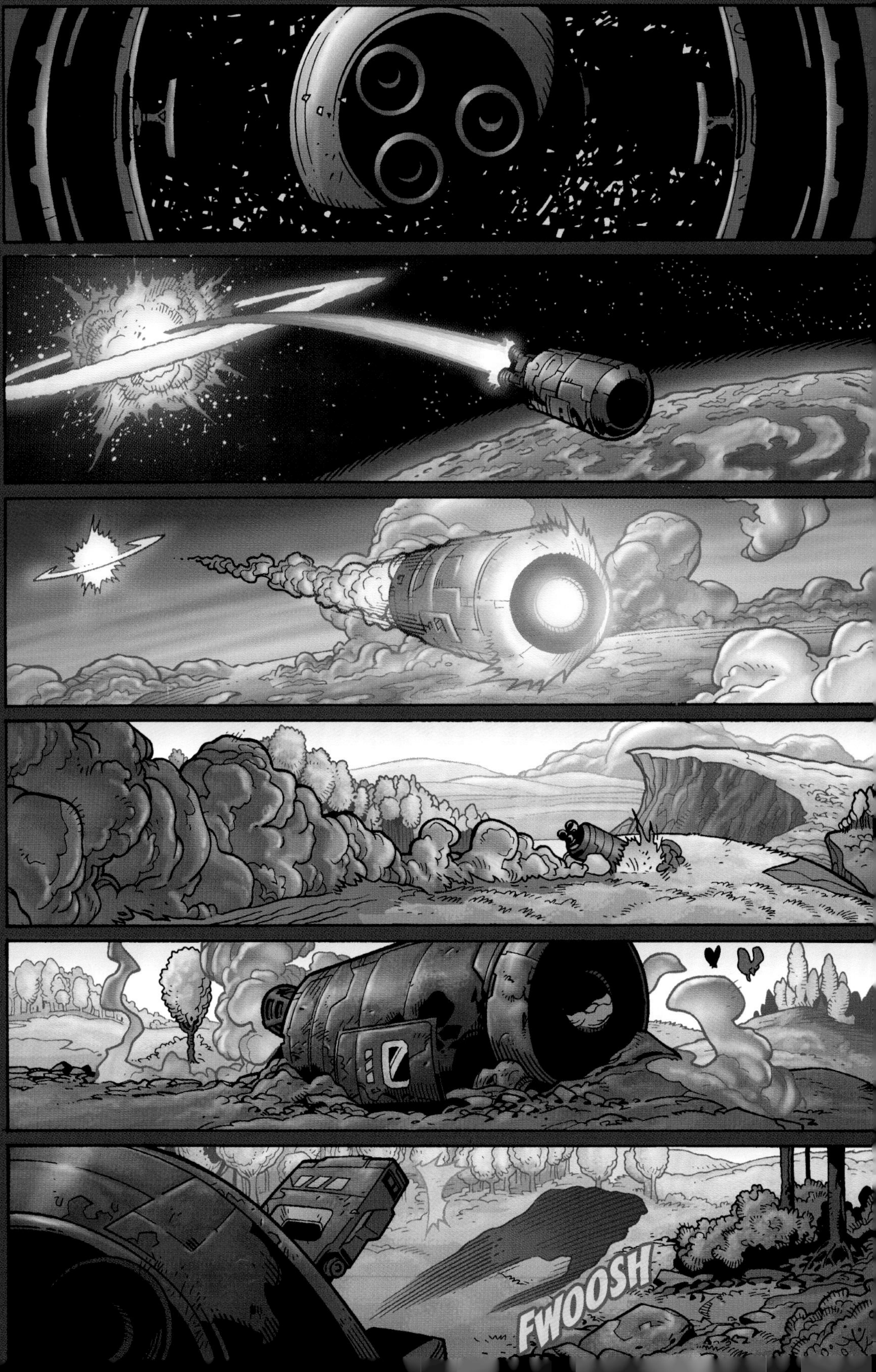
FWOOSH

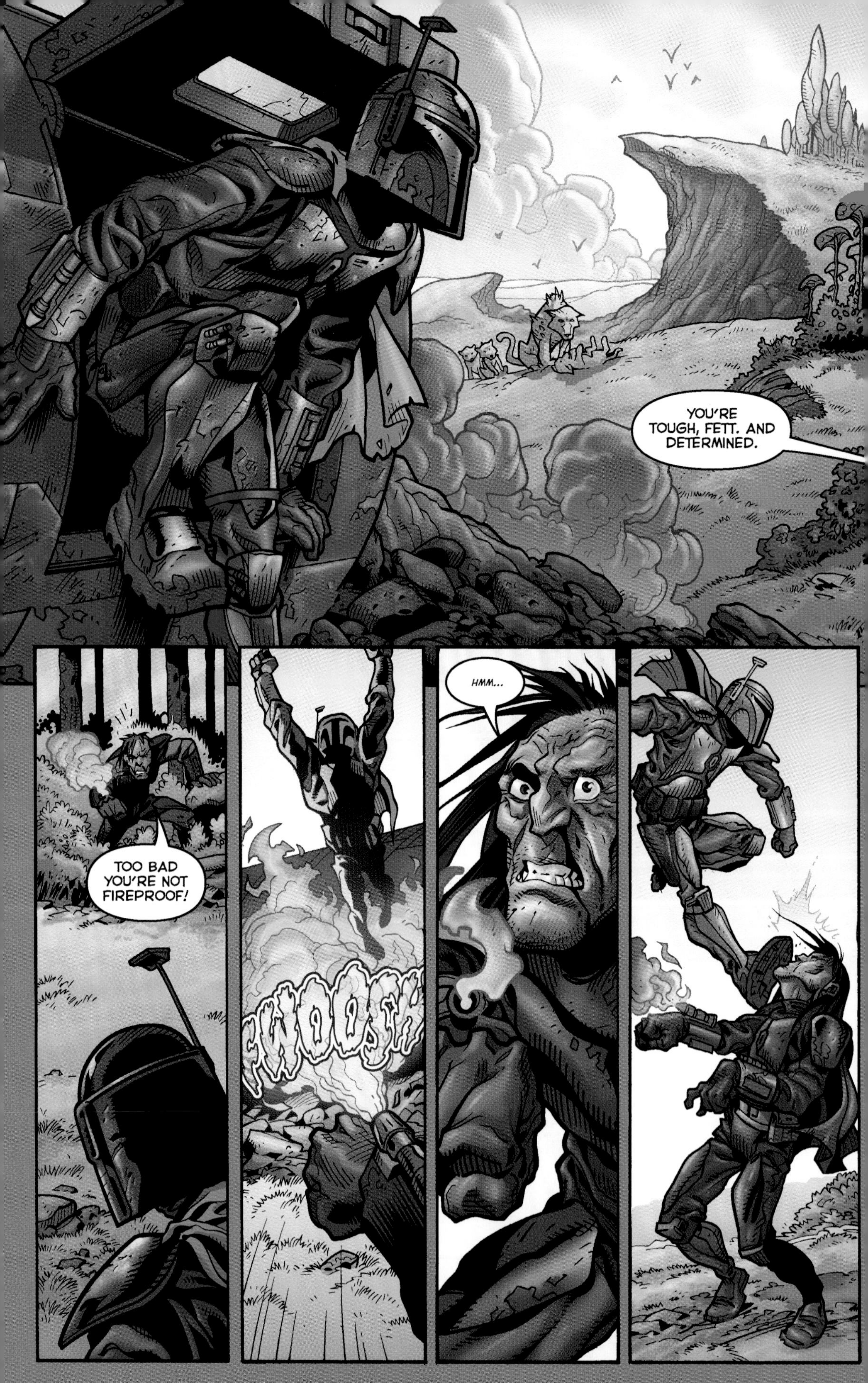
YOU'RE TOUGH, FETT. AND DETERMINED.
TOO BAD YOU'RE NOT FIREPROOF!
WHOOSH
HMM...

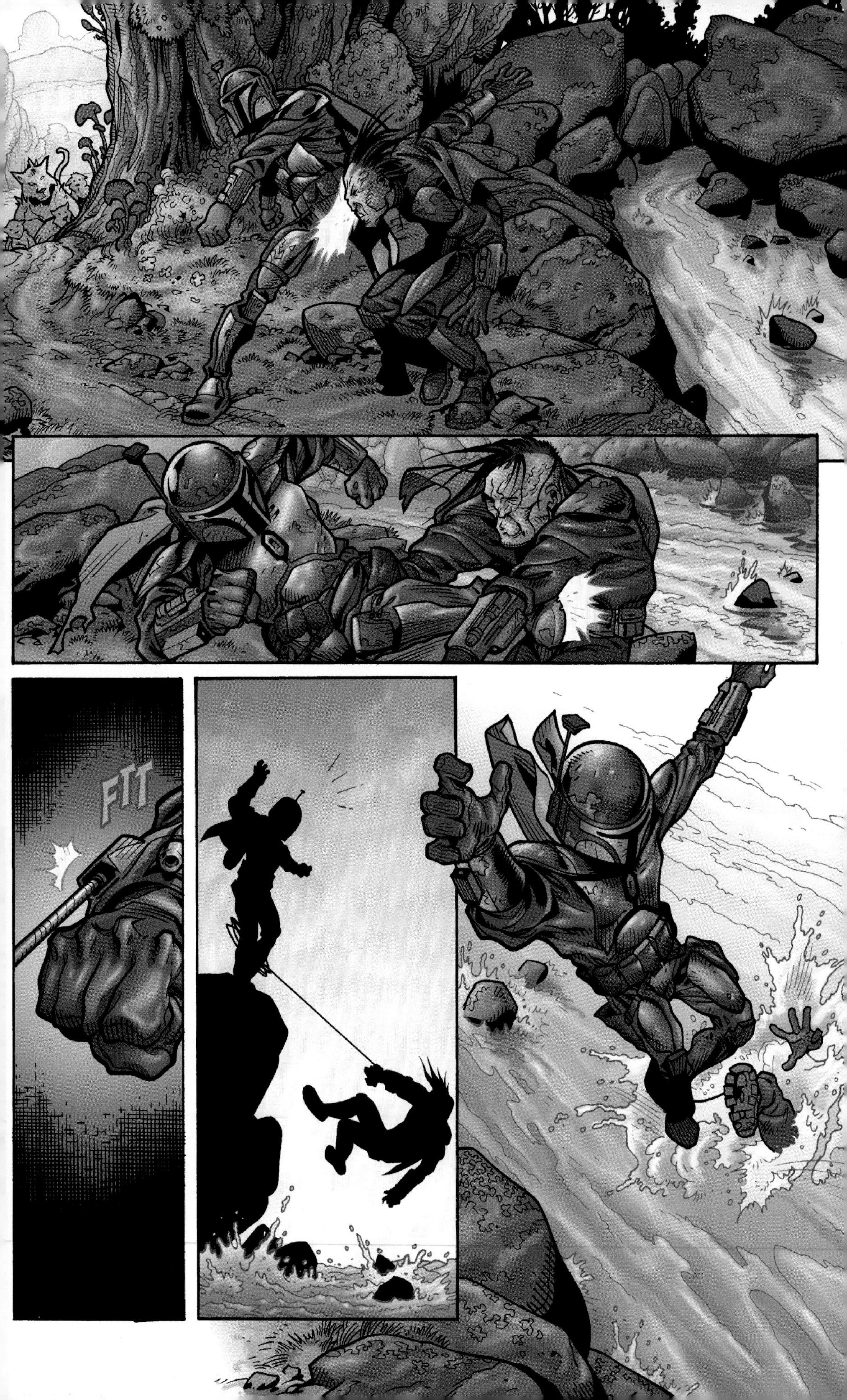
FTT

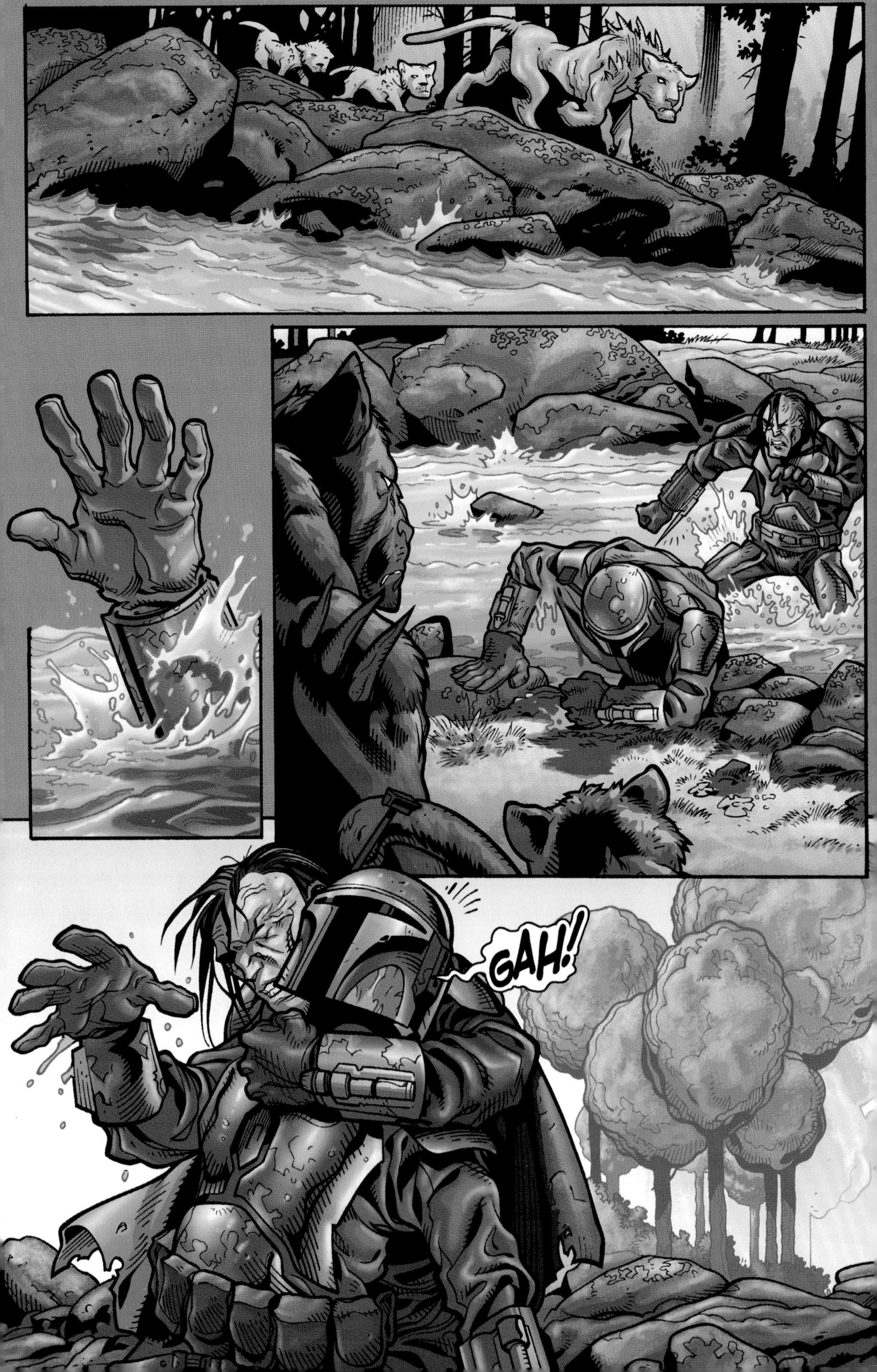
GAH!

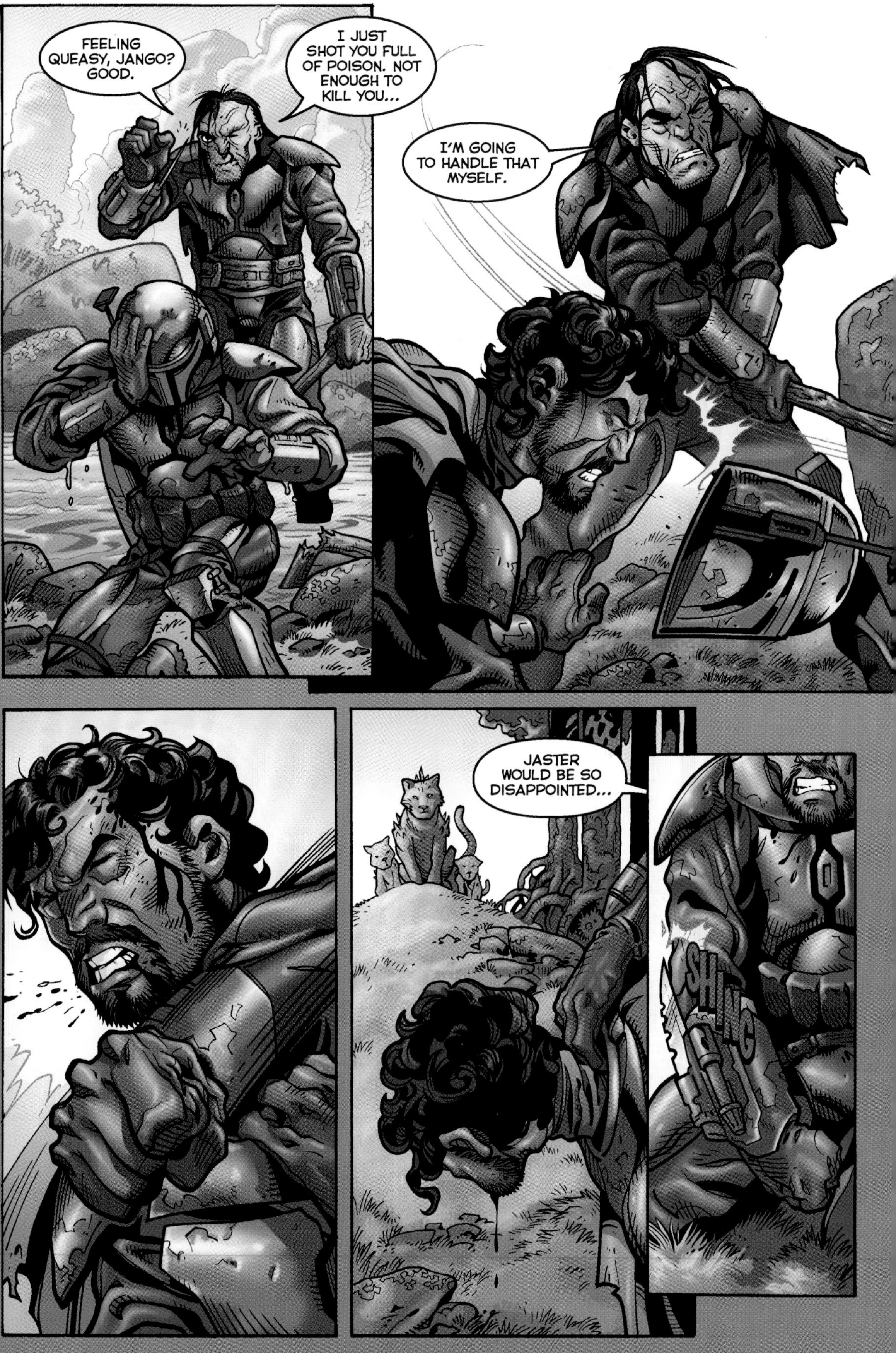
FEELING QUEASY, JANGO? GOOD.
I JUST SHOT YOU FULL OF POISON. NOT ENOUGH TO KILL YOU...
I'M GOING TO HANDLE THAT MYSELF.
JASTER WOULD BE SO DISAPPOINTED...
SHING

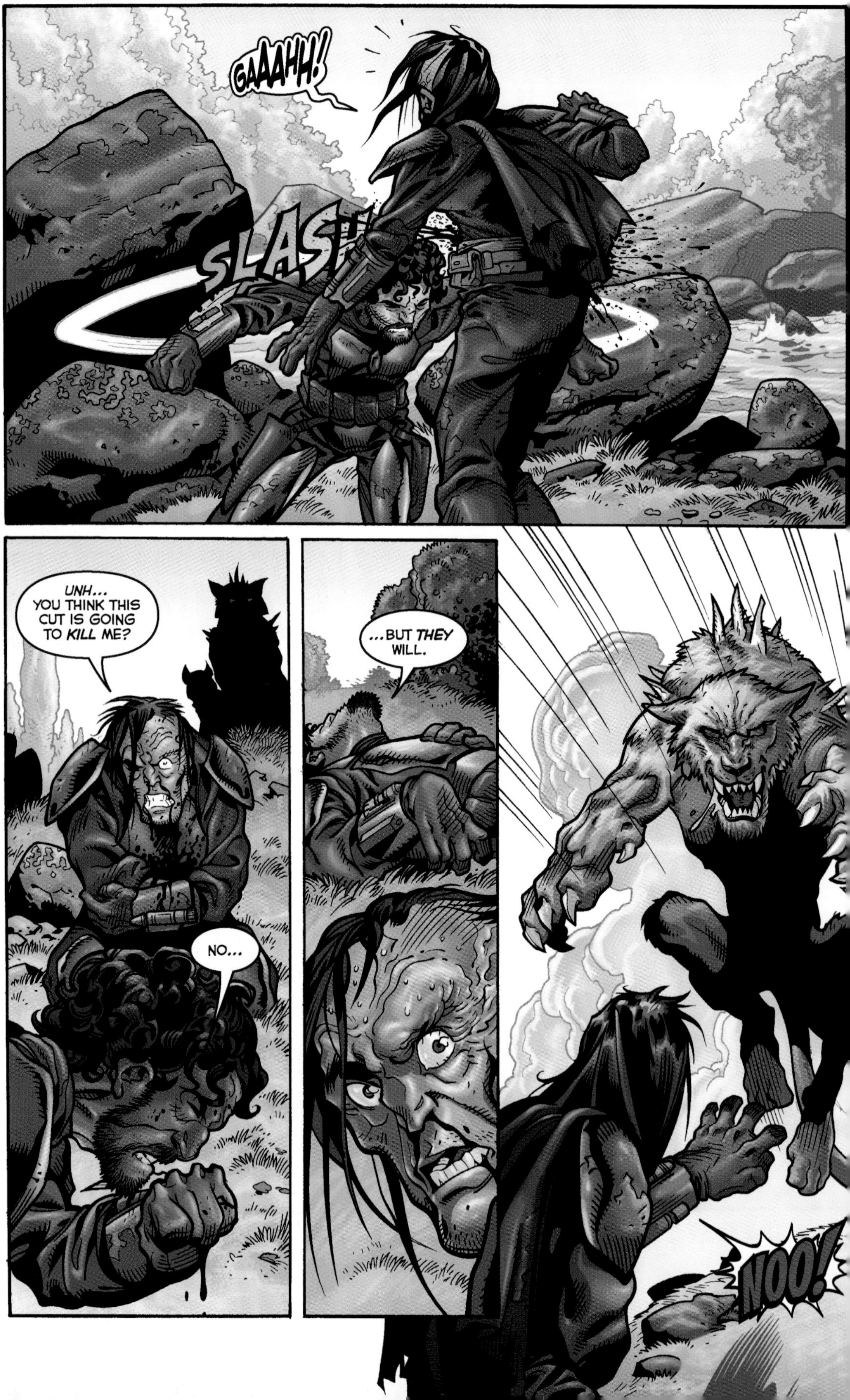

GAAAHH!
SLASH
UNH... YOU THINK THIS CUT IS GOING TO KILL ME?
NO...
...BUT THEY WILL.
NOO!

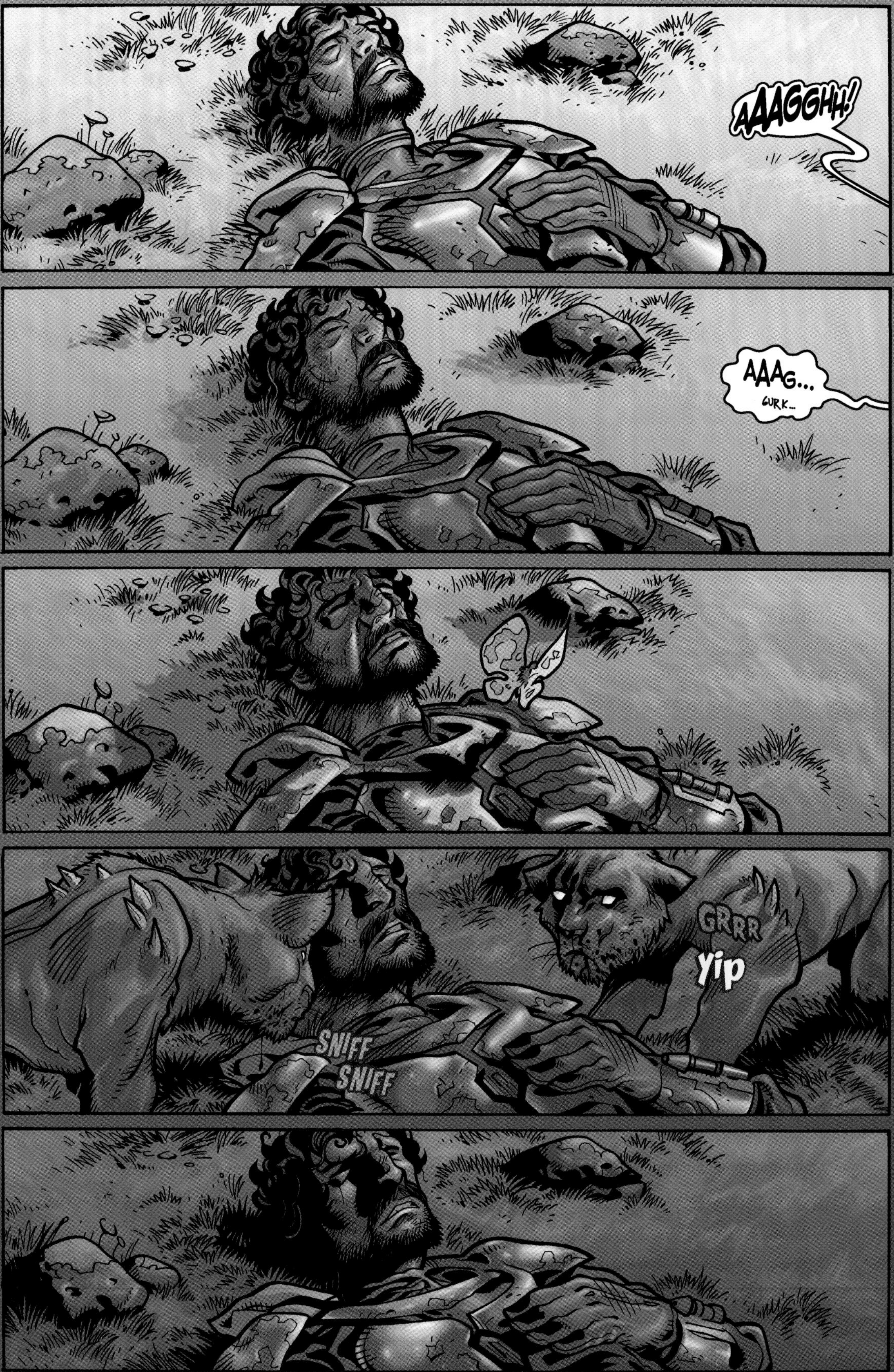
AAAGGHH!
AAAG...
GURK...
GRRR
YIP
SNIFF
SNIFF

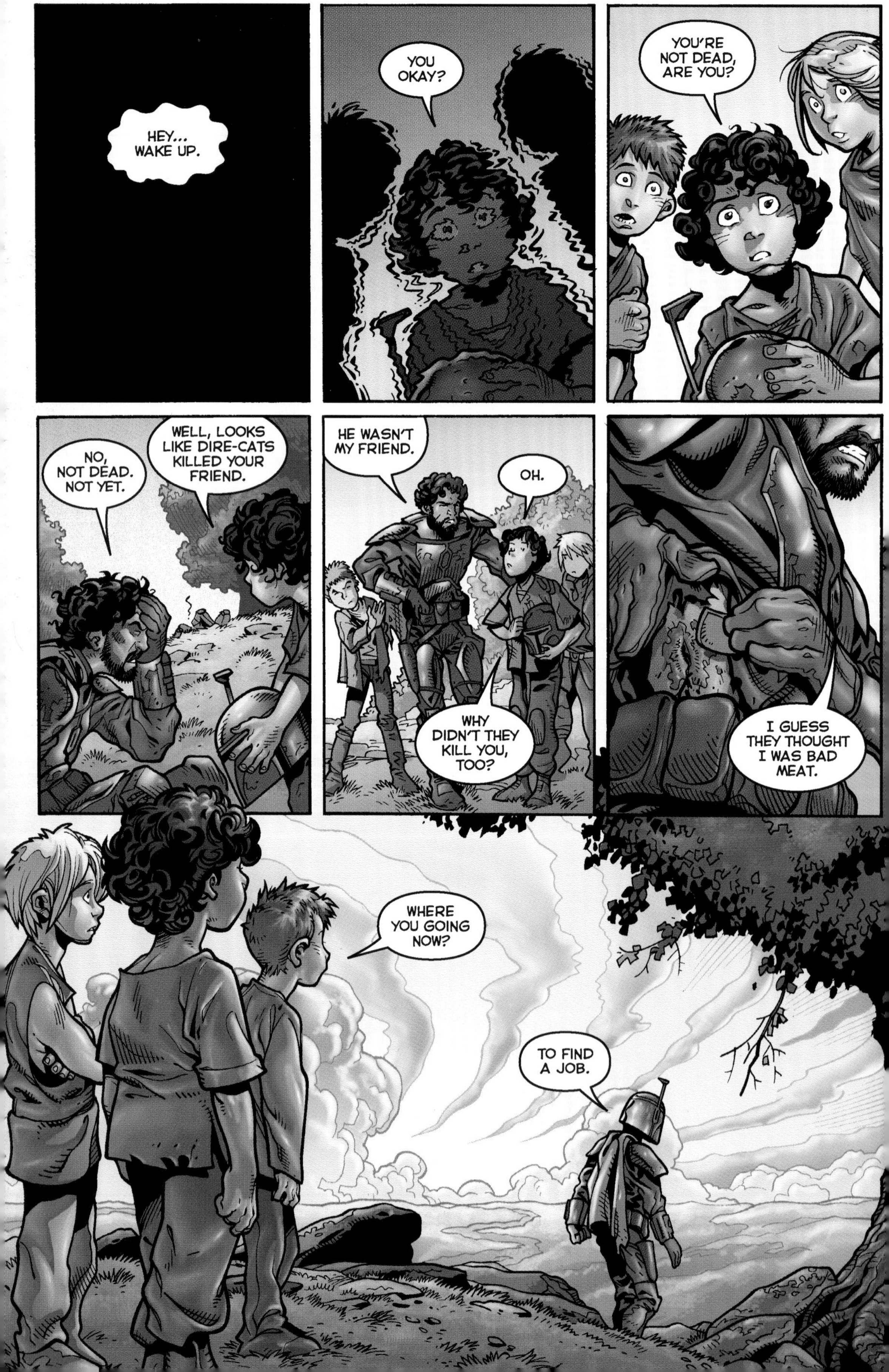
HEY... WAKE UP.
YOU OKAY?
YOU'RE NOT DEAD, ARE YOU?
NO, NOT DEAD. NOT YET.
WELL, LOOKS LIKE DIRE-CATS KILLED YOUR FRIEND.
HE WASN'T MY FRIEND.
OH.
WHY DIDN'T THEY KILL YOU, TOO?
I GUESS THEY THOUGHT I WAS BAD MEAT.
WHERE YOU GOING NOW?
TO FIND A JOB.

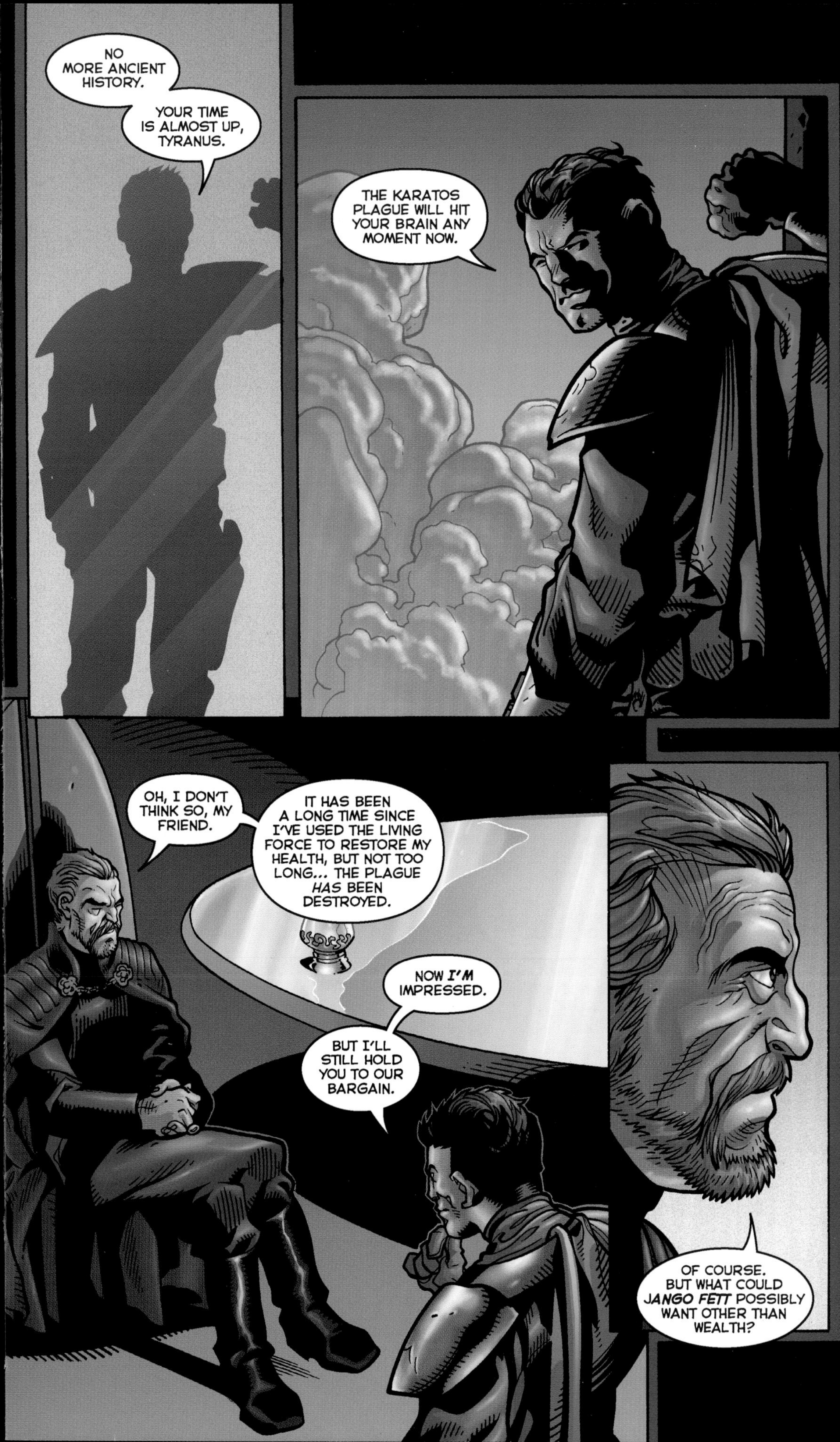

NO MORE ANCIENT HISTORY.
YOUR TIME IS ALMOST UP, TYRANUS.
THE KARATOS PLAGUE WILL HIT YOUR BRAIN ANY MOMENT NOW.
OH, I DON'T THINK SO, MY FRIEND.
IT HAS BEEN A LONG TIME SINCE I'VE USED THE LIVING FORCE TO RESTORE MY HEALTH, BUT NOT TOO LONG... THE PLAGUE *HAS* BEEN DESTROYED.
NOW *I'M* IMPRESSED.
BUT I'LL STILL HOLD YOU TO OUR BARGAIN.
OF COURSE. BUT WHAT COULD *JANGO FETT* POSSIBLY WANT OTHER THAN WEALTH?

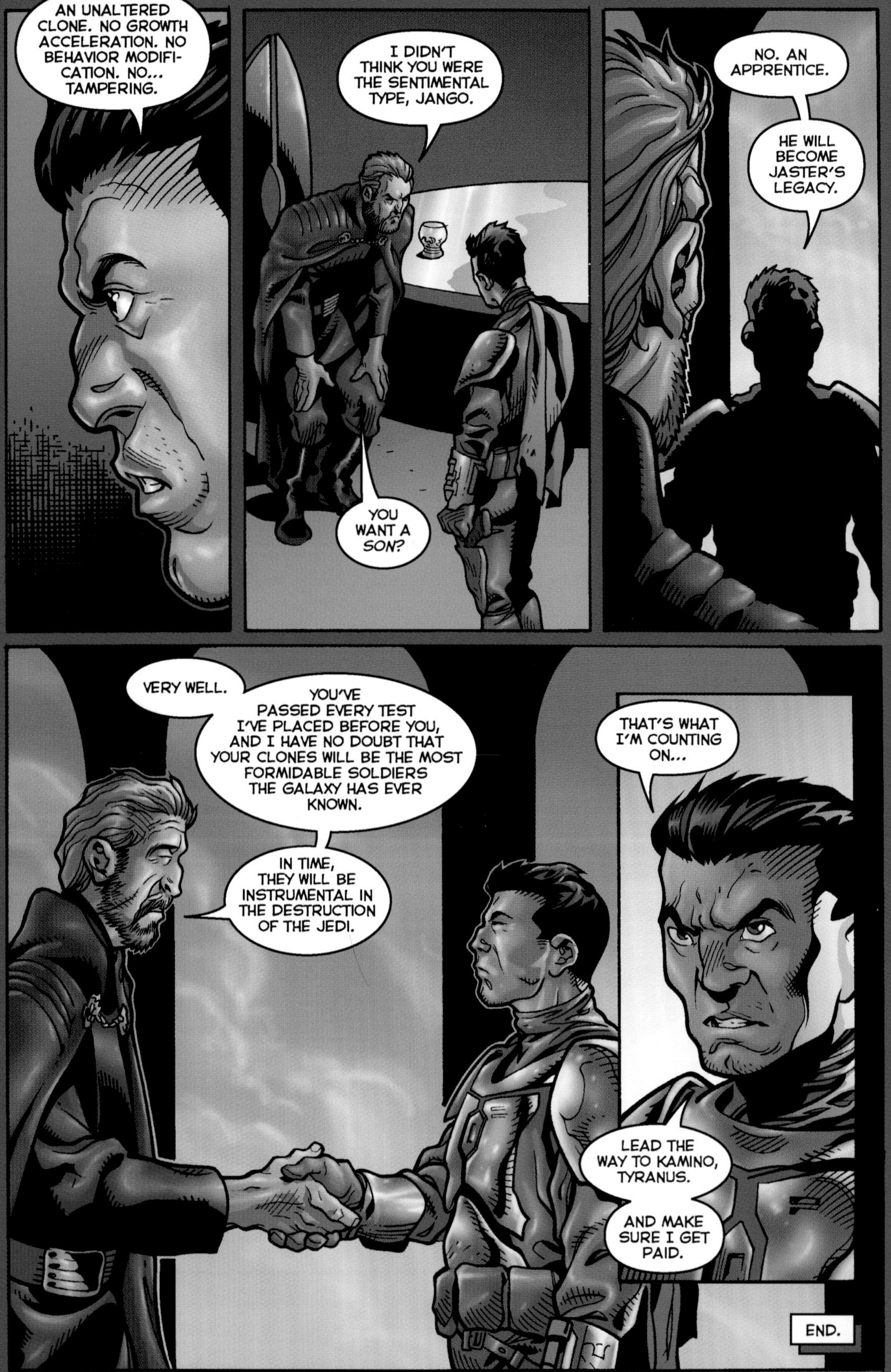
AN UNALTERED CLONE. NO GROWTH ACCELERATION. NO BEHAVIOR MODIFICATION. NO... TAMPERING.
I DIDN'T THINK YOU WERE THE SENTIMENTAL TYPE, JANGO.
YOU WANT A SON?
NO. AN APPRENTICE.
HE WILL BECOME JASTER'S LEGACY.
VERY WELL.
YOU'VE PASSED EVERY TEST I'VE PLACED BEFORE YOU, AND I HAVE NO DOUBT THAT YOUR CLONES WILL BE THE MOST FORMIDABLE SOLDIERS THE GALAXY HAS EVER KNOWN.
IN TIME, THEY WILL BE INSTRUMENTAL IN THE DESTRUCTION OF THE JEDI.
THAT'S WHAT I'M COUNTING ON...
LEAD THE WAY TO KAMINO, TYRANUS.
AND MAKE SURE I GET PAID.
END.

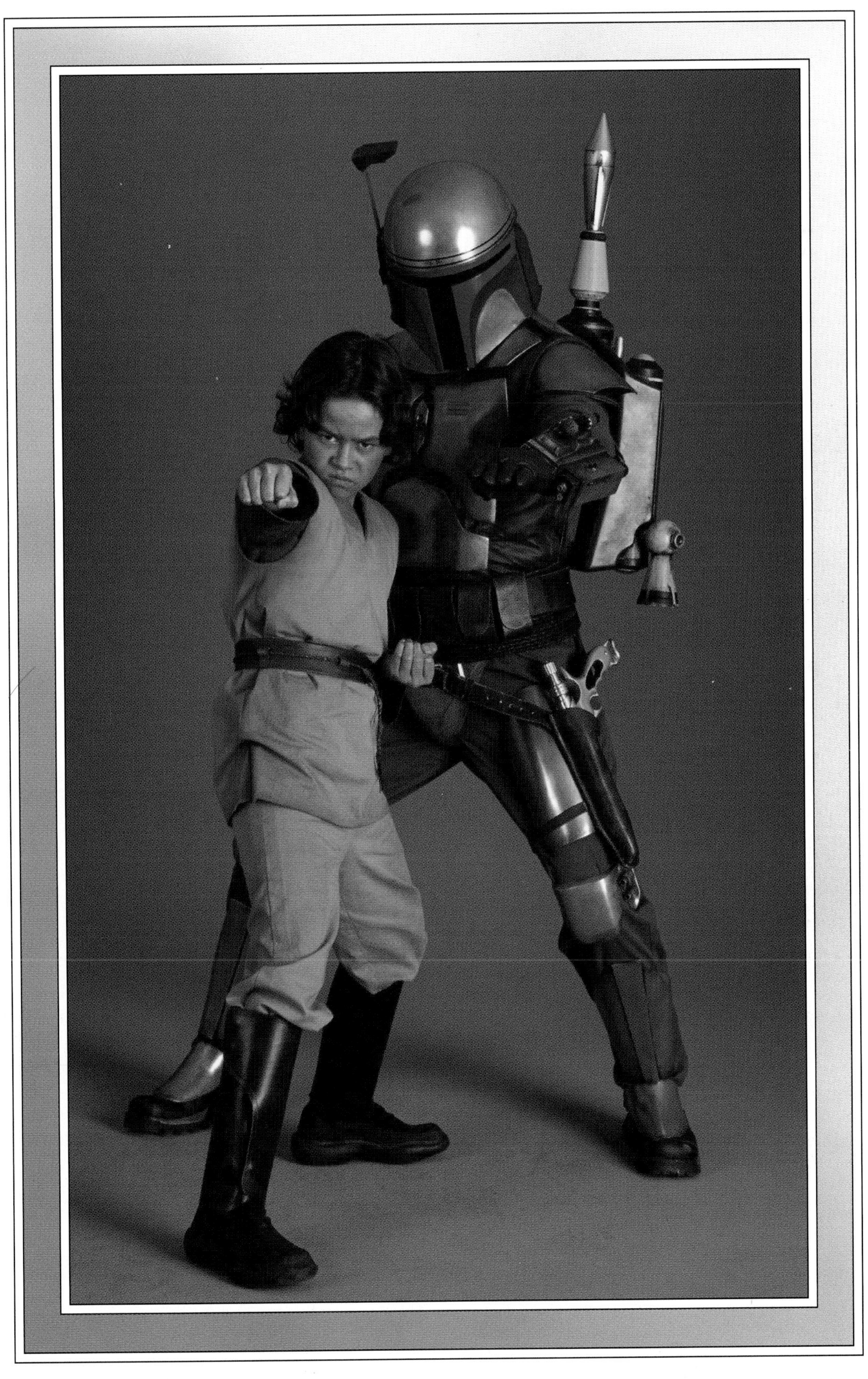

STAR WARS *TIMELINE*

GRAPHIC NOVELS AND TRADE PAPERBACKS FROM DARK HORSE COMICS

For more information go to www.darkhorse.com

TALES OF THE SITH ERA 25,000-1000 YEARS BEFORE STAR WARS: A NEW HOPE

TALES OF THE JEDI
THE GOLDEN AGE OF THE SITH
Anderson • Carrasco, Jr. • Gossett
ISBN: 1-56971-229-8 $16.95
FALL OF THE SITH EMPIRE
Anderson • Heike • Carrasco, Jr.
ISBN: 1-56971-320-0 $14 .95
KNIGHTS OF THE OLD REPUBLIC
Veitch • Gossett
ISBN: 1-56971-020-1 $14.95
THE FREEDON NADD UPRISING
Veitch • Akins • Rodier
ISBN: 1-56971-307-3 $5.95
DARK LORDS OF THE SITH
Veitch • Anderson • Gossett
ISBN: 1-56971-095-3 $17.95
THE SITH WAR
Anderson • Carrasco, Jr.
ISBN: 1-56971-173-9 $17.95

STAR WARS
TALES OF THE JEDI
REDEMPTION

****REDEMPTION***
Anderson • Gossett • Pepoy • McDaniel
ISBN: 1-56971-535-1 $14.95

STAR WARS

****JEDI VS. SITH***
Macan • Bachs • Fernandez
ISBN: 1-56971-649-8 $15.95

PREQUEL ERA 1000-0 YEARS BEFORE STAR WARS: A NEW HOPE

***JEDI COUNCIL**
ACTS OF WAR
Stradley • Fabbri • Vecchia
ISBN: 1-56971-539-4 $12.95

STAR WARS
JEDI COUNCIL
ACTS OF WAR

***DARTH MAUL**
Marz • Duursema • Magyar • Struzan
ISBN: 1-56971-542-4 $12.95

STAR WARS
DARTH MAUL

PRELUDE TO REBELLION
Strnad • Winn • Jones
ISBN: 1-56971-448-7 $14.95
OUTLANDER
Truman • Leonardi • Rio
ISBN: 1-56971-514-9 $14.95
***JEDI COUNCIL**
EMMISSARIES TO MALASTARE
Truman • Duursema • Others
ISBN: 1-56971-545-9 $15.95

STAR WARS

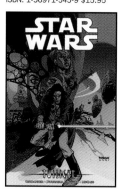

STAR WARS: TWILIGHT
Ostrander • Duursema • Magyar
ISBN: 1-56971-558-0 $12.95
EPISODE 1 —
THE PHANTOM MENACE
Gilroy • Damaggio • Williamson
ISBN: 1-56971-359-6 $12.95
EPISODE 1 —
THE PHANTOM MENACE ADVENTURES
ISBN: 1-56971-443-6 $12.95

MANGA EDITIONS
Translated into English
EPISODE 1 —
THE PHANTOM MENACE
George Lucas • Kia Asamiya
VOLUME 1
ISBN: 1-56971-483-5 $9.95
VOLUME 2
ISBN: 1-56971-484-3 $9.95

STAR WARS
JANGO FETT

***JANGO FETT**
Marz • Fowler
ISBN: 1-56971-623-4 $5.95

STAR WARS
ZAM WESELL

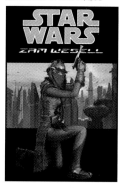

***ZAM WESELL**
Marz • Naifeh
ISBN: 1-56971-624-2 $5.95

STARWARS
EPISODE II
ATTACK OF THE CLONES

EPISODE 2 —
ATTACK OF THE CLONES
Gilroy • Duursema • Kryssing • McCaig
ISBN: 1-56971-609-9 $17.95
DROIDS
THE KALARBA ADVENTURES
Thorsland • Windham • Gibson
ISBN: 1-56971-064-3 $17.95
REBELLION
Windham • Gibson
ISBN: 1-56971-224-7 $14.95

JABBA THE HUTT
THE ART OF THE DEAL
Woodring • Wetherell • Sheldon
ISBN: 1-56971-310-3 $9.95
***UNDERWORLD**
THE YAVIN VASSILIKA
Kennedy • Meglia
ISBN: 1-56971-618-8 $14.95
CLASSIC STAR WARS
HAN SOLO AT STARS' END
Goodwin • Alcala
ISBN: 1-56971-254-9 $6.95
BOBA FETT
ENEMY OF THE EMPIRE
Wagner • Gibson • Nadeau • Ezquerra
ISBN: 1-56971-407-X $12.95

TRILOGY ERA 0-5 YEARS AFTER STAR WARS: A NEW HOPE

***A NEW HOPE* SPECIAL EDITION**
Jones • Barreto • Williamson
ISBN: 1-56971-213-1 $9.95
MANGA EDITIONS
Translated into English
A NEW HOPE
George Lucas • Hisao Tamaki
VOLUME 1
ISBN: 1-56971-362-6 $9.95
VOLUME 2
ISBN: 1-56971-363-4 $9.95
VOLUME 3
ISBN: 1-56971-364-2 $9.95
VOLUME 4
ISBN: 1-56971-365-0 $9.95
VADER'S QUEST
Macan • Gibbons
ISBN: 1-56971-415-0 $11.95

CLASSIC
STAR WARS
THE EARLY ADVENTURES

CLASSIC STAR WARS
THE EARLY ADVENTURES
Manning • Hoberg
ISBN: 1-56971-178-X $19.95
SPLINTER OF THE MIND'S EYE
Austin • Sprouse
ISBN: 1-56971-223-9 $14.95
CLASSIC STAR WARS
IN DEADLY PURSUIT
Goodwin • Williamson
ISBN: 1-56971-109-7 $16.95
THE EMPIRE STRIKES BACK SPECIAL EDITION
Goodwin • Williamson
ISBN: 1-56971-234-4 $9.95
MANGA EDITIONS
Translated into English
THE EMPIRE STRIKES BACK
George Lucas • Toshiki Kudo
VOLUME 1
ISBN: 1-56971-390-1 $9.95

AVAILABLE AT YOUR LOCAL COMICS SHOP OR BOOKSTORE
To find a comics shop in your area, call 1-888-266-4226
For more information or to order direct:
•On the web: www.darkhorse.com •E-mail: mailorder@darkhorse.com
•Phone: 1-800-862-0052 or (503) 652-9701 Mon.-Sat. 9 A.M. to 5 P.M. Pacific Time

THE EMPIRE STRIKES BACK
THE COMIC-BOOK ADAPTATION

VOLUME 2
ISBN: 1-56971-391-X $9.95
VOLUME 3
ISBN: 1-56971-392-8 $9.95
VOLUME 4
ISBN: 1-56971-393-6 $9.95
CLASSIC STAR WARS
THE REBEL STORM
Goodwin • Williamson
ISBN: 1-56971-106-2 $16.95
CLASSIC STAR WARS
ESCAPE TO HOTH
Goodwin • Williamson
ISBN: 1-56971-093-7 $16.95
SHADOWS OF THE EMPIRE
SHADOWS OF THE EMPIRE
Wagner • Plunkett • Russell
ISBN: 1-56971-183-6 $17.95
RETURN OF THE JEDI
SPECIAL EDITION
Goodwin • Williamson
ISBN: 1-56971-235-2 $9.95
MANGA EDITIONS
Translated into English
RETURN OF THE JEDI
George Lucas • Shin-ichi Hiromoto

STAR WARS
ジェダイの復讐
SHIN-ICHI HIROMOTO

VOLUME 1
ISBN: 1-56971-394-4 $9.95
VOLUME 2
ISBN: 1-56971-395-2 $9.95
VOLUME 3
ISBN: 1-56971-396-0 $9.95
VOLUME 4
ISBN: 1-56971-397-9 $9.95

CLASSIC SPIN-OFF ERA 5-25 YEARS AFTER STAR WARS: A NEW HOPE

MARA JADE
BY THE EMPEROR'S HAND
Zahn • Stackpole • Ezquerra
ISBN: 1-56971-401-0 $15.95

STAR WARS
Mara Jade
BY THE EMPEROR'S HAND

SHADOWS OF THE EMPIRE
EVOLUTION
Perry • Randall • Simmons
ISBN: 1-56971-441-X $14.95
X-WING ROGUE SQUADRON
THE PHANTOM AFFAIR
Stackpole • Macan • Biukovic
ISBN: 1-56971-251-4 $12.95

STAR WARS
X-WING
ROGUE SQUADRON
Battleground: Tatooine

BATTLEGROUND: TATOOINE
Stackpole • Strnad • Nadeau • Ensign
ISBN: 1-56971-276-X $12.95
THE WARRIOR PRINCESS
Stackpole • Tolson • Nadeau • Ensign
ISBN: 1-56971-330-8 $12.95

STAR WARS
X-WING
ROGUE SQUADRON
Requiem for a Rogue

REQUIEM FOR A ROGUE
Stackpole • Strnad • Barr • Erskine
ISBN: 1-56971-331-6 $12.95
IN THE EMPIRE'S SERVICE
Stackpole • Nadeau • Ensign
ISBN: 1-56971-383-9 $12.95
BLOOD AND HONOR
Stackpole • Crespo • Hall • Martin
ISBN: 1-56971-387-1 $12.95
MASQUERADE
Stackpole • Johnson • Martin
ISBN: 1-56971-487-8 $12.95

MANDATORY RETIREMENT
Stackpole • Crespo • Nadeau
ISBN: 1-56971-492-4 $12.95
THE THRAWN TRILOGY
HEIR TO THE EMPIRE
Baron • Vatine • Blanchard
ISBN: 1-56971-202-6 $19.95
DARK FORCE RISING
Baron • Dodson • Nowlan
ISBN: 1-56971-269-7 $17.95
THE LAST COMMAND
Baron • Biukovic • Shanower
ISBN: 1-56971-378-2 $17.95
DARK EMPIRE
DARK EMPIRE
Veitch • Kennedy
ISBN: 1-56971-073-2 $17.95
DARK EMPIRE II
Veitch • Kennedy
ISBN: 1-56971-119-4 $17.95
EMPIRE'S END
Veitch • Baikie
ISBN: 1-56971-306-5 $5.95

STAR WARS
BOBA FETT
Death, Lies, & Treachery

BOBA FETT
DEATH, LIES,
& TREACHERY
Wagner • Kennedy
ISBN: 1-56971-311-1 $12.95
CRIMSON EMPIRE
CRIMSON EMPIRE
Richardson • Stradley • Gulacy • Russell
ISBN: 1-56971-355-3 $17.95

STAR WARS
CRIMSON EMPIRE II
Council of Blood

COUNCIL OF BLOOD
Richardson • Stradley • Gulacy • Emberlin
ISBN: 1-56971-410-X $17.95
JEDI ACADEMY
LEVIATHAN
Anderson • Carrasco • Heike
ISBN: 1-56971-456-8 $11.95

THE NEW JEDI ORDER ERA 25+ YEARS AFTER STAR WARS: A NEW HOPE

UNION
Stackpole • Teranishi • Chuckry
ISBN: 1-56971-464-9 $12.95

STAR WARS
CHEWBACCA

CHEWBACCA
Macan • Duursema • Others
ISBN: 1-56971-515-7 $12.95

INFINITIES — DOES NOT APPLY TO TIMELINE

***TALES VOLUME 1**
Marz • Plunkett • Duursema • Others
ISBN: 1-56971-619-6 $19.95
***INFINITIES — A NEW HOPE**
Warner • Johnson • Snyder • Rio • Nelson
ISBN: 1-56971-648-X $12.95

BATTLE OF THE BOUNTY HUNTERS
POP-UP COMIC BOOK
Windham • Moeller
ISBN: 1-56971-129-1 $17.95
DARK FORCES
Prose novellas, heavily illustrated
SOLDIER FOR THE EMPIRE
Dietz • Williams
hardcover edition
ISBN: 1-56971-155-0 $24.95
paperback edition
ISBN: 1-56971-348-0 $14.95
REBEL AGENT
Dietz • Tucker
hardcover edition
ISBN: 1-56971-156-9 $24.95
paperback edition
ISBN: 1-56971-400-2 $14.95
JEDI KNIGHT
Dietz • Dorman
hardcover edition
ISBN: 1-56971-157-7 $24.95
paperback edition
ISBN: 1-56971-433-9 $14.95

SPANS MULTIPLE ERAS

BOUNTY HUNTERS
Truman • Schultz • Stradley • Mangels
ISBN: 1-56971-467-3 $12.95

** New*

•Prices and availability subject to change without notice

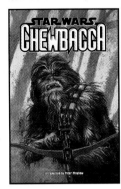

STAR WARS
TIMELINE OF TRADE PAPERBACKS AND GRAPHIC NOVELS!

TALES OF THE SITH ERA
25,000-1000 YEARS BEFORE
STAR WARS: A NEW HOPE

TALES OF THE JEDI
THE GOLDEN AGE OF THE SITH
ISBN: 1-56971-229-8 $16.95
FALL OF THE SITH EMPIRE
ISBN: 1-56971-320-0 $14.95
KNIGHTS OF THE OLD REPUBLIC
ISBN: 1-56971-020-1 $14.95
THE FREEDON NADD UPRISING
ISBN: 1-56971-307-3 $5.95
DARK LORDS OF THE SITH
ISBN: 1-56971-095-3 $17.95
THE SITH WAR
ISBN: 1-56971-173-9 $17.95
****REDEMPTION***
ISBN: 1-56971-535-1 $14.95
****JEDI VS. SITH***
ISBN: 1-56971-649-8 $15.95

PREQUEL ERA 1000-0 YEARS
BEFORE STAR WARS: A NEW HOPE

***JEDI COUNCIL**
ACTS OF WAR
ISBN: 1-56971-539-4 $12.95
***DARTH MAUL**
ISBN: 1-56971-542-4 $12.95
PRELUDE TO REBELLION
ISBN: 1-56971-448-7 $14.95
OUTLANDER
ISBN: 1-56971-514-9 $14.95
***JEDI COUNCIL**
EMMISSARIES TO MALASTARE
ISBN: 1-56971-545-9 $15.95
STAR WARS: TWILIGHT
ISBN: 1-56971-558-0 $12.95
***THE HUNT FOR AURRA SING**
ISBN: 1-56971-651-X $12.95
***DARKNESS**
ISBN: 1-56971-659-5 $12.95
EPISODE 1 —
THE PHANTOM MENACE
ISBN: 1-56971-359-6 $12.95
EPISODE 1 —
THE PHANTOM MENACE ADVENTURES
ISBN: 1-56971-443-6 $12.95
MANGA EDITIONS
Translated into English
EPISODE 1 — *THE PHANTOM MENACE*
VOLUME 1
ISBN: 1-56971-483-5 $9.95
VOLUME 2
ISBN: 1-56971-484-3 $9.95
***JANGO FETT**
ISBN: 1-56971-623-4 $5.95
***JANGO FETT: OPEN SEASONS**
ISBN: 1-56971-671-4 $12.95
***ZAM WESELL**
ISBN: 1-56971-624-2 $5.95
EPISODE 2 —
ATTACK OF THE CLONES
ISBN: 1-56971-609-9 $17.95
DROIDS
THE KALARBA ADVENTURES
ISBN: 1-56971-064-3 $17.95
REBELLION
ISBN: 1-56971-224-7 $14.95
JABBA THE HUTT
THE ART OF THE DEAL
ISBN: 1-56971-310-3 $9.95
***UNDERWORLD**
THE YAVIN VASSILIKA
ISBN: 1-56971-618-8 $14.95
CLASSIC STAR WARS
HAN SOLO AT STARS' END
ISBN: 1-56971-254-9 $6.95
BOBA FETT
ENEMY OF THE EMPIRE
ISBN: 1-56971-407-X $12.95

TRILOGY ERA 0-5 YEARS
AFTER STAR WARS: A NEW HOPE

A NEW HOPE SPECIAL EDITION
ISBN: 1-56971-213-1 $9.95
MANGA EDITIONS
Translated into English
A NEW HOPE
VOLUME 1
ISBN: 1-56971-362-6 $9.95
VOLUME 2
ISBN: 1-56971-363-4 $9.95
VOLUME 3
ISBN: 1-56971-364-2 $9.95
VOLUME 4
ISBN: 1-56971-365-0 $9.95
VADER'S QUEST
ISBN: 1-56971-415-0 $11.95
***A LONG TIME AGO VOLUME 1—**
ISBN: 1-56971-754-0 $29.95
***A LONG TIME AGO VOLUME 2—**
ISBN: 1-56971-785-0 $29.95
***A LONG TIME AGO VOLUME 3—**
RESURRECTION OF EVIL
ISBN: 1-56971-786-9 $29.95
***A LONG TIME AGO VOLUME 4—**
SCREAMS IN THE VOID
ISBN: 1-56971-787-7 $29.95
CLASSIC STAR WARS
THE EARLY ADVENTURES
ISBN: 1-56971-178-X $19.95
SPLINTER OF THE MIND'S EYE
ISBN: 1-56971-223-9 $14.95
CLASSIC STAR WARS
IN DEADLY PURSUIT
ISBN: 1-56971-109-7 $16.95
THE EMPIRE STRIKES BACK
SPECIAL EDITION
ISBN: 1-56971-234-4 $9.95
MANGA EDITIONS
Translated into English
THE EMPIRE STRIKES BACK
VOLUME 1
ISBN: 1-56971-390-1 $9.95
VOLUME 2
ISBN: 1-56971-391-X $9.95
VOLUME 3
ISBN: 1-56971-392-8 $9.95
VOLUME 4
ISBN: 1-56971-393-6 $9.95
CLASSIC STAR WARS
THE REBEL STORM
ISBN: 1-56971-106-2 $16.95
CLASSIC STAR WARS
ESCAPE TO HOTH
ISBN: 1-56971-093-7 $16.95
SHADOWS OF THE EMPIRE
SHADOWS OF THE EMPIRE
ISBN: 1-56971-183-6 $17.95
***RETURN OF THE JEDI* SPECIAL EDITION**
ISBN: 1-56971-235-2 $9.95
MANGA EDITIONS
Translated into English
RETURN OF THE JEDI
VOLUME 1
ISBN: 1-56971-394-4 $9.95
VOLUME 2
ISBN: 1-56971-395-2 $9.95
VOLUME 3
ISBN: 1-56971-396-0 $9.95
VOLUME 4
ISBN: 1-56971-397-9 $9.95

CLASSIC SPIN-OFF ERA 5-25 YEARS
AFTER STAR WARS: A NEW HOPE

MARA JADE
BY THE EMPEROR'S HAND
ISBN: 1-56971-401-0 $15.95
SHADOWS OF THE EMPIRE
EVOLUTION
ISBN: 1-56971-441-X $14.95
X-WING ROGUE SQUADRON
THE PHANTOM AFFAIR
ISBN: 1-56971-251-4 $12.95
BATTLEGROUND: TATOOINE
ISBN: 1-56971-276-X $12.95
THE WARRIOR PRINCESS
ISBN: 1-56971-330-8 $12.95
REQUIEM FOR A ROGUE
ISBN: 1-56971-331-6 $12.95
IN THE EMPIRE'S SERVICE
ISBN: 1-56971-383-9 $12.95
BLOOD AND HONOR
ISBN: 1-56971-387-1 $12.95
MASQUERADE
ISBN: 1-56971-487-8 $12.95
MANDATORY RETIREMENT
ISBN: 1-56971-492-4 $12.95
THE THRAWN TRILOGY
HEIR TO THE EMPIRE
ISBN: 1-56971-202-6 $19.95
DARK FORCE RISING
ISBN: 1-56971-269-7 $17.95
THE LAST COMMAND
ISBN: 1-56971-378-2 $17.95
DARK EMPIRE
DARK EMPIRE
ISBN: 1-56971-073-2 $17.95
DARK EMPIRE II
ISBN: 1-56971-119-4 $17.95
EMPIRE'S END
ISBN: 1-56971-306-5 $5.95
BOBA FETT
DEATH, LIES, & TREACHERY
ISBN: 1-56971-311-1 $12.95
CRIMSON EMPIRE
CRIMSON EMPIRE
ISBN: 1-56971-355-3 $17.95
COUNCIL OF BLOOD
ISBN: 1-56971-410-X $17.95
JEDI ACADEMY
LEVIATHAN
ISBN: 1-56971-456-8 $11.95

THE NEW JEDI ORDER ERA
25+ YEARS AFTER STAR WARS:
A NEW HOPE

UNION
ISBN: 1-56971-464-9 $12.95
CHEWBACCA
ISBN: 1-56971-515-7 $12.95

INFINITIES —
DOES NOT APPLY TO TIMELINE

***TALES VOLUME 1**
ISBN: 1-56971-619-6 $19.95
***TALES VOLUME 2**
ISBN: 1-56971-757-5 $19.95
***INFINITIES**
A NEW HOPE
ISBN: 1-56971-648-X $12.95
BATTLE OF THE BOUNTY HUNTERS
POP-UP COMIC BOOK
ISBN: 1-56971-129-1 $17.95
DARK FORCES
Prose novellas, heavily illustrated
SOLDIER FOR THE EMPIRE
hardcover edition
ISBN: 1-56971-155-0 $24.95
paperback edition
ISBN: 1-56971-348-0 $14.95
REBEL AGENT
hardcover edition
ISBN: 1-56971-156-9 $24.95
paperback edition
ISBN: 1-56971-400-2 $14.95
JEDI KNIGHT
hardcover edition
ISBN: 1-56971-157-7 $24.95
paperback edition
ISBN: 1-56971-433-9 $14.95

** New •Prices and availability subject to change without notice.*

Available from your local comics shop or bookstore!

To find a comics shop in your area, call 1-888-266-4226
For more information or to order direct:
•On the web: www.darkhorse.com •E-mail: mailorder@darkhorse.com
•Phone: 1-800-862-0052 or (503) 652-9701 Mon.-Sat. 9 A.M. to 5 P.M. Pacific Time
*Prices and availability subject to change without notice

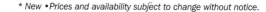

Dark Horse Comics: **Mike Richardson** *publisher* • **Neil Hankerson** *executive vice president* • **Tom Weddle** *vice president of finance* • **Randy Stradley** *vice president of publishing* • **Chris Warner** *senior editor* • **Sara Perrin** *vice president of marketing* • **Michael Martens** *vice president of business development* • **Anita Nelson** *vice president of sales & licensing* • **David Scroggy** *vice president of product development* • **Mark Cox** *art director* • **Dale LaFountain** *vice president of information technology* • **Kim Haines** *director of human resources* • **Darlene Vogel** *director of purchasing* • **Ken Lizzi** • *general counsel*